THE STANDARD FOR PROJECT MANAGEMENT

and

A GUIDE TO THE PROJECT MANAGEMENT BODY OF KNOWLEDGE

(PMBOK® GUIDE)
Seventh Edition

Library of Congress Cataloging-in-Publication Data

Names: Project Management Institute, publisher.

Title: The standard for project management and a guide to the project management body of knowledge (PMBOK guide).

Other titles: Guide to the project management body of knowledge (PMBOK guide) | PMBOK guide

Description: Seventh edition. | Newtown Square, Pennsylvania: Project Management Institute, Inc., [2021] | Includes bibliographical references and index. | Summary: "Over the past few years, emerging technology, new approaches, and rapid market changes disrupted our ways of working, driving the project management profession to evolve. Each industry, organization and project face unique challenges, and team members must adapt their approaches to successfully manage projects and deliver results. With this in mind, A Guide to the Project Management Body of Knowledge (PMBOK® Guide) - Seventh Edition takes a deeper look into the fundamental concepts and constructs of the profession. Including both The Standard for Project Management and the PMBOK® Guide, this edition presents 12 principles of project management and eight project performance domains that are critical for effectively delivering project outcomes. This edition of the PMBOK® Guide: Reflects the full range of development approaches (predictive, traditional, adaptive, agile, hybrid, etc.); Devotes an entire section to tailoring development approaches and processes; Expands the list of tools and techniques in a new section, "Models, Methods, and Artifacts"; Focuses on project outcomes, in addition to deliverables; and Integrates with PMIstandards+, giving users access to content that helps them apply the PMBOK® Guide on the job. The result is a modern guide that betters enables project team members to be proactive, innovative, and nimble in delivering project outcomes." – Provided by publisher.

Identifiers: LCCN 2021011107 (print) | LCCN 2021011108 (ebook) | ISBN 9781628256642 (paperback) | ISBN 9781628256659 (epub) | ISBN 9781628256666 (kindle edition) | ISBN 9781628256673 (pdf)

Subjects: LCSH: Project management–Standards

Classification: LCC HD69.P75 G845 2021 (print) | LCC HD69.P75 (ebook) | DDC 658.4/04–dc23

LC record available at https://lccn.loc.gov/2021011107

LC ebook record available at https://lccn.loc.gov/2021011108

A Guide to the Project Management Body of Knowledge (PMBOK Guide) -- Seventh Edition
and The Standard for Project Management

ISBN: 978-1-62825-664-2

Published by:
    Project Management Institute, Inc.
    14 Campus Boulevard
    Newtown Square, Pennsylvania 19073-3299 USA
    Phone: +1 610 356 4600
    Email: customercare@pmi.org
    Internet: www.PMI.org

To place an order or for pricing information, please contact Independent Publishers Group:
    Independent Publishers Group
    Order Department
    814 North Franklin Street
    Chicago, IL 60610 USA
    Phone: 800 888 4741
    Fax: +1 312 337 5985
    Email: orders@ipgbook.com (For orders only)

10 9 8 7 6 5 4 3 2 1

Notice

The Project Management Institute, Inc. (PMI) standards and guideline publications, of which the document contained herein is one, are developed through a voluntary consensus standards development process. This process brings together volunteers and/or seeks out the views of persons who have an interest in the topic covered by this publication. While PMI administers the process and establishes rules to promote fairness in the development of consensus, it does not write the document and it does not independently test, evaluate, or verify the accuracy or completeness of any information or the soundness of any judgments contained in its standards and guideline publications.

PMI disclaims liability for any personal injury, property or other damages of any nature whatsoever, whether special, indirect, consequential or compensatory, directly or indirectly resulting from the publication, use of application, or reliance on this document. PMI disclaims and makes no guaranty or warranty, expressed or implied, as to the accuracy or completeness of any information published herein, and disclaims and makes no warranty that the information in this document will fulfill any of your particular purposes or needs. PMI does not undertake to guarantee the performance of any individual manufacturer or seller's products or services by virtue of this standard or guide.

In publishing and making this document available, PMI is not undertaking to render professional or other services for or on behalf of any person or entity, nor is PMI undertaking to perform any duty owed by any person or entity to someone else. Anyone using this document should rely on his or her own independent judgment or, as appropriate, seek the advice of a competent professional in determining the exercise of reasonable care in any given circumstances. Information and other standards on the topic covered by this publication may be available from other sources, which the user may wish to consult for additional views or information not covered by this publication.

PMI has no power, nor does it undertake to police or enforce compliance with the contents of this document. PMI does not certify, test, or inspect products, designs, or installations for safety or health purposes. Any certification or other statement of compliance with any health or safety-related information in this document shall not be attributable to PMI and is solely the responsibility of the certifier or maker of the statement.

Preface

Each time work begins on a new edition of *The Standard for Project Management* and the *PMBOK® Guide*, there is an opportunity to consider global perspectives on changes in project management and the approaches used for realizing benefits and value from project outputs. In the time between every edition, a world of change has occurred. Some organizations have ceased to exist, and new organizations have emerged. Older technologies have reached end of life while technologies offering completely new capabilities have evolved. People who continue in the workforce have advanced their thinking, skills, and capabilities as new entrants focus on quickly understanding their professional language, building their skills, developing their business acumen, and contributing to the objectives of their employers.

Even in the midst of such changes, though, there are fundamental concepts and constructs that remain in place. The understanding that collective thinking produces more holistic solutions than the thoughts of one individual continues. And the fact that organizations use projects as a vehicle for delivering a unique result or output endures.

CUSTOMER- AND END-USER-CENTERED DESIGN

While the Sixth Edition of the *PMBOK® Guide* was under development and throughout development of this Seventh Edition, PMI has actively engaged with a broad range of global stakeholders on their experiences with using *The Standard for Project Management* and the *PMBOK® Guide*. These engagements have included:

- ▶ Online surveys to representative samples of PMI stakeholders;
- ▶ Focus groups with PMO leaders, project managers, agile practitioners, project team members, and educators and trainers; and
- ▶ Interactive workshops with practitioners at various PMI events around the globe.

The feedback and inputs collectively emphasized four key points:

▶ Maintain and enhance the credibility and relevance of the *PMBOK® Guide*.

▶ Improve the readability and usefulness of the *PMBOK® Guide* while avoiding overstuffing it with new content.

▶ Sense stakeholder information and content needs and provide vetted supplemental content supporting practical application.

▶ Recognize that there is continued value for some stakeholders in the structure and content of previous editions so that any shifts enhance without negating that value.

SUSTAINING THE RELEVANCE OF THE *PMBOK® GUIDE*

Since its inception as the *Project Management Body of Knowledge (PMBOK)* in 1987, *A Guide to the Project Management Body of Knowledge (PMBOK® Guide)* has evolved while recognizing that fundamental elements of project management endure. Its evolution has not just involved an increase in the page count, it has also involved significant and substantive changes in the nature of the content. A sampling of some of those key changes is reflected in the following table:

Evolution of Key Changes in the *PMBOK® Guide*

PMBOK® Guide Edition	Key Evolutionary Changes
1996	• Distinguished as "a guide to the body of knowledge," rather than the body of knowledge for project management. • Reflected the subset of the project management body of knowledge that is "generally accepted," meaning applicable to most projects most of the time with widespread consensus that practices have value and usefulness. • Defined project management as "the application of knowledge, skills, tools, and techniques to project activities **in order to meet or exceed stakeholder needs and expectations** [emphasis added] from a project." • Specific decision to shift to a process-based standard driven by a desire to show interactions among Knowledge Areas; create a robust and flexible structure; and recognize that ISO and other standards organizations were establishing process-based standards.
Third (2004)	• First edition to incorporate the "ANSI Standard" logo on the cover. • First edition to formally designate *The Standard for Project Management of a Project* separate and distinct from the Project Management Framework and Body of Knowledge. • Included material "generally recognized as good practice on most projects most of the time." • Defined project management as "the application of knowledge, skills, tools, and techniques to project activities **to meet the project requirements**."
Sixth (2017)	• First edition to make a distinct separation between the ANSI standard and the guide. • First time "agile" content is incorporated into the text, not just referenced in examples. • Expansion of Knowledge Area front material, including key concepts, trends and emerging practices, tailoring considerations, and considerations for agile/adaptive environments.

Like previous editions of *The Standard for Project Management* and the *PMBOK® Guide*, this edition recognizes that the project management landscape continues to evolve and adapt. Over the past 10 years alone, the advancement of software into all types of products, services, and solutions has grown exponentially. What software can enable continues to change as artificial intelligence, cloud-based capabilities, and new business models drive innovation and new ways of working. Transformed organizational models have yielded new project work and team structures, the need for a broad range of approaches to project and product delivery, and a stronger focus on outcomes rather than deliverables. Individual contributors can join project teams from anywhere in the world, serve in a broader array of roles, and enable new ways of thinking and working collaboratively. These changes and more have created this opportunity to reconsider perspectives to support the continued evolution of *The Standard for Project Management* and the *PMBOK® Guide*.

SUMMARY OF CHANGES

Since 1987, *The Standard for Project Management* has represented a process-based standard. *The Standard for Project Management* included in the *PMBOK® Guide* aligned the project management discipline and function around a collection of business processes. Those business processes enabled consistent and predictable practices:

▶ That could be documented;

▶ Through which performance against the processes could be assessed; and

▶ Through which improvements to the process could be made to maximize efficiency and minimize threats.

While effective in supporting good practice, process-based standards are prescriptive by their very nature. With project management evolving more rapidly than ever before, the process-based orientation of past editions cannot be maintained in a manner conducive to reflecting the full value delivery landscape. Therefore, this edition shifts to a principles-based standard to support effective project management and to focus more on intended outcomes rather than deliverables.

A global community of practitioners from different industries and organizations, in different roles, and working on different types of projects have developed and/or provided feedback on drafts of the standard as it has evolved for this edition. In addition, the *PMBOK® Guide* – Seventh Edition coleaders and staff reviewed other bodies of knowledge and works focused on project management to identify principle concepts embedded in those texts. These combined efforts showed strong alignment and supported the validation that the guiding principles in this edition of the standard apply across the spectrum of project management.

To date, the global project management community has embraced the shift of this standard toward a set of principle statements. The principle statements capture and summarize generally accepted objectives for the practice of project management and its core functions. The principle statements provide broad parameters within which project teams can operate and offer many ways to remain aligned with the intent of the principles.

Using these principle statements, PMI can reflect effective management of projects across the full value delivery landscape: predictive to adaptive and everything in between. This principles-based approach is also consistent with the evolution of *The Standard for Program Management* (Third and Fourth Editions) and *The Standard for Portfolio Management* – Fourth Edition. *The Standard for Risk Management in Portfolios, Programs, and Projects* and *Benefits Realization Management: A Practice Guide* represent new standard products intentionally developed with a principles-based focus by global teams of subject matter experts.

Nothing in this edition of *The Standard for Project Management* or *A Guide to the Project Management Body of Knowledge* negates alignment with the process-based approach of past editions. Many organizations and practitioners continue to find that approach useful for guiding their project management capabilities, aligning their methodologies, and evaluating their project management capabilities. That approach remains relevant in the context of this new edition.

Another significant change with this edition of the *PMBOK® Guide* is a systems view of project management. This shift begins with a systems view of value delivery as part of *The Standard for Project Management* and continues with the presentation of the *PMBOK® Guide* content. A systems focus for value delivery changes the perspective from one of governing portfolios, programs, and projects to focusing on the value chain that links those and other business capabilities to advancing organizational strategy, value, and business objectives. In the context of project management, *The Standard for Project Management* and the *PMBOK® Guide* emphasize that projects do not simply produce outputs, but more importantly, enable those outputs to drive outcomes that ultimately deliver value to the organization and its stakeholders.

This systems view reflects a shift from the Knowledge Areas in past editions of the *PMBOK® Guide* to eight project performance domains. A performance domain is a group of related activities that are critical for the effective delivery of project outcomes. Collectively, the performance domains represent a project management system of interactive, interrelated, and interdependent management capabilities that work in unison to achieve desired project outcomes. As the performance domains interact and react to each other, change occurs. Project teams continuously review, discuss, adapt, and respond to such changes with the whole system in mind—not just the specific performance domain in which the change occurred. Aligned with the concept of a system for value delivery in *The Standard for Project Management*, teams evaluate effective performance in each performance domain through outcomes-focused measures, rather than through adherence to processes or the production of artifacts, plans, etc.

Previous editions of the *PMBOK® Guide* emphasized the importance of tailoring the project management approach to the unique characteristics of each project and its context. The Sixth Edition specifically incorporated considerations to help project teams think about how to tailor their approach to project management. That content was included in the front matter of each of the Knowledge Areas and provided considerations for all types of project environments. This edition further expands upon that work with a dedicated section on Tailoring in the *PMBOK® Guide*.

A new section on Models, Methods, and Artifacts provides a high-level grouping of models, methods, and artifacts that support project management. This section maintains linkages to tools, techniques, and outputs from previous editions that support project management without prescribing when, how, or which tools teams should use.

The final change reflects the most significant advancement in the *PMBOK® Guide's* history—the creation of PMIstandards+™, an interactive digital platform that incorporates current, emerging, and future practices, methods, artifacts, and other useful information. The digital content better reflects the dynamic nature of a body of knowledge. PMIstandards+ provides project practitioners and other stakeholders with access to a richer and broader range of information and resources that can more quickly accommodate advances and changes in project management. The content explains how specific practices, methods, or artifacts apply to projects based on industry segments, project types, or other characteristics. Starting with the inputs, tools and techniques, and outputs from the *PMBOK® Guide* – Sixth Edition, PMIstandards+ will continue to incorporate new resources that support continued evolution in project management. Going forward, users of *The Standard for Project Management* and the *PMBOK® Guide* can find information in PMIstandards+ that will supplement the information included in the printed publication.

The following figure illustrates the revision to *The Standard for Project Management* and migration from the Sixth to the Seventh Edition of the *PMBOK® Guide*, along with the connection to the PMIstandards+ digital platform.

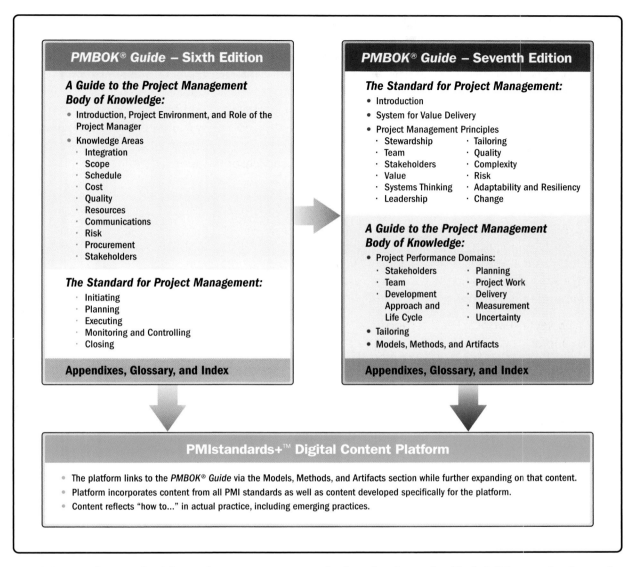

PMBOK® Guide – Sixth Edition

A Guide to the Project Management Body of Knowledge:
- Introduction, Project Environment, and Role of the Project Manager
- Knowledge Areas
  · Integration
  · Scope
  · Schedule
  · Cost
  · Quality
  · Resources
  · Communications
  · Risk
  · Procurement
  · Stakeholders

The Standard for Project Management:
  · Initiating
  · Planning
  · Executing
  · Monitoring and Controlling
  · Closing

Appendixes, Glossary, and Index

PMBOK® Guide – Seventh Edition

The Standard for Project Management:
- Introduction
- System for Value Delivery
- Project Management Principles
  · Stewardship   · Tailoring
  · Team   · Quality
  · Stakeholders   · Complexity
  · Value   · Risk
  · Systems Thinking   · Adaptability and Resiliency
  · Leadership   · Change

A Guide to the Project Management Body of Knowledge:
- Project Performance Domains:
  · Stakeholders   · Planning
  · Team   · Project Work
  · Development   · Delivery
    Approach and   · Measurement
    Life Cycle   · Uncertainty
- Tailoring
- Models, Methods, and Artifacts

Appendixes, Glossary, and Index

PMIstandards+™ Digital Content Platform

- The platform links to the *PMBOK® Guide* via the Models, Methods, and Artifacts section while further expanding on that content.
- Platform incorporates content from all PMI standards as well as content developed specifically for the platform.
- Content reflects "how to..." in actual practice, including emerging practices.

Revision to *The Standard for Project Management* and Migration from the Sixth Edition to the Seventh Edition of the *PMBOK® Guide* and the PMIstandards+™ Digital Content Platform

CONCLUSION

The Standard for Project Management and the *PMBOK® Guide* – Seventh Edition respond to all four elements that stakeholders have emphasized in their feedback. The revision maintains and enhances the credibility and relevance of the *PMBOK® Guide*. It improves the readability and usefulness of the *PMBOK® Guide*. It recognizes that there is continued value for some stakeholders in the structure and content of previous editions and enhances the content in this edition without negating that value. Most importantly, it links with the PMIstandards+ digital content platform to respond to stakeholders' needs with vetted supplemental content that supports practical application.

Table of Contents

THE STANDARD FOR PROJECT MANAGEMENT

A GUIDE TO THE PROJECT MANAGEMENT BODY OF KNOWLEDGE (PMBOK® GUIDE)

List of Figures and Tables

THE STANDARD FOR PROJECT MANAGEMENT

THE
STANDARD FOR
PROJECT MANAGEMENT

Introduction

The Standard for Project Management identifies project management principles that guide the behaviors and actions of project professionals and other stakeholders who work on or are engaged with projects.

This introductory section describes the purpose of this standard, defines key terms and concepts, and identifies the audience for the standard.

The Standard for Project Management consists of the following sections:

▶ **Section 1 Introduction**

▶ **Section 2 A System for Value Delivery**

▶ **Section 3 Project Management Principles**

1.1 PURPOSE OF *THE STANDARD FOR PROJECT MANAGEMENT*

The Standard for Project Management provides a basis for understanding project management and how it enables intended outcomes. This standard applies regardless of industry, location, size, or delivery approach, for example, predictive, hybrid, or adaptive. It describes the system within which projects operate, including governance, possible functions, the project environment, and considerations for the relationship between project management and product management.

1.2 KEY TERMS AND CONCEPTS

The Standard for Project Management reflects the progression of the profession. Organizations expect projects to deliver outcomes in addition to outputs and artifacts. Project managers are expected to deliver projects that create value for the organization and stakeholders within the organization's system for value delivery. The following terms are defined to provide context for the content in this standard.

▶ **Outcome.** An end result or consequence of a process or project. Outcomes can include outputs and artifacts, but have a broader intent by focusing on the benefits and value that the project was undertaken to deliver.

▶ **Portfolio.** Projects, programs, subsidiary portfolios, and operations managed as a group to achieve strategic objectives.

▶ **Product.** An artifact that is produced, is quantifiable, and can be either an end item in itself or a component item.

▶ **Program.** Related projects, subsidiary programs, and program activities that are managed in a coordinated manner to obtain benefits not available from managing them individually.

▶ **Project.** A temporary endeavor undertaken to create a unique product, service, or result. The temporary nature of projects indicates a beginning and an end to the project work or a phase of the project work. Projects can stand alone or be part of a program or portfolio.

▶ **Project management.** The application of knowledge, skills, tools, and techniques to project activities to meet project requirements. Project management refers to guiding the project work to deliver the intended outcomes. Project teams can achieve the outcomes using a broad range of approaches (e.g., predictive, hybrid, and adaptive).

▶ **Project manager.** The person assigned by the performing organization to lead the project team that is responsible for achieving the project objectives. Project managers perform a variety of functions, such as facilitating the project team work to achieve the outcomes and managing the processes to deliver intended outcomes. Additional functions are identified in Section 2.3.

- **Project team.** A set of individuals performing the work of the project to achieve its objectives.

- **System for value delivery.** A collection of strategic business activities aimed at building, sustaining, and/or advancing an organization. Portfolios, programs, projects, products, and operations can all be part of an organization's system for value delivery.

- **Value.** The worth, importance, or usefulness of something. Different stakeholders perceive value in different ways. Customers can define value as the ability to use specific features or functions of a product. Organizations can focus on business value as determined with financial metrics, such as the benefits less the cost of achieving those benefits. Societal value can include the contribution to groups of people, communities, or the environment.

For other terms used in this standard, refer to the Glossary and the *PMI Lexicon of Project Management Terms* [1].[1]

1.3 AUDIENCE FOR THIS STANDARD

This standard provides a foundational reference for stakeholders participating in a project. This includes, but is not limited to, project practitioners, consultants, educators, students, sponsors, stakeholders, and vendors who:

- Are responsible or accountable for delivering project outcomes;

- Work on projects full or part time;

- Work in portfolio, program, or project management offices (PMOs);

- Are involved in project sponsorship, product ownership, product management, executive leadership, or project governance;

- Are involved with portfolio or program management;

- Provide resources for project work;

- Focus on value delivery for portfolios, programs, and projects;

- Teach or study project management; and

- Are involved in any aspect of the project value delivery chain.

_____

[1] The numbers in brackets refer to the list of references at the end of this standard.

2

A System for Value Delivery

The information in this section provides a context for value delivery, governance, project functions, the project environment, and product management.

▶ **Section 2.1 Creating Value.** This section describes how projects operate within a system to produce value for organizations and their stakeholders.

▶ **Section 2.2 Organizational Governance Systems.** This section describes how governance supports a system for value delivery.

▶ **Section 2.3 Functions Associated with Projects.** This section identifies the functions that support projects.

▶ **Section 2.4 The Project Environment.** This section identifies internal and external factors that influence projects and the delivery of value.

▶ **Section 2.5 Product Management Considerations.** This section identifies the ways portfolios, programs, projects, and products relate.

2.1 CREATING VALUE

Projects exist within a larger system, such as a governmental agency, organization, or contractual arrangement. For the sake of brevity, this standard uses the term *organization* when referring to government agencies, enterprises, contractual arrangements, joint ventures, and other arrangements. Organizations create value for stakeholders. Examples of ways that projects produce value include, but are not limited to:

- ▶ Creating a new product, service, or result that meets the needs of customers or end users;

- ▶ Creating positive social or environmental contributions;

- ▶ Improving efficiency, productivity, effectiveness, or responsiveness;

- ▶ Enabling the changes needed to facilitate organizational transition to its desired future state; and

- ▶ Sustaining benefits enabled by previous programs, projects, or business operations.

2.1.1 VALUE DELIVERY COMPONENTS

There are various components, such as portfolios, programs, projects, products, and operations, that can be used individually and collectively to create value. Working together, these components comprise a system for delivering value that is aligned with the organization's strategy. Figure 2-1 shows an example of a system to deliver value that has two portfolios comprised of programs and projects. It also shows a stand-alone program with projects and stand-alone projects not associated with portfolios or programs. Any of the projects or programs could include products. Operations can directly support and influence portfolios, programs, and projects, as well as other business functions, such as payroll, supply chain management, and so forth. Portfolios, programs, and projects influence each other as well as operations.

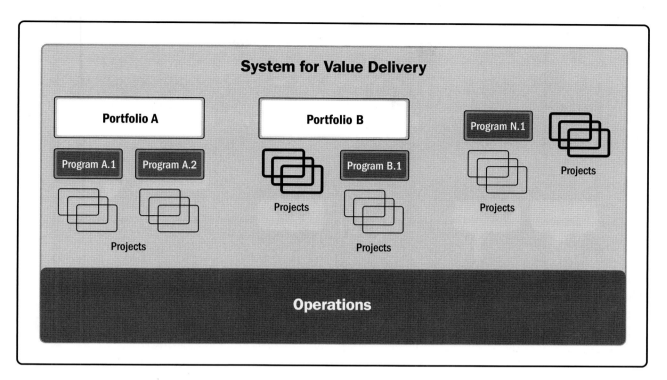

Figure 2-1. Example of a System for Value Delivery

As shown in Figure 2-2, a system for value delivery is part of an organization's internal environment that is subject to policies, procedures, methodologies, frameworks, governance structures, and so forth. That internal environment exists within the larger external environment, which includes the economy, the competitive environment, legislative constraints, etc. Section 2.4 provides more detail on internal and external environments.

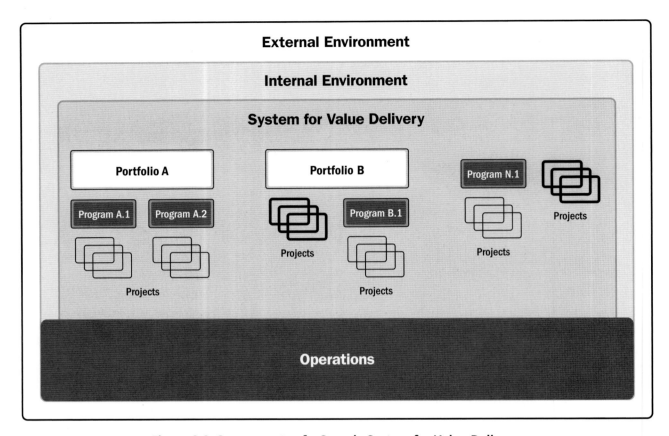

Figure 2-2. Components of a Sample System for Value Delivery

The components in a value delivery system create deliverables used to produce outcomes. An outcome is the end result or consequence of a process or a project. Focusing on outcomes, choices, and decisions emphasizes the long-range performance of the project. The outcomes create benefits, which are gains realized by the organization. Benefits, in turn, create value, which is something of worth, importance, or usefulness.

2.1.2 INFORMATION FLOW

A value delivery system works most effectively when information and feedback are shared consistently among all components, keeping the system aligned with strategy and attuned to the environment.

Figure 2-3 shows a model of the flow of information where black arrows represent information from senior leadership to portfolios, portfolios to programs and projects, and then to operations. Senior leadership shares strategic information with portfolios. Portfolios share the desired outcomes, benefits, and value with programs and projects. Deliverables from programs and projects are passed on to operations along with information on support and maintenance for the deliverables.

The light gray arrows in Figure 2-3 represent the reverse flow of information. Information from operations to programs and projects suggests adjustments, fixes, and updates to deliverables. Programs and projects provide performance information and progress on achieving the desired outcomes, benefits, and value to portfolios. Portfolios provide evaluations on portfolio performance with senior leadership. Additionally, operations provide information on how well the organization's strategy is advancing.

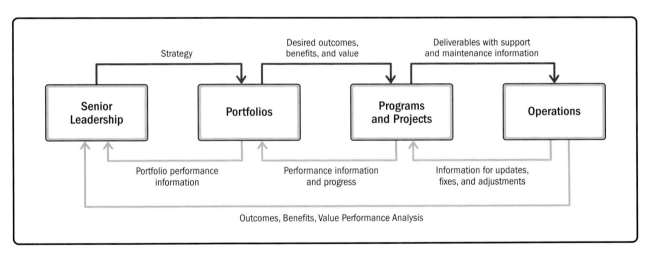

Figure 2-3. Example of Information Flow

2.2 ORGANIZATIONAL GOVERNANCE SYSTEMS

The governance system works alongside the value delivery system to enable smooth workflows, manage issues, and support decision making. Governance systems provide a framework with functions and processes that guide activities. A governance framework can include elements of oversight, control, value assessment, integration among components, and decision-making capabilities.

Governance systems provide an integrated structure for evaluating changes, issues, and risks associated with the environment and any component in the value delivery system. This includes portfolio objectives, program benefits, and deliverables produced by projects.

Projects can operate within a program or portfolio or as a stand-alone activity. In some organizations, a project management office might support programs and projects within a portfolio. Project governance includes defining the authority to approve changes and make other business decisions related to the project. Project governance is aligned with program and/or organizational governance.

2.3 FUNCTIONS ASSOCIATED WITH PROJECTS

People drive project delivery. They do so by fulfilling functions necessary for the project to run effectively and efficiently. Functions related to the project can be fulfilled by one person, by a group of people, or combined into defined roles.

Coordinating a collective work effort is extremely important to the success of any project. There are different types of coordination suitable for different contexts. Some projects benefit from decentralized coordination in which project team members self-organize and self-manage. Other projects benefit from centralized coordination with the leadership and guidance of a designated project manager or similar role. Some projects with centralized coordination can also benefit from including self-organized project teams for portions of the work. Regardless of how coordination takes place, supportive leadership models and meaningful, continuous engagements between project teams and other stakeholders underpin successful outcomes.

Regardless of how projects are coordinated, the collective effort of the project team delivers the outcomes, benefits, and value. The project team may be supported by additional functions depending on the deliverables, industry, organization, and other variables. Sections 2.3.1 through 2.3.8 provide examples of functions that are often found on projects, though these are not a comprehensive list. In addition to these functions, other functions may be necessary to enable project deliverables that produce the desired outcomes. The needs of the project, organization, and environment influence which functions are used on a project and how those functions are carried out.

2.3.1 PROVIDE OVERSIGHT AND COORDINATION

People in this function help the project team achieve the project objectives, typically by orchestrating the work of the project. The specifics of how this function is carried out within the project team can vary among organizations, but can include leading the planning, monitoring, and controlling activities. In some organizations, this function may involve some evaluation and analysis activities as part of pre-project activities. This function includes monitoring and working to improve the health, safety, and overall well-being of project team members.

Coordination includes consulting with executive and business unit leaders on ideas for advancing objectives, improving project performance, or meeting customer needs. It can also include assisting in business analysis, tendering and contract negotiations, and business case development.

Oversight can be involved in follow-on activities related to benefits realization and sustainment after the project deliverables are finalized but before formal closure of the project. This function can support portfolios and programs within which the project is initiated. Ultimately, the function is tailored to fit the organization.

2.3.2 PRESENT OBJECTIVES AND FEEDBACK

People in this function contribute perspectives, insights, and clear direction from customers and end users. The customer and end user are not always synonymous. For the purpose of this standard, the customer is defined as the individual or group who has requested or is funding the project. The end user is the individual or group who will experience the direct use of the project deliverable.

Projects need clear direction from customers and end users regarding project requirements, outcomes, and expectations. In adaptive and hybrid project environments, the need for ongoing feedback is greater because the project teams are exploring and developing product elements within specific increments. In some project environments, the customer or end user engages with the project team for periodic review and feedback. In some projects, a representative of the customer or client participates on the project team. The customer and end user input and feedback needs are determined by the nature of the project and the guidance or direction required.

2.3.3 FACILITATE AND SUPPORT

The function of facilitation and support may be closely related to providing oversight and coordination, depending on the nature of the project. The work involves encouraging project team member participation, collaboration, and a shared sense of responsibility for the work output. Facilitation helps the project team create consensus around solutions, resolve conflicts, and make decisions. Facilitation is also required to coordinate meetings and contribute in an unbiased way to the advancement of project objectives.

Supporting people through change and helping address obstacles that can prevent success is also required. This can include evaluating performance and providing individuals and project teams with feedback to help them learn, adapt, and improve.

2.3.4 PERFORM WORK AND CONTRIBUTE INSIGHTS

This group of people provides the knowledge, skills, and experience necessary to produce the products and realize the outcomes of the project. Work can be full time or part time for the duration of the project or for a limited period, and the work can be colocated or virtual, depending on the environmental factors. Some work can be highly specialized, while other work can be done by project team members who have broad skill sets.

Gaining insights from cross-functional project team members representing different parts of the organization can provide a mix of internal perspectives, establish alliances with key business units, and encourage project team members to act as change agents within their functional areas. This work can extend into support functions (during or after the project) as the project deliverables are implemented or transitioned into operations.

2.3.5 APPLY EXPERTISE

People in this function provide the knowledge, vision, and expertise in a specific subject for a project. They offer advice and support throughout the organization, and contribute to the project team's learning process and work accuracy. These people can be external to the organization or can be internal project team members. They can be required for the whole project or during a specific time frame.

2.3.6 PROVIDE BUSINESS DIRECTION AND INSIGHT

People in this function guide and clarify the direction of the project or product outcome. This function involves prioritizing the requirements or backlog items based on business value, dependencies, and technical or operational risk. People in this function provide feedback to project teams and set direction for the next increment or element to be developed or delivered. The function involves interacting with other stakeholders, customers, and their project teams to define the product direction. The goal is to maximize the value of the project deliverable.

In adaptive and hybrid environments, direction and insight can be provided using a specific cadence. In predictive environments, there can be designated checkpoints for presentation of and feedback on project progress. In some instances, business direction can interact with funding and resourcing functions.

2.3.7 PROVIDE RESOURCES AND DIRECTION

People in this function promote the project and communicate the organization's vision, goals, and expectations to the project team and broader stakeholder community. They advocate for the project and the project team by helping to secure the decisions, resources, and authority that allow project activities to progress.

People in this function serve as liaisons between senior management and the project team, play a supporting role in keeping projects aligned to business objectives, remove obstacles, and address issues outside the bounds of the project team's decision authority. People in this function provide an escalation path for problems, issues, or risks that project teams cannot resolve or manage on their own, such as a shortage of funding or other resources, or deadlines that cannot be met.

This function can facilitate innovation by identifying opportunities that arise within the project and communicating these to senior management. People in this function may monitor project outcomes after project closure to ensure the intended business benefits are realized.

2.3.8 MAINTAIN GOVERNANCE

People who fill a governance function approve and support recommendations made by the project team and monitor project progress in achieving the desired outcomes. They maintain linkages between project teams and strategic or business objectives that can change over the course of the project.

2.4 THE PROJECT ENVIRONMENT

Projects exist and operate within internal and external environments that have varying degrees of influence on value delivery. Internal and external environments can influence planning and other project activities. These influences can yield a favorable, unfavorable, or neutral impact on project characteristics, stakeholders, or project teams.

2.4.1 INTERNAL ENVIRONMENT

Factors internal to the organization can arise from the organization itself, a portfolio, a program, another project, or a combination of these. They include artifacts, practices, or internal knowledge. Knowledge includes lessons learned as well as completed artifacts from previous projects. Examples include but are not limited to:

- ▶ **Process assets.** Process assets may include tools, methodologies, approaches, templates, frameworks, patterns, or PMO resources.

- ▶ **Governance documentation.** This documentation includes policies and processes.

- ▶ **Data assets.** Data assets may include databases, document libraries, metrics, data, and artifacts from previous projects.

- ▶ **Knowledge assets.** Knowledge assets may include tacit knowledge among project team members, subject matter experts, and other employees.

- ▶ **Security and safety.** Security and safety measures may include procedures and practices for facility access, data protection, levels of confidentiality, and proprietary secrets.

- ▶ **Organizational culture, structure, and governance.** These aspects of an organization include the vision, mission, values, beliefs, cultural norms, leadership style, hierarchy and authority relationships, organizational style, ethics, and code of conduct.

- ▶ **Geographic distribution of facilities and resources.** These resources include work locations, virtual project teams, and shared systems.

- ▶ **Infrastructure.** Infrastructure consists of existing facilities, equipment, organizational and telecommunications channels, information technology hardware, availability, and capacity.

- ▶ **Information technology software.** Examples include scheduling software, configuration management systems, web interfaces to online automated systems, collaboration tools, and work authorization systems.

- ▶ **Resource availability.** Examples include contracting and purchasing constraints, approved providers and subcontractors, and collaboration agreements. Availability related to both people and materials includes contracting and purchasing constraints, approved providers and subcontractors, and time lines.

- ▶ **Employee capability.** Examples include general and specialized expertise, skills, competencies, techniques, and knowledge.

2.4.2 EXTERNAL ENVIRONMENT

Factors external to the organization can enhance, constrain, or have a neutral influence on project outcomes. Examples include but are not limited to:

▶ **Marketplace conditions.** Marketplace conditions include competitors, market share, brand recognition, technology trends, and trademarks.

▶ **Social and cultural influences and issues.** These factors include political climate, regional customs and traditions, public holidays and events, codes of conduct, ethics, and perceptions.

▶ **Regulatory environment.** The regulatory environment may include national and regional laws and regulations related to security, data protection, business conduct, employment, licensing, and procurement.

▶ **Commercial databases.** Databases include standardized cost estimating data and industry risk study information.

▶ **Academic research.** This research can include industry studies, publications, and benchmarking results.

▶ **Industry standards.** These standards are related to products, production, environment, quality, and workmanship.

▶ **Financial considerations.** These considerations include currency exchange rates, interest rates, inflation, taxes, and tariffs.

▶ **Physical environment.** The physical environment pertains to working conditions and weather.

2.5 PRODUCT MANAGEMENT CONSIDERATIONS

The disciplines of portfolio, program, project, and product management are becoming more interlinked. While portfolio, program, and product management are beyond the scope of this standard, understanding each discipline and the relationships between them provides a useful context for projects whose deliverables are products.

A product is an artifact that is produced, is quantifiable, and can be either an end item itself or a component item. Product management involves the integration of people, data, processes, and business systems to create, maintain, and develop a product or service throughout its life cycle. The product life cycle is a series of phases that represents the evolution of a product, from introduction through growth, maturity, and to retirement.

Product management may initiate programs or projects at any point in the product life cycle to create or enhance specific components, functions, or capabilities (see Figure 2-4). The initial product may begin as a deliverable of a program or project. Throughout its life cycle, a new program or project may add or improve specific components, attributes, or capabilities that create additional value for customers and the sponsoring organization. In some instances, a program can encompass the full life cycle of a product or service to manage the benefits and create value for the organization more directly.

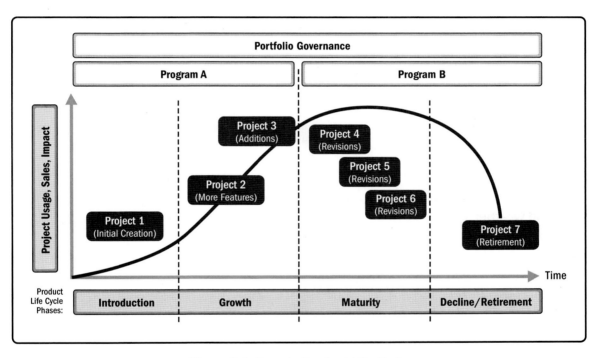

Figure 2-4. Sample Product Life Cycle

Product management can exist in different forms, including but not limited to:

▶ **Program management within a product life cycle.** This approach incorporates related projects, subsidiary programs, and program activities. For very large or long-running products, one or more product life cycle phases may be sufficiently complex to merit a set of programs and projects working together.

▶ **Project management within a product life cycle.** This approach oversees development and maturing of product capabilities as an ongoing business activity. Portfolio governance charters individual projects as needed to perform enhancements and improvements or to produce other unique outcomes.

▶ **Product management within a program.** This approach applies the full product life cycle within the purview and boundaries of a given program. A series of subsidiary programs or projects will be chartered to achieve specific benefits for a product. Those benefits can be enhanced by applying product management competencies like competitive analysis, customer acquisition, and customer advocacy.

While product management is a separate discipline with its own body of knowledge, it represents a key integration point within the program management and project management disciplines. Programs and projects with deliverables that include products use a tailored and integrated approach that incorporates all of the relevant bodies of knowledge and their related practices, methods, and artifacts.

Project Management Principles

3

Principles for a profession serve as foundational guidelines for strategy, decision making, and problem solving. Professional standards and methodologies are often based on principles. In some professions, principles serve as laws or rules, and are therefore prescriptive in nature. The principles of project management are not prescriptive in nature. They are intended to guide the behavior of people involved in projects. They are broadly based so there are many ways individuals and organizations can maintain alignment with the principles.

Principles can, but do not necessarily, reflect morals. A code of ethics is related to morals. A code of ethics for a profession can be adopted by an individual or profession to establish expectations for moral conduct. The *PMI Code of Ethics and Professional Conduct* [2] is based on four values that were identified as most important to the project management community:

▶   Responsibility,

▶   Respect,

▶   Fairness, and

▶   Honesty.

The 12 principles of project management are aligned with the values identified in the *PMI Code of Ethics and Professional Conduct.* They do not follow the same format, and they are not duplicative, rather the principles and the *Code of Ethics* are complementary.

The principles of project management were identified and developed by engaging a global community of project practitioners. The practitioners represent different industries, cultural backgrounds, and organizations in different roles and with experience in various types of projects. Multiple rounds of feedback resulted in 12 principles that provide guidance for effective project management.

Because the principles of project management provide guidance, the degree of application and the way in which they are applied are influenced by the context of the organization, project, deliverables, project team, stakeholders, and other factors. The principles are internally consistent, meaning that no principle contradicts any other principle. However, in practice there may be times when the principles can overlap. For example, guidance for navigating complexity can present information that is useful in recognizing, evaluating, and responding to system interactions or optimizing risk responses.

Principles of project management can also have areas of overlap with general management principles. For example, both projects and business in general focus on delivering value. The methods may be somewhat different in projects as opposed to operations, but the underlying principle associated with focusing on value can apply to both. Figure 3-1 demonstrates this overlap.

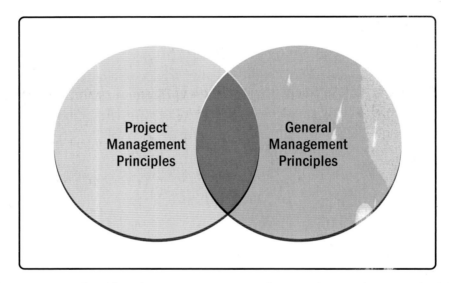

Figure 3-1. Overlap of Project Management and General Management Principles

The principle labels are listed here without any specific weighting or order. The principle statements are presented and described in Sections 3.1 through 3.12. Each section begins with a figure that provides the principle label across the top with the principle and key points under the label. Following the figure, each principle is elaborated in the text. The principle labels are:

- ▶ Be a diligent, respectful, and caring steward (see Section 3.1).
- ▶ Create a collaborative project team environment (see Section 3.2).
- ▶ Effectively engage with stakeholders (see Section 3.3).
- ▶ Focus on value (see Section 3.4).
- ▶ Recognize, evaluate, and respond to system interactions (see Section 3.5).
- ▶ Demonstrate leadership behaviors (see Section 3.6).
- ▶ Tailor based on context (see Section 3.7).
- ▶ Build quality into processes and deliverables (see Section 3.8).
- ▶ Navigate complexity (see Section 3.9).
- ▶ Optimize risk responses (see Section 3.10).
- ▶ Embrace adaptability and resiliency (see Section 3.11).
- ▶ Enable change to achieve the envisioned future state (see Section 3.12).

3.1 BE A DILIGENT, RESPECTFUL, AND CARING STEWARD

STEWARDSHIP

Stewards act responsibly to carry out activities with integrity, care, and trustworthiness while maintaining compliance with internal and external guidelines. They demonstrate a broad commitment to financial, social, and environmental impacts of the projects they support.

▶ Stewardship encompasses responsibilities within and external to the organization.

▶ Stewardship includes:
  • Integrity,
  • Care,
  • Trustworthiness, and
  • Compliance.

▶ A holistic view of stewardship considers financial, social, technical, and sustainable environmental awareness.

Figure 3-2. Be a Diligent, Respectful, and Caring Steward

Stewardship has slightly different meanings and applications in different contexts. One aspect of stewardship involves being entrusted with the care of something. Another aspect focuses on the responsible planning, use, and management of resources. Yet another aspect means upholding values and ethics.

Stewardship encompasses responsibilities both within and external to the organization. Within the organization, stewardship includes:

▶ Operating in alignment with the organization, its objectives, strategy, vision, mission, and sustainment of its long-term value;

▶ Commitment to and respectful engagement of project team members, including their compensation, access to opportunity, and fair treatment;

▶ Diligent oversight of organizational finances, materials, and other resources used within a project; and

▶ Understanding the appropriate use of authority, accountability, and responsibility, particularly in leadership positions.

Stewardship outside the organization includes responsibilities in areas such as:

▶ Environmental sustainability and the organization's use of materials and natural resources;

▶ Organization's relationship with external stakeholders such as its partners and channels;

▶ Impact of the organization or project on the market, social community, and regions in which it operates; and

▶ Advancing the state of practice in professional industries.

Stewardship reflects understanding and acceptance of trust as well as actions and decisions that engender and sustain that trust. Stewards also adhere to both implicit and explicit duties. These can include the following:

▶ **Integrity.** Stewards behave honestly and ethically in all engagements and communications. Stewards hold themselves to the highest standards and reflect the values, principles, and behaviors expected of those in their organization. Stewards serve as role models, building trust by living and demonstrating personal and organizational values in their engagements, work activities, and decisions. In the project management context, this duty often requires stewards to challenge team members, peers, and other stakeholders to consider their words and actions; and to be empathetic, self-reflective, and open to feedback.

▶ **Care.** Stewards are fiduciaries of the organizational matters in their charge, and they diligently oversee them. Higher-performing projects feature professionals who diligently oversee those matters, beyond the confines of strictly defined responsibilities. Stewards pay close attention and exercise the same level of care over those matters as they would for their personal matters. Care relates to the internal business affairs of the organization. Care for the environment, sustainable use of natural resources, and concern for the conditions of people across the planet should be reflected in the organizational policies and principles.

Projects bring about changes that may have unanticipated or unwanted consequences. Project practitioners should identify, analyze, and manage the potential downsides of project outcomes so that stakeholders are aware and informed.

Care includes creating a transparent working environment, open communication channels, and opportunities for stakeholders to raise concerns without penalty or fear of retribution.

- ▶ **Trustworthiness.** Stewards represent themselves, their roles, their project team, and their authority accurately, both inside and outside of the organization. This behavior allows people to understand the degree to which an individual can commit resources, make decisions, or approve something. Trustworthiness also entails individuals proactively identifying conflicts between their personal interests and those of their organization or clients. Such conflicts can undermine trust and confidence, result in unethical or illegal behaviors, create confusion, or contribute to suboptimal outcomes. Stewards protect projects from such breaches of trust.

- ▶ **Compliance.** Stewards comply with laws, rules, regulations, and requirements that are properly authorized within or outside of their organization. However, high-performing projects seek ways to integrate compliance more fully into the project culture, creating more alignment with diverse and potentially conflicting guidelines. Stewards strive for compliance with guidelines intended to protect them, their organization, their stakeholders, and the public at large. In instances where stewards face conflicting guidelines or questions regarding whether or not actions or plans align with established guidelines, stewards seek appropriate counsel and direction.

Stewardship requires leadership with transparency and trustworthiness. Projects affect the lives of the people who deliver them as well as those who are affected by the project deliverables and outcomes. Projects can have effects, such as easing traffic congestion, producing new medications, or creating opportunities for people to interact. Those effects can produce negative impacts and consequences, such as reduced green space, side effects from medications, or disclosure of personal information. Project teams and their organizational leaders carefully consider such factors and impacts so they can make responsible decisions by balancing organizational and project objectives with the larger needs and expectations of global stakeholders.

Increasingly, organizations are taking a holistic view to business that considers financial, technical, social, and environmental performance simultaneously instead of sequentially. Since the world is interconnected now more than ever and has finite resources and a shared environment, stewardship decisions have ramifications beyond the project.

3.2 CREATE A COLLABORATIVE PROJECT TEAM ENVIRONMENT

TEAM	

Project teams are made up of individuals who wield diverse skills, knowledge, and experience. Project teams that work collaboratively can accomplish a shared objective more effectively and efficiently than individuals working on their own.	▶ Projects are delivered by project teams.
	
	▶ Project teams work within organizational and professional cultures and guidelines, often establishing their own "local" culture.
	
	▶ A collaborative project team environment facilitates:
	  • Alignment with other organizational cultures and guidelines,
	  • Individual and team learning and development, and
	  • Optimal contributions to deliver desired outcomes.

Figure 3-3. Create a Collaborative Project Team Environment

Creating a collaborative project team environment involves multiple contributing factors, such as team agreements, structures, and processes. These factors support a culture that enables individuals to work together and provide synergistic effects from interactions.

- ▶ **Team agreements.** Team agreements represent a set of behavioral parameters and working norms established by the project team and upheld through individual and project team commitment. The team agreement should be created at the beginning of a project and will evolve over time as the project team continues to work together and identify norms and behaviors that are necessary in order to continue to work together successfully.

- ▶ **Organizational structures.** Project teams use, tailor, and implement structures that help coordinate the individual effort associated with project work. Organizational structures are any arrangement of or relation between the elements of project work and organizational processes.

  These structures can be based on roles, functions, or authority. They can be defined as being external to the project, tailored to fit the project context, or newly designed to meet a unique project need. An authority figure may formally impose a structure, or project team members may contribute to its design in alignment with organizational structures.

  Examples of organizational structures that can improve collaboration include, but are not limited to:

  - ▷ Definitions of roles and responsibilities,
  - ▷ Allocation of employees and vendors into project teams,
  - ▷ Formal committees tasked with a specific objective, and
  - ▷ Standing meetings that regularly review a given topic.

- ▶ **Processes.** Project teams define processes that enable completion of tasks and work assignments. For example, project teams may agree to a decomposition process using a work breakdown structure (WBS), backlog, or task board.

Project teams are influenced by the culture of the organizations involved in the project, the nature of the project, and the environment in which they operate. Within these influences, project teams establish their own team cultures. Project teams can tailor their structure to best accomplish the project objective.

By fostering inclusive and collaborative environments, knowledge and expertise are more freely exchanged, which in turn enable better project outcomes.

Clarity on roles and responsibilities can improve team cultures. Within project teams, specific tasks may be delegated to individuals or selected by project team members themselves. This includes the authority, accountability, and responsibility related to tasks:

▶ **Authority.** The condition of having the right, within a given context, to make relevant decisions, establish or improve procedures, apply project resources, expend funds, or give approvals. Authority is conferred from one entity to another, whether done explicitly or implicitly.

▶ **Accountability.** The condition of being answerable for an outcome. Accountability is not shared.

▶ **Responsibility.** The condition of being obligated to do or fulfill something. Responsibility can be shared.

Regardless of who is accountable or responsible for specific project work, a collaborative project team takes collective ownership of the project outcomes.

A diverse project team can enrich the project environment by bringing together different perspectives. The project team can be comprised of internal organizational staff, contracted contributors, volunteers, or external third parties. Additionally, some project team members join the project on a short-term basis to work on a specific deliverable while other members are assigned to the project on a longer-term basis. Integrating these individuals with a project team can challenge everyone involved. A team culture of respect allows for differences and finds ways to leverage them productively, encouraging effective conflict management.

Another aspect of a collaborative project team environment is the incorporation of practice standards, ethical codes, and other guidelines that are part of the professional work within the project team and the organization. Project teams consider how these guides can support their efforts to avoid possible conflict among the disciplines and the established guidelines they use.

A collaborative project team environment fosters the free exchange of information and individual knowledge. This, in turn, increases shared learning and individual development while delivering outcomes. A collaborative project team environment enables everyone to contribute their best efforts to deliver the desired outcomes for an organization. The organization, in turn, will benefit from deliverables and outcomes that respect and enhance its fundamental values, principles, and culture.

3.3 EFFECTIVELY ENGAGE WITH STAKEHOLDERS

STAKEHOLDERS

Engage stakeholders proactively and to the degree needed to contribute to project success and customer satisfaction.

- ▶ Stakeholders influence projects, performance, and outcomes.
- ▶ Project teams serve other stakeholders by engaging with them.
- ▶ Stakeholder engagement proactively advances value delivery.

Figure 3-4. Effectively Engage with Stakeholders

Stakeholders can be individuals, groups, or organizations that may affect, be affected by, or perceive themselves to be affected by a decision, activity, or outcome of a portfolio, program, or project. Stakeholders also directly or indirectly influence a project, its performance, or outcome in either a positive or negative way.

Stakeholders can affect many aspects of a project, including but not limited to:

▶ *Scope/requirements,* by revealing the need to add, adjust, or remove elements of the scope and/or project requirements;

▶ *Schedule,* by offering ideas to accelerate delivery or by slowing down or stop delivery of key project activities;

▶ *Cost,* by helping to reduce or eliminate planned expenditures or by adding steps, requirements, or restrictions that increase cost or require additional resources;

▶ *Project team,* by restricting or enabling access to people with the skills, knowledge, and experience needed to deliver the intended outcomes, and promote a learning culture;

▶ *Plans,* by providing information for plans or by advocating for changes to agreed activities and work;

▶ *Outcomes,* by enabling or blocking work required for the desired outcomes;

▶ *Culture,* by establishing or influencing—or even defining—the level and character of engagement of the project team and broader organization;

▶ *Benefits realization,* by generating and identifying long-term goals so that the project delivers the intended identified value;

▶ *Risk,* by defining the risk thresholds of the project, as well as participating in subsequent risk management activities;

▶ *Quality,* by identifying and requiring quality requirements; and

▶ *Success,* by defining success factors and participating in the evaluation of success.

Stakeholders may come and go throughout the life cycle of the project. Additionally, the degree of a stakeholder's interest, influence, or impact may change over time. Stakeholders, especially those with a high degree of influence and who have an unfavorable or neutral view about a project, need to be effectively engaged so that their interests, concerns, and rights are understood. The project team can then address these concerns through effective engagement and support leading to the probability of a successful project outcome.

Identifying, analyzing, and proactively engaging with stakeholders from the start to the end of the project helps to enable success.

Project teams are a group of stakeholders. This group of stakeholders engages other stakeholders to understand, consider, communicate, and respond to their interests, needs, and opinions.

Effective and efficient engagement and communication include determining how, when, how often, and under what circumstances stakeholders want to be—and should be—engaged. Communication is a key part of engagement; however, engagement delves deeper to include awareness of the ideas of others, assimilation of other perspectives, and collective shaping of a shared solution. Engagement includes building and maintaining solid relationships through frequent, two-way communication. It encourages collaboration through interactive meetings, face-to-face meetings, informal dialogue, and knowledge-sharing activities.

Stakeholder engagement relies heavily on interpersonal skills, including taking initiative, integrity, honesty, collaboration, respect, empathy, and confidence. These skills and attitudes can help everyone adapt to the work and to each other, increasing the likelihood of success.

Engagement helps project teams detect, collect, and evaluate information, data, and opinions. This creates shared understanding and alignment, which enables project outcomes. Additionally, these activities help the project team to tailor the project to identify, adjust, and respond to changing circumstances.

Project teams actively engage other stakeholders throughout the project to minimize potential negative impacts and maximize positive impacts. Stakeholder engagements also enable opportunities for stronger project performance and outcomes in addition to increasing stakeholder satisfaction. Finally, engaging other stakeholders helps the project team to find solutions that may be more acceptable to a broader range of stakeholders.

3.4 FOCUS ON VALUE

VALUE	
Continually evaluate and adjust project alignment to business objectives and intended benefits and value.	▶ Value is the ultimate indicator of project success. ▶ Value can be realized throughout the project, at the end of the project, or after the project is complete. ▶ Value, and the benefits that contribute to value, can be defined in quantitative and/or qualitative terms. ▶ A focus on outcomes allows project teams to support the intended benefits that lead to value creation. ▶ Project teams evaluate progress and adapt to maximize the expected value.

Figure 3-5. Focus on Value

Value, including outcomes from the perspective of the customer or end user, is the ultimate success indicator and driver of projects. Value focuses on the outcome of the deliverables. The value of a project may be expressed as a financial contribution to the sponsoring or receiving organization. Value may be a measure of public good achieved, for example, social benefit or the customer's perceived benefit from the project result. When the project is a component of a program, the project's contribution to program outcomes can represent value.

Many projects, though not all, are initiated based on a business case. Projects may be initiated due to any identified need to deliver or modify a process, product, or service, such as contracts, statements of work, or other documents. In all cases, the project intent is to provide the desired outcome that addresses the need with a valued solution. A business case can contain information about strategic alignment, assessment of risk exposure, economic feasibility study, return on investments, expected key performance measures, evaluations, and alternative approaches. The business case may state the intended value contribution of the project outcome in qualitative or quantitative terms, or both. A business case contains at least these supporting and interrelated elements:

The Standard for Project Management

- ▶ **Business need.** Business provides the rationale for the project, explaining why the project is undertaken. It originates with the preliminary business requirements, which are reflected in the project charter or other authorizing document. It provides details about the business goals and objectives. The business need may be intended for the performing organization, a client organization, a partnership of organizations, or public welfare. A clear statement of the business need helps the project team understand the business drivers for the future state and allows the project team to identify opportunities or problems to increase the potential value from the project outcome.

- ▶ **Project justification.** Project justification is connected to business need. It explains why the business need is worth the investment and why it should be addressed at this time. The project justification is accompanied by a cost-benefit analysis and assumptions.

- ▶ **Business strategy.** Business strategy is the reason for the project and all needs are related to the strategy to achieve the value.

Together, the business need, project justification, and business strategy, in addition to benefits and possible agreements, provide the project team with information that allows them to make informed decisions to meet or exceed the intended business value.

Desired outcomes should be clearly described, iteratively assessed, and updated throughout the project. During its life cycle, a project may undergo change and the project team then adapts in response. The project team continuously evaluates project progress and direction against the desired outputs, baselines, and business case to confirm that the project remains aligned to the need and will deliver its intended outcomes. Alternatively, the business case is updated to capture an opportunity or minimize a problem identified by the project team and other stakeholders. If the project or its stakeholders are no longer aligned with the business need or if the project seems unlikely to provide the intended value, the organization may choose to terminate the effort.

Value is the worth, importance, or usefulness of something. Value is subjective, in the sense that the same concept can have different values for different people and organizations. This occurs because what is considered a benefit depends on organizational strategies, ranging from short-term financial gains, long-term gains, and even nonfinancial elements. Because all projects have a range of stakeholders, different values generated for each group of stakeholders have to be considered and balanced with the whole, while placing a priority on the customer perspective.

Within the context of some projects, there may be different forms of value engineering that maximize value to the customer, to the performing organization, or other stakeholders. An example of this includes delivering the required functionality and level of quality with an acceptable risk exposure, while using as few resources as possible, and by avoiding waste. Sometimes, especially in adaptive projects that do not have a fixed, up-front scope, the project team can optimize value by working with the customer to determine which features are worth investment and which may not be valuable enough to be added to the output.

To support value realization from projects, project teams shift focus from deliverables to the intended outcomes. Doing so allows project teams to deliver on the vision or purpose of the project, rather than simply creating a specific deliverable. While the deliverable may support the intended project outcome, it may not fully achieve the vision or purpose of the project. For example, customers may want a specific software solution because they think that the solution resolves the business need for higher productivity. The software is the output of the project, but the software itself does not enable the productivity outcome that is intended. In this case, adding a new deliverable of training and coaching on the use of the software can enable a better productivity outcome. If the project's output fails to enable higher productivity, stakeholders may feel that the project has failed. Thus, project teams and other stakeholders understand both the deliverable and the intended outcome from the deliverable.

The value contribution of project work could be a short- or long-term measure. Because value contribution may be mixed with contributions from operational activities, it may be difficult to isolate. When the project is a component of a program, evaluation of value at the program level may also be necessary to properly direct the project. A reliable evaluation of value should consider the whole context and the entire life cycle of the project's output. While value is realized over time, effective processes can enable early benefit realization. With efficient and effective implementation, project teams may demonstrate or achieve such outcomes as prioritized delivery, better customer service, or an improved work environment. By working with organizational leaders who are responsible for putting project deliverables into use, project leaders can make sure that the deliverables are positioned to realize the planned outcomes.

3.5 RECOGNIZE, EVALUATE, AND RESPOND TO SYSTEM INTERACTIONS

SYSTEMS THINKING	
Recognize, evaluate, and respond to the dynamic circumstances within and surrounding the project in a holistic way to positively affect project performance.	▶ A project is a system of interdependent and interacting domains of activity. ▶ Systems thinking entails taking a holistic view of how project parts interact with each other and with external systems. ▶ Systems are constantly changing, requiring consistent attention to internal and external conditions. ▶ Being responsive to system interactions allows project teams to leverage positive outcomes.

Figure 3-6. Recognize, Evaluate, and Respond to System Interactions

A *system* is a set of interacting and interdependent components that function as a unified whole. Taking a holistic view, a project is a multifaceted entity that exists in dynamic circumstances, exhibiting the characteristics of a system. Project teams should acknowledge this holistic view of a project, seeing the project as a system with its own working parts.

A project works within other larger systems, and a project deliverable may become part of a larger system to realize benefits. For example, projects may be part of a program which, in turn, may also be part of a portfolio. These interconnected structures are known as a *system of systems*. Project teams balance inside/out and outside/in perspectives to support alignment across the system of systems.

The project may also have subsystems that are required to integrate effectively to deliver the intended outcome. For example, when individual project teams develop separate components of a deliverable, all components should integrate effectively. This requires project teams to interact and align subsystem work on a regular basis.

Systems thinking also considers timing elements of systems, such as what the project delivers or enables over time. For example, if project deliverables are released incrementally, each increment expands the cumulative outcomes or capabilities of previous versions. Project teams should think beyond the end of the project to the operational state of the project's deliverable, so that intended outcomes are realized.

As projects unfold, internal and external conditions are continuously changing. A single change can create several impacts. For example, on a large construction project, a change in requirements can cause contractual changes with the primary contractor, subcontractors, suppliers, or others. In turn, those changes can create an impact on project cost, schedule, scope, and performance. Subsequently, these changes could invoke a change control protocol for obtaining approvals from entities in external systems, such as the service providers, regulators, financiers, and government authorities.

While it is possible to predict some of the changes in advance, many of the changes that can impact the project during its life cycle emerge in real time. With systems thinking, including constant attention to internal and external conditions, the project team can navigate a wide spectrum of changes and impacts to keep the project in agreement with the relevant stakeholders.

Systems thinking also applies to how the project team views itself and its interactions within the project system. The project system often brings together a diverse project team engaged in working for a common objective. This diversity brings value to project teams, but they need to consider how to leverage those differences effectively, so that the project team works cohesively. For example, if a government agency contracts with a private company for development of a new technology, the development team may consist of project team members from both organizations. Those project team members may have assumptions, ways of working, and mental models related to how they function within their home organization. In this new project system, which combines the cultures of a private company and a government agency, the project team members can establish a synthesized team culture that creates a common vision, language, and toolset. This can help project team members to engage and contribute effectively and help to increase the probability that the project system works.

Because of the interactivity among systems, project teams should operate with awareness of, and vigilance toward, changing system dynamics. The following skills support a systems view of the project:

- Empathy with the business areas;

- Critical thinking with a big picture focus;

- Challenging of assumptions and mental models;

- Seeking external review and advice;

- Use of integrated methods, artifacts, and practices so there is a common understanding of project work, deliverables, and outcomes;

- Use of modeling and scenarios to envision how system dynamics may interact and react; and

- Proactive management of the integration to help achieve business outcomes.

Recognizing, evaluating, and responding to system interactions can lead to the following positive outcomes:

- Early consideration of uncertainty and risk within the project, exploration of alternatives, and consideration of unintended consequences;

- Ability to adjust assumptions and plans throughout the project life cycle;

- Provision of ongoing information and insights that inform planning and delivery;

- Clear communication of plans, progress, and projections to relevant stakeholders;

- Alignment of project goals and objectives to the customer organization's goals, objectives, and vision;

- Ability to adjust to the changing needs of the end user, sponsor, or customer of the project deliverables;

- Ability to see synergies and savings between aligned projects or initiatives;

- Ability to exploit opportunities not otherwise captured or see threats posed to or by other projects or initiatives;

- Clarity regarding the best project performance measurement and their influence on the behavior of the people involved in the project;

- Decisions that benefit the organization as a whole; and

- More comprehensive and informed identification of risks.

3.6 DEMONSTRATE LEADERSHIP BEHAVIORS

LEADERSHIP	
Demonstrate and adapt leadership behaviors to support individual and team needs.	▶ Effective leadership promotes project success and contributes to positive project outcomes.
	▶ Any project team member can demonstrate leadership behaviors.
	▶ Leadership is different than authority.
	▶ Effective leaders adapt their style to the situation.
	▶ Effective leaders recognize differences in motivation among project team members.
	▶ Leaders demonstrate desired behavior in areas of honesty, integrity, and ethical conduct.

Figure 3-7. Demonstrate Leadership Behaviors

Projects create a unique need for effective leadership. Unlike general business operations, where roles and responsibilities are often established and consistent, projects often involve multiple organizations, departments, functions, or vendors that do not interact on a regular basis. Moreover, projects may carry higher stakes and expectations than regular operational functions. As a result, a broader array of managers, executives, senior contributors, and other stakeholders attempt to influence a project. This often creates higher degrees of confusion and conflict. Consequently, higher-performing projects demonstrate effective leadership behaviors more frequently, and from more people than most projects.

A project environment that prioritizes vision, creativity, motivation, enthusiasm, encouragement, and empathy can support better outcomes. These traits are often associated with leadership. Leadership comprises the attitude, talent, character, and behaviors to influence individuals within and outside the project team toward the desired outcomes.

Leadership is not exclusive to any specific role. High-performing projects may feature multiple people exhibiting effective leadership skills, for example, the project manager, sponsors, stakeholders, senior management, or even project team members. Anyone working on a project can demonstrate effective leadership traits, styles, and skills to help the project team perform and deliver the required results.

It is important to note that more conflict and confusion can emerge when too many participants attempt to exert project influence in multiple, misaligned directions. However, higher-performing projects show a paradoxical combination of more influencers, each contributing more leadership skills in a complementary fashion. For example: if a sponsor articulates clear priorities, then a technical lead opens the discussion for delivery options, where individual contributors assert pros and cons until the project manager brings the conversation to a consensus strategy. Successful leadership enables someone to influence, motivate, direct, and coach people under any condition. It also incorporates characteristics derived from an organization's culture and practices.

Leadership should not be confused with *authority*, which is the position of control given to individuals within an organization to foster overall effective and efficient function. Authority is the right to exercise power. Authority is usually delegated to a person by formal means such as a charter document or designated title. This person may then have a role or position description that indicates their authority. Authority denotes accountability for certain activities, actions of individuals, or decision making in certain circumstances. While individuals may use their authority to influence, motivate, direct others, or act when others do not perform or act as directed or requested, this is not the same as leadership. For example, organizational executives may grant someone the authority to form a project team to deliver an outcome. However, authority alone is insufficient. It takes leadership to motivate a group toward a common goal, influence them to align their individual interests in favor of collective effort, and achieve success as a project team rather than as individuals.

Effective leadership draws from or combines elements of various styles of leadership. Documented leadership styles range from autocratic, democratic, laissez-faire, directive, participative, assertive, supportive, and autocratic to consensus. Of all these, no single leadership style has proven to be the universally best or recommended approach. Instead, effective leadership is shown when it best fits a given situation. For example:

- In moments of chaos, directive action creates more clarity and momentum than collaborative problem solving.

- For environments with highly competent and engaged staff, empowered delegation elicits more productivity than centralized coordination.

When senior managers suffer conflict over priorities, neutral facilitation helps more than detailed recommendations. Effective leadership skill is grown. It can be learned and developed so that it becomes a professional asset to the individual, as well as a benefit to the project and its stakeholders. High-performing projects show a pervasive pattern of continuous improvement down to the personal level. A project team member deepens leadership acumen by adding or practicing a combination of various skills or techniques, including but not limited to:

- ▶ Focusing a project team around agreed goals,
- ▶ Articulating a motivating vision for the project outcomes,
- ▶ Seeking resources and support for the project,
- ▶ Generating consensus on the best way forward,
- ▶ Overcoming obstacles to project progress,
- ▶ Negotiating and resolving conflict within the project team and between the project team and other stakeholders,
- ▶ Adapting communication style and messaging so that they are relevant to the audience,
- ▶ Coaching and mentoring fellow project team members,
- ▶ Appreciating and rewarding positive behaviors and contributions,
- ▶ Providing opportunities for skill growth and development,
- ▶ Facilitating collaborative decision making,
- ▶ Employing effective conversations and active listening,
- ▶ Empowering project team members and delegating responsibilities to them,
- ▶ Building a cohesive project team that takes responsibility,
- ▶ Showing empathy for project team and stakeholder perspectives,
- ▶ Having self-awareness of one's own bias and behaviors,
- ▶ Managing and adapting to change during the project life cycle,
- ▶ Facilitating a fail-fast/learn quickly mindset by acknowledging mistakes, and
- ▶ Role modeling of desired behaviors.

Personal character matters in a leader. A person may have strong ability in leadership skills but then have their influence undermined by the perception of being self-serving or untrustworthy. Effective leaders seek to be a role model in areas of honesty, integrity, and ethical conduct. Effective leaders focus on being transparent, behave unselfishly, and are able to ask for help. Effective leaders understand that project team members scrutinize and emulate the values, ethics, and behaviors that leaders exhibit. Therefore, leaders have an additional responsibility to demonstrate expected behaviors through their actions.

Projects work best when leaders understand what motivates people. Project teams can thrive when project team members use appropriate leadership traits, skills, and characteristics that match the specific needs and expectations of stakeholders. Knowing how to best communicate with or motivate people, or take action when required, can help improve project team performance and manage obstacles to project success. When practiced by more than one person on a project, leadership can foster shared responsibility toward the project goal, which in turn can foster a healthy and vibrant environment. Motivators include such forces as finances, recognition, autonomy, compelling purpose, growth opportunity, and personal contribution.

Effective leadership promotes project success and contributes to positive project outcomes. Project teams, individual project team members, and other stakeholders are engaged throughout a well-led project. Each project team member can focus on delivering results using a common vision and working toward shared outcomes. Effective leadership is essential in helping project teams maintain an ethical and adaptable environment.

Additionally, business obligations can be fulfilled based on delegated responsibility and authority. Shared leadership does not undermine or diminish the role or authority of a leader designated by the organization, nor does it diminish the need for that leader to apply the right leadership style and skills at the right time.

By blending styles, continuing skill growth, and leveraging motivators, any project team member or stakeholder can motivate, influence, coach, and grow the project team, regardless of role or position.

3.7 TAILOR BASED ON CONTEXT

TAILORING	
Design the project development approach based on the context of the project, its objectives, stakeholders, governance, and the environment using "just enough" process to achieve the desired outcome while maximizing value, managing cost, and enhancing speed.	▶ Each project is unique. ▶ Project success is based on adapting to the unique context of the project to determine the most appropriate methods of producing the desired outcomes. ▶ Tailoring the approach is iterative, and therefore is a continuous process throughout the project.

Figure 3-8. Tailor Based on Context

Adapting to the unique objectives, stakeholders, and complexity of the environment contributes to project success. Tailoring is the deliberate adaptation of approach, governance, and processes to make them more suitable for the given environment and the work at hand. Project teams tailor the appropriate framework that will enable the flexibility to consistently produce positive outcomes within the context of the life cycle of the project. The business environment, team size, degree of uncertainty, and complexity of the project all factor into how project systems are tailored. Project systems can be tailored with a holistic perspective, including the consideration of interrelated complexities. Tailoring aims to maximize value, manage constraints, and improve performance by using "just enough" processes, methods, templates, and artifacts to achieve the desired outcome from the project.

Together with the PMO and considering governance, project teams discuss and decide on the delivery approach and resources required for producing outcomes on a project-by-project basis. This includes the selection of the processes to use, development approach, methods, and artifacts needed to deliver the project outcomes. Tailoring decisions can be an implicit action of accepting an established methodology. Conversely, tailoring can be an explicit action of selecting and mixing specific elements to suit the unique characteristics of the project and the project environment. Tailoring is necessary to some degree in every project, because each project exists in a particular context.

Projects are often unique, even when the deliverable of the project does not seem unique. This is because project contexts differ in that the organization, its customers, its channels, and its environment are dynamic elements. Those changes and ongoing learning may cause project teams to use or develop different methods or approaches in pursuit of success. The project team should examine the unique set of conditions for each project, so that they can determine the most appropriate methods of producing the desired outcomes.

An existing methodology or common way of working can inform the way in which a project is tailored. A methodology is a system of practices, techniques, procedures, and rules used by those who work in a discipline. Project teams may be required to assume the methodology of the parent organization. That is, the project team adopts a system of processes, governance, methods, and templates that provide guidance on how to run the project. While this provides a degree of consistency to projects within an organization, the methodology itself may still need tailoring to suit each project. Organizational policies and procedures prescribe authorized boundaries within which the project team can tailor.

Project teams can also factor in the time and cost of project management processes. Processes that are not tailored may add little value to the project or its outcomes while increasing cost and lengthening schedule. Tailoring the approach along with appropriate processes, methods, and artifacts can help project teams make decisions about process-related costs and the related value contribution to project outcomes.

In addition to deciding on how to tailor an approach, project teams communicate the tailoring decisions to stakeholders associated with that approach. Each member of the project team is aware of the chosen methods and processes that relate to those stakeholders and their role.

Tailoring the project approach to suit the unique characteristics of the project and its environment can contribute to a higher level of project performance and an increased probability of success. A tailored project approach can produce direct and indirect benefits to organizations, such as:

▶ Deeper commitment from project team members because they took part in defining the approach,

▶ Reduction in waste in terms of actions or resources,

▶ Customer-oriented focus, as the needs of the customer and other stakeholders are an important influencing factor in the tailoring of the project, and

▶ More efficient use of project resources, as project teams are conscious of the weight of project processes.

Tailoring projects can lead to the following positive outcomes:

▶ Increased innovation, efficiency, and productivity;

▶ Lessons learned, so that improvements from a specific delivery approach can be shared and applied to the next round of work or future projects;

▶ Further improvement of an organization's methodology, with new practices, methods, and artifacts;

▶ Discovery of improved outcomes, processes, or methods through experimentation;

▶ Effective integration within multidisciplinary project teams of methods and practices used to deliver project results; and

▶ Increased adaptability for the organization in the long term.

Tailoring an approach is iterative in nature, and therefore is a constant process itself during the project life cycle. Project teams collect feedback from all stakeholders on how the methods and tailored processes are working for them as the project progresses to evaluate their effectiveness and add value to the organization.

3.8 BUILD QUALITY INTO PROCESSES AND DELIVERABLES

<table>
<tr><td colspan="2">**QUALITY**</td></tr>
<tr>
<td>Maintain a focus on quality that produces deliverables that meet project objectives and align to the needs, uses, and acceptance requirements set forth by relevant stakeholders.</td>
<td>
▶ Project quality entails satisfying stakeholders' expectations and fulfilling project and product requirements.

▶ Quality focuses on meeting acceptance criteria for deliverables.

▶ Project quality entails ensuring project processes are appropriate and as effective as possible.
</td>
</tr>
</table>

Figure 3-9. Build Quality into Processes and Deliverables

Quality is the degree to which a set of inherent characteristics of a product, service, or result fulfills the requirements. Quality includes the ability to satisfy the customer's stated or implied needs. The product, service, or result of a project (referred to here as deliverables) is measured for the quality of both the conformance to acceptance criteria and fitness for use.

Quality may have several different dimensions, including but not limited to the following:

▶ **Performance.** Does the deliverable function as the project team and other stakeholders intended?

▶ **Conformity.** Is the deliverable fit for use, and does it meet the specifications?

▶ **Reliability.** Does the deliverable produce consistent metrics each time it is performed or produced?

▶ **Resilience.** Is the deliverable able to cope with unforeseen failures and quickly recover?

▶ **Satisfaction.** Does the deliverable elicit positive feedback from end users? This includes usability and user experience?

▶ **Uniformity.** Does the deliverable show parity with other deliverables produced in the same manner?

▶ **Efficiency.** Does the deliverable produce the greatest output with the least amount of inputs and effort?

▶ **Sustainability.** Does the deliverable produce a positive impact on economic, social, and environmental parameters?

Project teams measure quality using metrics and acceptance criteria based on requirements. A requirement is a condition or capability that is necessary to be present in a product, service, or result to satisfy a need. Requirements, either explicit or implicit, may come from stakeholders, a contract, organizational policies, standards, or regulatory bodies, or a combination of these. Quality is closely linked to the product acceptance criteria, as described in the statement of work or other design documents. These criteria should be updated as experimentation and prioritization occur and validated as part of the acceptance process.

Quality is also relevant to the project approaches and activities used to produce the project's deliverables. While project teams evaluate the quality of a deliverable through inspection and testing, project activities and processes are assessed through reviews and audits. In both instances, quality activities may focus on detection and prevention of errors and defects.

The objective of quality activities is to help ensure that what is delivered meets the objectives of the customer and other relevant stakeholders in the most straightforward path. The intention is to minimize the waste of resources and maximize the probability of attaining the desired outcome. This results in:

- ▶ Moving the deliverables to the point of delivery quickly, and
- ▶ Preventing defects in the deliverables or identifying them early to avoid or reduce the need for rework and scrap.

The objective of quality activities is the same whether dealing with an up-front, well-defined set of requirements or a set of requirements that are progressively elaborated and incrementally delivered.

Quality management processes and practices help produce deliverables and outcomes that meet project objectives and align to the expectations, uses, and acceptance criteria expressed by the organization and relevant stakeholders. Close attention to quality in project processes and deliverables creates positive outcomes, including:

- ▶ Project deliverables that are fit for purpose, as defined by acceptance criteria,
- ▶ Project deliverables that meet stakeholder expectations and business objectives,
- ▶ Project deliverables with minimal or no defects,
- ▶ Timely or expedited delivery,
- ▶ Enhanced cost control,
- ▶ Increased quality of product delivery,
- ▶ Reduced rework and scrap,
- ▶ Reduced customer complaints,
- ▶ Good supply chain integration,
- ▶ Improved productivity,
- ▶ Increased project team morale and satisfaction,
- ▶ Robust service delivery,
- ▶ Improved decision making, and
- ▶ Continually improved processes.

3.9 NAVIGATE COMPLEXITY

COMPLEXITY

Continually evaluate and navigate project complexity so that approaches and plans enable the project team to successfully navigate the project life cycle.

▶ Complexity is the result of human behavior, system interactions, uncertainty, and ambiguity.

▶ Complexity can emerge at any point during the project.

▶ Complexity can be introduced by events or conditions that affect value, scope, communications, stakeholders, risk, and technological innovation.

▶ Project teams can stay vigilant in identifying elements of complexity and use a variety of methods to reduce the amount or impact of complexity.

Figure 3-10. Navigate Complexity

A project is a system of elements that interact with each other. Complexity is a characteristic of a project or its environment that is difficult to manage due to human behavior, system behavior, and ambiguity. The nature and number of the interactions determine the degree of complexity in a project. Complexity emerges from project elements, interactions between project elements, and interactions with other systems and the project environment. Though complexity cannot be controlled, project teams can modify their activities to address impacts that occur as a result of complexity.

Project teams often cannot foresee complexity emerging because it is the result of many interactions such as risks, dependencies, events, or relationships. Alternatively, a few causes may converge to produce a single complex effect, which makes isolating a specific cause of complexity difficult.

Project complexity occurs as the result of individual elements within the project and project system as a whole. For example, complexity within a project may be amplified with a greater number or diversity of stakeholders, such as regulatory agencies, international financial institutions, multiple vendors, numerous specialty subcontractors, or local communities. These stakeholders can have a significant impact on the complexity of a project, both individually and collectively.

Some of the more common sources of complexity are:

▶ **Human behavior.** Human behavior is the interplay of conduct, demeanors, attitudes, and experience of people. Human behavior can also contribute to complexity by introducing elements of subjectivity such as personal agendas that conflict with the project's goals and objectives. Stakeholders located in remote locations may have different time zones, speak different languages, and have different cultural norms.

▶ **System behavior.** System behavior is the result of dynamic interdependencies within and among project elements. For example, the integration of different technology systems may cause threats that could impact project outcomes and success. The interactions among components of the project system may lead to interconnected risk, create emerging or unforeseeable issues, and produce unclear and disproportional cause-and-effect relationships.

▶ **Uncertainty and ambiguity.** *Ambiguity* is a state of being unclear, of not knowing what to expect or how to comprehend a situation. Ambiguity can arise from having many options or a lack of clarity on the optimal choice. Unclear or misleading events, emerging issues, or subjective situations can also lead to ambiguity.

Uncertainty is the lack of understanding and awareness of issues, events, paths to follow, or solutions to pursue. Uncertainty deals with the probabilities of alternative actions, reactions, and outcomes. Uncertainty includes unknown unknowns and black swans, which are emerging factors that are completely outside of existing knowledge or experience.

Within a complex environment, uncertainty and ambiguity can combine to blur causal relationships to the point where probabilities and impacts are ill defined. It becomes difficult to reduce uncertainty and ambiguity to the point where relationships can be well defined and therefore addressed effectively.

▶ **Technological innovation.** Technological innovation can cause disruption to products, services, ways of working, processes, tools, techniques, procedures, and more. The introduction of desktop computing and social media are examples of technological innovations that have fundamentally changed the way project work is performed. New technology, along with the uncertainty of how that technology will be used, contributes to complexity. Innovation has the potential to help move projects toward a solution, or to disrupt the project when associated uncertainties are not defined, leading to increased complexity.

Complexity may emerge and impact the project in any area and at any point in the project life cycle. Project teams can identify elements of complexity throughout the project by continually looking at the project component as well as the project as a whole for signs of complexity. Knowledge of systems thinking, complex adaptive systems, experience from past project work, experimentation, and continuous learning related to system interaction leads to the project team's increased ability to navigate complexity when it emerges. Being vigilant for indications of complexity allows project teams to adapt their approaches and plans to navigate potential disruption to effective project delivery.

3.10 OPTIMIZE RISK RESPONSES

RISK	
Continually evaluate exposure to risk, both opportunities and threats, to maximize positive impacts and minimize negative impacts to the project and its outcomes.	▶ Individual and overall risks can impact projects.
	▶ Risks can be positive (opportunities) or negative (threats).
	▶ Risks are addressed continually throughout the project.
	▶ An organization's risk attitude, appetite, and threshold influence how risk is addressed.
	▶ Risk responses should be: • Appropriate for the significance of the risk, • Cost effective, • Realistic within the project context, • Agreed to by relevant stakeholders, and • Owned by a responsible person.

Figure 3-11. Optimize Risk Responses

A *risk* is an uncertain event or condition that, if it occurs, can have a positive or negative effect on one or more objectives. Identified risks may or may not materialize in a project. Project teams endeavor to identify and evaluate known and emergent risks, both internal and external to the project, throughout the life cycle.

Project teams seek to maximize positive risks (opportunities) and decrease exposure to negative risks (threats). Threats may result in issues such as delay, cost overrun, technical failure, performance shortfall, or loss of reputation. Opportunities can lead to benefits such as reduced time and cost, improved performance, increased market share, or enhanced reputation.

Project teams also monitor the overall project risk. Overall project risk is the effect of uncertainty on the project as a whole. Overall risk arises from all sources of uncertainty, including individual risks, and represents the exposure of the stakeholders to the implications of variations in project outcome, both positive and negative. Management of overall project risk aims to keep project risk exposure within an acceptable range. Management strategies include reducing drivers of threats, promoting drivers of opportunities, and maximizing the probability of achieving overall project objectives.

Project team members engage with relevant stakeholders to understand their risk appetite and risk thresholds. *Risk appetite* describes the degree of uncertainty an organization or individual is willing to accept in anticipation of a reward. *Risk threshold* is the measure of acceptable variation around an objective that reflects the risk appetite of the organization and stakeholders. The risk threshold reflects the risk appetite. Therefore, a risk threshold of ±5% around a cost objective reflects a lower risk appetite than a risk threshold of ±10%. The risk appetite and risk threshold inform how the project team navigates risk in a project.

Effective and appropriate risk responses can reduce individual and overall project threats and increase individual and overall opportunities. Project teams should consistently identify potential risk responses with the following characteristics in mind:

▶ Appropriate and timely to the significance of the risk,

▶ Cost effective,

▶ Realistic within the project context,

▶ Agreed to by relevant stakeholders, and

▶ Owned by a responsible person.

Risks can exist within the enterprise, portfolio, program, project, and product. The project may be a component of a program in which the risk can potentially enhance or diminish benefits realization and, therefore, value. The project may be a component of a portfolio of related or unrelated work in which the risk can potentially enhance or diminish overall value of the portfolio and realization of business objectives.

Organizations and project teams that employ consistent risk evaluation, planning, and proactive risk implementation often find the effort to be less costly than reacting to issues when the risk materializes.

More information on risk management may be found in *The Standard for Risk Management in Portfolios, Programs, and Projects* [3].

3.11 EMBRACE ADAPTABILITY AND RESILIENCY

ADAPTABILITY AND RESILIENCY

Build adaptability and resiliency into the organization's and project team's approaches to help the project accommodate change, recover from setbacks, and advance the work of the project.

▶ Adaptability is the ability to respond to changing conditions.

▶ Resiliency is the ability to absorb impacts and to recover quickly from a setback or failure.

▶ A focus on outcomes rather than outputs facilitates adaptability.

Figure 3-12. Embrace Adaptability and Resiliency

Most projects encounter challenges or obstacles at some stage. The combined attributes of adaptability and resiliency in the project team's approach to a project help the project accommodate impacts and thrive. *Adaptability* refers to the ability to respond to changing conditions. *Resiliency* consists of two complementary traits: the ability to absorb impacts and the ability to recover quickly from a setback or failure. Both adaptability and resiliency are helpful characteristics for anyone working on projects.

A project rarely performs exactly as initially planned. Projects are influenced by internal and external factors—new requirements, issues, stakeholder influences, among other factors—which exist in a system of interactions. Some elements within a project may fail or fall short of expectations, requiring the project team to regroup, rethink, and replan. On an infrastructure project, for example, a court decision during project execution could change the designs and plans. In a technology project, a computerized model of the technology might show that the components work together properly, but the real-world application fails. In both cases, the project team will need to address the situation in order to move the project forward. The view that projects should hold firm to plans and commitments made during the early stages, even after new or unforeseen factors emerge, is not beneficial to stakeholders, including customers and end users, as this limits the potential for generating value. However, adapting should be done with a holistic view, such as a proper change control process, to avoid problems such as scope creep. In a project environment, capabilities that support adaptability and resilience include:

- Short feedback loops to adapt quickly;
- Continuous learning and improvement;
- Project teams with broad skill sets, coupled with individuals having extensive knowledge in each required skill area;
- Regular inspection and adaptation of project work to identify improvement opportunities;
- Diverse project teams to capture a broad range of experiences;
- Open and transparent planning that engages internal and external stakeholders;
- Small-scale prototypes and experiments to test ideas and try new approaches;
- Ability to leverage new ways of thinking and working;
- Process design that balances velocity of work and stability of requirements;
- Open organizational conversations;
- Diverse project teams with broad skill sets, cultures, and experience, coupled with subject matter experts in each required skill area;
- Understanding from past learning of the same or similar endeavors;

- ▶ Ability and willingness to anticipate multiple potential scenarios and prepare for multiple eventualities;

- ▶ Deferring decision making to the last responsible moment;

- ▶ Management support; and

- ▶ Open-ended design that balances speed and stability.

Envisioning outcomes rather than deliverables can enable solutions, harnessing a better result than the one originally planned. For example, a project team may find an alternative solution that would provide stronger outcomes than the original defined deliverable. While exploration of alternatives is usually the purview of the business case, technologies and other capabilities are evolving so rapidly that a solution could emerge at any time between completion of the business case and project closure. Opportunities for adaptation may emerge during a project, at which time the project team should make a case to the project sponsor, product owner, or customer for capturing the opportunity. Depending on the type of contract, the customer's approval may be needed for some of the changes that result from the adaptation. The project team should be prepared to adapt its plans and activities to take advantage of the opportunity, with the support of the project sponsor, product owner, or customer.

Unexpected changes and circumstances in a project system can also present opportunities. To optimize value delivery, project teams should use problem solving as well as a holistic-thinking approach to changes and unplanned events. When an unplanned event occurs, project teams should look for potential positive outcomes that might be gained. For example, incorporating a change that occurs late in a project time line could add competitive advantage by being the first product in the market to offer the feature.

Building adaptability and resiliency in a project keeps project teams focused on the desired outcome when internal and external factors change, and it helps them recover from setbacks. These characteristics also help project teams learn and improve so that they can quickly recover from failures or setbacks and continue making progress toward delivering value.

3.12 ENABLE CHANGE TO ACHIEVE THE ENVISIONED FUTURE STATE

CHANGE	
Prepare those impacted for the adoption and sustainment of new and different behaviors and processes required for the transition from the current state to the intended future state created by the project outcomes.	▶ A structured approach to change helps individuals, groups, and the organization transition from the current state to a future desired state. ▶ Change can originate from internal influences or external sources. ▶ Enabling change can be challenging as not all stakeholders embrace change. ▶ Attempting too much change in a short time can lead to change fatigue and/or resistance. ▶ Stakeholder engagement and motivational approaches assist in change adoption.

Figure 3-13. Enable Change to Achieve the Envisioned Future State

Remaining relevant in today's business environment is a fundamental challenge for all organizations. Relevance entails being responsive to stakeholder needs and desires. This requires continually evaluating offerings for the benefit of stakeholders, rapidly responding to changes, and acting as agents for change. Project managers are uniquely poised to keep an organization prepared for changes. Projects, by their very definition, create something new: they are agents of change.

Change management, or enablement, is a comprehensive, cyclic, and structured approach for transitioning individuals, groups, and organizations from a current state to a future state in which they realize desired benefits. It is different from project change control, which is a process whereby modifications to documents, deliverables, or baselines associated with the project are identified and documented, and then are approved or rejected.

Change in an organization can originate from internal sources, such as the need for a new capability or in response to a performance gap. Change can also originate from external sources such as technological advances, demographic changes, or socioeconomic pressures. Any type of change involves some level of adaptability or assimilation by the group experiencing the change as well as the industries with which the group interacts.

Change may be implemented by and have consequences for stakeholders. Enabling stakeholder change is part of facilitating the project to provide the required deliverable as well as the intended outcome.

Enabling change in an organization can be challenging. Some people may seem inherently resistant to change or risk averse, and environments may display a conservative culture, among other reasons. Effective change management uses a motivational strategy rather than a forceful one. Engagement and two-way communication create an environment in which adoption and assimilation of change can occur or identify some valid concerns from the resistant users that may need to be addressed.

Project team members and project managers can work with relevant stakeholders to address resistance, fatigue, and change absorption to increase the probability that change will be adopted or assimilated successfully by customers or recipients of project deliverables. This includes communicating the vision and goals associated with the change early in the project to achieve buy-in for the change. The benefits of the change and the impact on work processes should be communicated to all levels of the organization throughout the project.

It is also important to adapt the speed of change to the change appetite, cost, and ability of the stakeholders and the environment to assimilate change. Attempting to create too many changes in too short a time can lead to resistance because of change saturation. Even when stakeholders unanimously agree that change will produce more value or enhance outcomes, they often still have difficulty working through the actions that will deliver enhanced benefits. To foster benefits realization, the project may also include activities to reinforce the change after its implementation in order to avoid people returning to the initial state.

Recognizing and addressing the needs of stakeholders to embrace change throughout the project life cycle helps to integrate the resulting change in the project work, making a successful outcome more likely.

More information on organizational change management may be found in *Managing Change in Organizations: A Practice Guide* [4].

REFERENCES

[1] Project Management Institute. 2016. *PMI Lexicon of Project Management Terms.* Available from http://www.pmi.org/lexiconterms

[2] Project Management Institute. 2006. *PMI Code of Ethics and Professional Conduct.* Available from http://www.pmi.org/codeofethics

[3] Project Management Institute. 2019. *The Standard for Risk Management in Portfolios, Programs, and Projects.* Newtown Square, PA: Author.

[4] Project Management Institute. 2013. *Managing Change in Organizations: A Practice Guide.* Newtown Square, PA: Author.

H

High-performing projects, 42
Holistic thinking approach, 57
Holistic view, 27, 37, 44, 56
Human behavior, 51
Hybrid environments
    direction, insight and, 15
    feedback and, 14

I

Improvement, continuous, 42
Industry standards, 18
Influence
    leadership and, 41
    stakeholders and, 31, 32
Information flow, value delivery system, 11
Information technology software, 17
Infrastructure, 17
Innovation
    facilitation of, 16
    technological, 51
Insights
    business direction and, 15
    contributing, 14
Inspection, 48, 56
Integrity, 26
Internal environment, 16–17
Interpersonal skills
    stakeholder engagement and, 33

K

Key concepts, 4–5
Key terms, 4–5
Knowledge assets, 17

L

Leadership.
    authority contrasted with, 41
    character and, 43
    motivation and, 43
    shared, 43
    styles and, 41

Leadership behaviors, principle, 40–43
    authority contrasted with, 41
    motivators and, 43
    neutral facilitation and, 42
    personal character and, 43
    styles of leadership, 41
Leadership skills and techniques, 42

M

Management. *See also* Product management;
    Program management; Project management
    change, 58
    risk, 32
    supply chain, 8
Manager(s). *See also* Project manager
Methodology, definition, 45
Monitoring
    project risk and, 54
Motivation
    change management and, 59
    leadership and, 43

N

Navigate complexity, principle, 50
Negative risks (threats), 53

O

Objectives
    feedback and, 13–14
Opportunities
    adaptation and, 57
    identification of, 16
    maximizing, 53, 54
Organization(s)
    definition, 7
Organizational culture, 17
Organizational governance
    systems, 12
Organizational structure(s)
    collaborative project team environment and, 29

A GUIDE TO THE PROJECT MANAGEMENT BODY OF KNOWLEDGE

(PMBOK® GUIDE)

Introduction

1

This section describes important information about *A Guide to the Project Management Body of Knowledge (PMBOK® Guide)* – Seventh Edition. It describes the relationship of the *PMBOK® Guide* to *The Standard for Project Management* [1],[1] changes to the *PMBOK® Guide*, the relationship to PMIstandards+™ (PMI's digital platform for standards), and provides a brief overview of the content.

1.1 STRUCTURE OF THE *PMBOK® GUIDE*

In addition to this Introduction, this edition of the *PMBOK® Guide* contains three sections:

▶ **Section 2 Project Performance Domains.** This section identifies and describes eight project performance domains that form an integrated system to enable successful delivery of the project and intended outcomes.

▶ **Section 3 Tailoring.** This section describes what tailoring is and presents an overview of what to tailor and how to go about tailoring individual projects.

▶ **Section 4 Models, Methods, and Artifacts.** This section presents a brief description of commonly used models, methods, and artifacts. These models, methods, and artifacts illustrate the range of options project teams can use to produce deliverables, organize work, and enable communication and collaboration.

---

[1] The numbers in brackets refer to the list of references at the end of the *PMBOK® Guide*.

1.2 RELATIONSHIP OF THE *PMBOK® GUIDE* AND *THE STANDARD FOR PROJECT MANAGEMENT*

Work in the project performance domains is guided by the principles of project management. As described in *The Standard for Project Management* [1], a principle is a fundamental norm, truth, or value. The principles for project management provide guidance for the behavior of people involved in projects as they influence and shape the performance domains to produce the intended outcomes. While there is conceptual overlap between the principles and the performance domains, the principles guide behavior, while the performance domains present broad areas of focus in which to demonstrate that behavior. Figure 1-1 shows how the project management principles sit above the performance domains, providing guidance to activities in each performance domain.

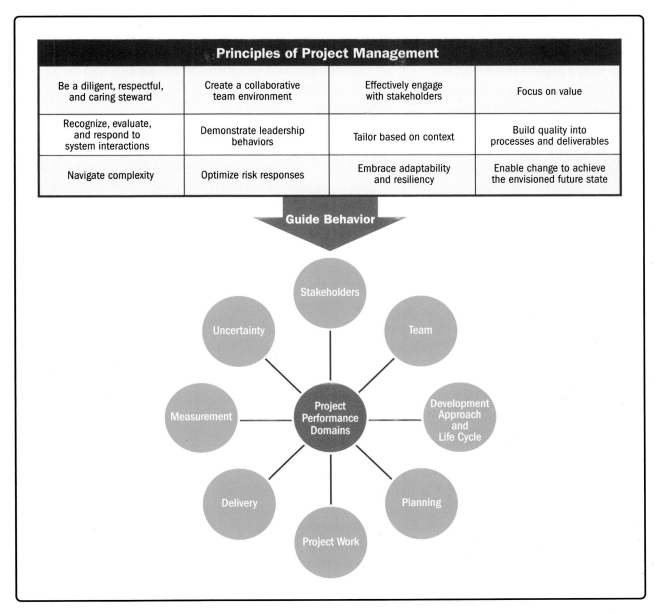

Figure 1-1. Relationship between Project Management Principles and Project Performance Domains

1.3 CHANGES TO THE *PMBOK® GUIDE*

This edition of the *PMBOK® Guide* focuses on delivering outcomes regardless of the approach used by the project team. However, project practitioners using the *PMBOK® Guide* also benefit from some level of understanding of how to deliver projects.

This edition is very different from the inputs, tools/techniques, and outputs (ITTOs) from previous editions of the *PMBOK® Guide*. In the previous editions, the ITTOs supported implementation of various processes used in project management. The shift from a process-based standard to one based on principles necessitates a different approach for thinking about the various aspects of project management. Thus, the project performance domains represent a group of related activities that are critical for the effective delivery of project outcomes. There are eight project performance domains in this guide.

Tailoring is the deliberate adaptation of the project management approach, governance, and processes to make them more suitable for the given environment and the work at hand. The tailoring process is driven by the guiding project management principles, organizational values, and organizational culture.

In embracing the full spectrum of project approaches, this edition of the *PMBOK® Guide* recognizes that no publication can capture every tool, technique, or practice that project teams might use. Therefore, this edition presents an array of commonly used models, methods, and artifacts that project practitioners can use to accomplish their work.

1.4 RELATIONSHIP TO PMIstandards+

Information in this guide is further elaborated on PMIstandards+, PMI's digital content platform. The digital platform encompasses current and emerging practices and other useful information related to PMI's library of standards products. It also includes practical examples of application within various contexts and industry segments. PMIstandards+ evolved in response to advances and changes in how projects can be delivered. It offers a dynamic body of knowledge with real-time access and in-depth information that is aligned to PMI standards and carefully vetted by a panel of subject matter experts representing a wide range of expertise.

2

Project Performance Domains

A project performance domain is a group of related activities that are critical for the effective delivery of project outcomes. Project performance domains are interactive, interrelated, and interdependent areas of focus that work in unison to achieve desired project outcomes. There are eight project performance domains:

- ▶ Stakeholders,
- ▶ Team,
- ▶ Development Approach and Life Cycle,
- ▶ Planning,
- ▶ Project Work,
- ▶ Delivery,
- ▶ Measurement, and
- ▶ Uncertainty.

Together the performance domains form a unified whole. In this way, the performance domains operate as an integrated system, with each performance domain being interdependent of the other performance domains to enable successful delivery of the project and its intended outcomes.

Performance domains run concurrently throughout the project, regardless of how value is delivered (frequently, periodically, or at the end of the project). For example, project leads spend time focused on stakeholders, the project team, the project life cycle, the project work, and so forth, from the outset of the project to its closure. These areas of focus are not addressed as siloed efforts because they overlap and interconnect. The ways in which the performance domains relate are different for each project, but they are present in every project.

The specific activities undertaken within each of the performance domains are determined by the context of the organization, the project, deliverables, the project team, stakeholders, and other factors. The performance domains are presented in the following sections without specific weighting or order.

2.1 STAKEHOLDER PERFORMANCE DOMAIN

STAKEHOLDER PERFORMANCE DOMAIN

The Stakeholder Performance Domain addresses activities and functions associated with stakeholders.

Effective execution of this performance domain results in the following desired outcomes:

▶ A productive working relationship with stakeholders throughout the project.

▶ Stakeholder agreement with project objectives.

▶ Stakeholders who are project beneficiaries are supportive and satisfied while stakeholders who may oppose the project or its deliverables do not negatively impact project outcomes.

Figure 2-1. Stakeholder Performance Domain

The following definitions are relevant to the Stakeholder Performance Domain:

Stakeholder. An individual, group, or organization that may affect, be affected by, or perceive itself to be affected by a decision, activity, or outcome of a project, program, or portfolio.

Stakeholder Analysis. A method of systematically gathering and analyzing quantitative and qualitative information to determine whose interests should be taken into account throughout the project.

Projects are performed by people and for people. This performance domain entails working with stakeholders to maintain alignment and engaging with them to foster positive relationships and satisfaction.

Stakeholders include individuals, groups, and organizations (see Figure 2-2). A project can have a small group of stakeholders or potentially millions of stakeholders. There may be different stakeholders in different phases of the project, and the influence, power, or interests of stakeholders may change as the project unfolds.

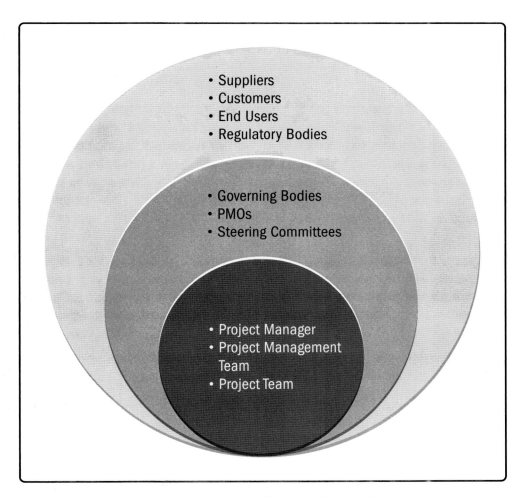

Figure 2-2. Examples of Project Stakeholders

Effective stakeholder identification, analysis, and engagement includes stakeholders who are internal and external to the organization, those who are supportive of the project, and those who may not be supportive or are neutral. While having relevant technical project management skills is an important aspect of successful projects, having the interpersonal and leadership skills to work effectively with stakeholders is just as important, if not more so.

2.1.1 STAKEHOLDER ENGAGEMENT

Stakeholder engagement includes implementing strategies and actions to promote productive involvement of stakeholders. Stakeholder engagement activities start before or when the project starts and continue throughout the project.

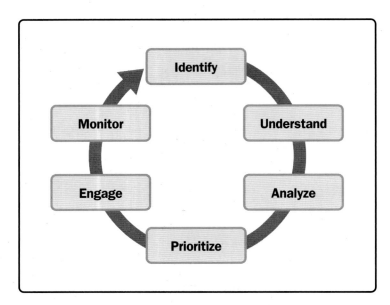

Figure 2-3. Navigating Effective Stakeholder Engagement

Defining and sharing a clear vision at the start of the project can enable good relationships and alignment throughout the project. Establishing a clear vision that key stakeholders agree on can entail some challenging negotiations, especially with stakeholders who are not necessarily in favor of the project or its intended outcomes. As shown in Figure 2-3, there are several steps to engage stakeholders effectively.

2.1.1.1 Identify

High-level stakeholder identification may be carried out prior to forming the project team. Detailed stakeholder identification progressively elaborates the initial work and is a continuous activity throughout the project. Some stakeholders are easy to identify, such as the customer, sponsor, project team, end users, and so forth, but others can be difficult to identify when they are not directly connected to the project.

2.1.1.2 Understand and Analyze

Once stakeholders are identified, the project manager and the project team should seek to understand stakeholders' feelings, emotions, beliefs, and values. These elements can lead to additional threats or opportunities for the project outcomes. They can also change quickly, and as such, understanding and analyzing stakeholders is an ongoing action.

Related to understanding the project stakeholders is the need to analyze aspects of each stakeholder's position on and perspective of the project. Analyzing stakeholders considers several stakeholder aspects, such as:

▶ Power,

▶ Impact,

▶ Attitude,

▶ Beliefs,

▶ Expectations,

▶ Degree of influence,

▶ Proximity to the project,

▶ Interest in the project, and

▶ Other aspects surrounding stakeholder interaction with the project.

This information helps the project team consider interactions that may influence the motivations, actions, and behaviors of stakeholders. In addition to individual analysis, the project team should consider how stakeholders interact with each other, as they often form alliances that help or hinder the project's objectives. For example, if the project team believes a key business manager is highly influential but has negative perceptions related to the project, they can explore how to detect the business manager's perceptions and respond appropriately as the project unfolds. In all cases, the analysis work should be held in confidence by the project team since the information could be misinterpreted outside the context for the analysis.

2.1.1.3 Prioritize

On many projects, there are too many stakeholders involved for the project team to engage directly or effectively with all of them. Based on its analysis, the project team can complete an initial prioritization of stakeholders. It is common to focus on stakeholders with the most power and interest as one way to prioritize engagement. As events unfold throughout the project, the project team may need to reprioritize based on new stakeholders or evolving changes in the stakeholder landscape.

2.1.1.4 Engage

Stakeholder engagement entails working collaboratively with stakeholders to introduce the project, elicit their requirements, manage expectations, resolve issues, negotiate, prioritize, problem solve, and make decisions. Engaging stakeholders requires the application of soft skills, such as active listening, interpersonal skills, and conflict management, as well as leadership skills such as establishing the vision and critical thinking.

Communication with stakeholders can take place via written or verbal means, and it can be formal or informal. Examples of each type of communication are shown in Table 2-1.

Table 2-1. Types of Communication

Type	Formal	Informal
Verbal	Presentations Project reviews Briefings Product demos Brainstorming	Conversations Ad hoc discussions
Written	Progress reports Project documents Business case	Brief notes Email Instant messaging/texting Social media

Communication methods include push, pull, and interactive communication:

▶ **Push.** Communication sent to stakeholders such as memos, emails, status reports, voice mail, and so forth. Push communication is used for one-way communications with individual stakeholders or groups of stakeholders. Push communication inhibits the ability to immediately gauge reaction and assess understanding; therefore, it should be used deliberately.

▶ **Pull.** Information sought by the stakeholder, such as a project team member going to an intranet to find communication policies or templates, running internet searches, and using online repositories. Pulling information is used for indirect sensing of stakeholder concerns.

Engagement goes deeper than pushing or pulling communication. Engagement is interactive. It includes an exchange of information with one or more stakeholders such as conversations, phone calls, meetings, brainstorming, product demos, and the like.

With all forms of communication, quick feedback loops provide useful information to:

▶ Confirm the degree to which the stakeholder(s) heard the message.

▶ Determine if stakeholders agree with the message.

▶ Identify nuanced or other unintended messages the recipient detected.

▶ Gain other helpful insights.

2.1.1.5 Monitor

Throughout the project, stakeholders will change as new stakeholders are identified and others cease to be stakeholders. As the project progresses, the attitude or power of some stakeholders may change. In addition to identifying and analyzing new stakeholders, there is an opportunity to assess whether the current engagement strategy is effective or if it needs to be adjusted. Therefore, the amount and effectiveness of stakeholder engagement is monitored throughout the project.

The degree of stakeholder satisfaction can often be determined by having a conversation with stakeholders to gauge their satisfaction with the project deliverables and the overall management of the project. Project and iteration reviews, product reviews, stage gates, and other methods are ways to obtain periodic feedback. For large groups of stakeholders, a survey can be used to assess the degree of satisfaction. Where necessary, the stakeholder engagement approach can be updated to achieve higher stakeholder satisfaction.

2.1.2 INTERACTIONS WITH OTHER PERFORMANCE DOMAINS

Stakeholders permeate all aspects of the project. They define and prioritize the requirements and scope for the project team. They participate in and shape the planning. They determine acceptance and quality criteria for the project deliverables and outcomes. Much of the project work is around engaging and communicating with stakeholders. Throughout the project or at its closure, they use the project deliverables and influence the realization of project outcomes.

Some stakeholders can assist in lowering the amount of uncertainty present on a project while others may cause an increase in uncertainty. Stakeholders such as customers, senior management, project management office leads, or program managers will focus on measures of performance for the project and its deliverables. These interactions are samples of how the Stakeholder Performance Domain integrates and interweaves with other performance domains, though they are not inclusive of all the ways stakeholder concerns interact throughout the performance domains.

2.1.3 CHECKING RESULTS

Table 2-2 identifies the outcomes on the left and ways of checking them on the right.

Table 2-2. Checking Outcomes—Stakeholder Performance Domain

Outcome	Check
A productive working relationship with stakeholders throughout the project	Productive working relationships with stakeholders can be observed. However, the movement of stakeholders along a continuum of engagement can indicate the relative level of satisfaction with the project.
Stakeholder agreement with project objectives	A significant number of changes or modifications to the project and product requirements in addition to the scope may indicate stakeholders are not engaged or aligned with the project objectives.
Stakeholders who are project beneficiaries are supportive and satisfied; stakeholders who may oppose the project or its deliverables do not negatively impact project results	Stakeholder behavior can indicate whether project beneficiaries are satisfied and supportive of the project or whether they oppose it. Surveys, interviews, and focus groups are also effective ways to determine if stakeholders are satisfied and supportive or if they oppose the project and its deliverables. A review of the project issue register and risk register can identify challenges associated with individual stakeholders.

2.2 TEAM PERFORMANCE DOMAIN

<table>
<tr><td colspan="2">TEAM PERFORMANCE DOMAIN</td></tr>
<tr>
<td>The Team Performance Domain addresses activities and functions associated with the people who are responsible for producing project deliverables that realize business outcomes.</td>
<td>Effective execution of this performance domain results in the following desired outcomes:

▶ Shared ownership.

▶ A high-performing team.

▶ Applicable leadership and other interpersonal skills demonstrated by all team members.</td>
</tr>
</table>

Figure 2-4. Team Performance Domain

This performance domain entails establishing the culture and environment that enables a collection of diverse individuals to evolve into a high-performing project team. This includes recognizing the activities needed to foster project team development and encouraging leadership behaviors from all project team members.

● ● ●

The following definitions are relevant to the Team Performance Domain:

Project Manager. The person assigned by the performing organization to lead the project team that is responsible for achieving the project objectives.

Project Management Team. The members of the project team who are directly involved in project management activities.

Project Team. A set of individuals performing the work of the project to achieve its objectives.

● ● ●

2.2.1 PROJECT TEAM MANAGEMENT AND LEADERSHIP

Project management entails applying knowledge, skills, tools, and techniques for management activities as well as leadership activities. Management activities focus on the means of meeting project objectives, such as having effective processes, planning, coordinating, measuring, and monitoring work, among others. Leadership activities focus on people. Leadership includes influencing, motivating, listening, enabling, and other activities having to do with the project team. Both are important in delivering the intended outcomes.

2.2.1.1 Centralized Management and Leadership

While leadership activities should be practiced by all project team members, management activities may be centralized or distributed. In an environment where management activities are centralized, accountability (being answerable for an outcome), is usually assigned to one individual, such as the project manager or similar role. In these situations, a project charter or other authorizing document can provide approval for the project manager to form a project team to achieve the project outcomes.

2.2.1.2 Distributed Management and Leadership

Sometimes project management activities are shared among a project management team, and project team members are responsible for completing the work. There are also situations where a project team may self-organize to complete a project. Rather than having a designated project manager, someone within the project team may serve as facilitator to enable communication, collaboration, and engagement. This role may shift among project team members.

Servant leadership is a style of leadership that focuses on understanding and addressing the needs and development of project team members in order to enable the highest possible project team performance. Servant leaders place emphasis on developing project team members to their highest potential by focusing on addressing questions, such as:

▶ Are project team members growing as individuals?

▶ Are project team members becoming healthier, wiser, freer, and more autonomous?

▶ Are project team members more likely to become servant leaders?

Servant leaders allow project teams to self-organize when possible and increase levels of autonomy by passing appropriate decision-making opportunities to project team members. Servant leadership behaviors include:

- **Obstacle removal.** Since it is the project team who generates the majority of business value, a critical role for the servant leader is to maximize delivery by removing impediments to their progress. This includes solving problems and removing obstacles that may be hampering the project team's work. By solving or easing these impediments, the project team can deliver value to the business faster.

- **Diversion shield.** Servant leaders protect the project team from internal and external diversions that redirect the project team from the current objectives. Time fragmentation reduces productivity, so shielding the project team from noncritical, external demands helps the project team stay focused.

- **Encouragement and development opportunities.** The servant leader also provides tools and encouragement to keep the project team satisfied and productive. Learning what motivates project team members as individuals and finding ways to reward them for good work helps keep project team members satisfied.

2.2.1.3 Common Aspects of Team Development

Regardless of how the management activities are structured, there are common aspects of project team development that are relevant for most project teams. These include:

- **Vision and objectives.** It is essential that everyone is aware of the project vision and objectives. The vision and objectives are communicated throughout the project. This includes referencing the intended outcomes when the project team is engaged in making decisions and solving problems.

- **Roles and responsibilities.** It is important to make sure project team members understand and fulfill their roles and responsibilities. This can include identifying gaps in knowledge and skills as well as strategies to address those gaps through training, mentoring, or coaching.

▶ **Project team operations.** Facilitating project team communication, problem solving, and the process of coming to consensus may include working with the project team to develop a project team charter and a set of operating guidelines or project team norms.

▶ **Guidance.** Guidance can be directed to the overall project team to keep everyone headed in the right direction. Individual project team members may also provide guidance on a particular task or deliverable.

▶ **Growth.** Identifying areas where the project team is performing well and pointing out areas where the project team can improve helps the project team to grow. Working collaboratively, the project team can identify goals for its improvement and take steps to meet those goals. This also applies to each individual on the project team. Individuals may want to grow their skills and experience in certain areas, and the project manager can assist with that.

There are several models that describe the stages of project team growth included in Section 4.

● ● ● ●

When project teams form across different organizations based on a contract, strategic partnership, or other business relationship, specific roles that perform various functions may be more formalized and less flexible depending on the contract or other terms. Such arrangements often require more up-front work to establish a "one team" mindset, ensure project team members understand how everyone contributes to the project, and establish other enablers that integrate skills, capabilities, and processes.

● ● ● ●

2.2.2 PROJECT TEAM CULTURE

Each project team develops its own team culture. The project team's culture may be established deliberately by developing project team norms, or informally through the behaviors and actions of its project team members. The project team culture operates within the organization's culture but reflects the project team's individual ways of working and interacting.

Human beings have a set of biases, some of them unconscious and some of them conscious. For example, one person may feel that unless a schedule is displayed using a software-generated Gantt chart, that it is not a true or valid schedule. Another person may have a contrasting bias that detailed planning any further out than 30 days is a waste of time. Being open and transparent about biases up front establishes a culture of openness and trust that can enable consensus and collaboration.

The project manager is key in establishing and maintaining a safe, respectful, nonjudgmental environment that allows the project team to communicate openly. One way to accomplish this is by modeling desired behaviors, such as:

▶ **Transparency.** Being transparent in how one thinks, makes choices, and processes information helps others identify and share their own processes. This can extend to being transparent about biases as well.

▶ **Integrity.** Integrity is comprised of ethical behavior and honesty. Individuals demonstrate honesty by surfacing risks, communicating their assumptions and basis of estimates, delivering bad news early, ensuring status reports provide an accurate depiction of the project's status, and in many other ways. Ethical behavior can include surfacing potential defects or negative effects in product design, disclosing potential conflicts of interest, ensuring fairness, and making decisions based on environmental, stakeholder, and financial impacts.

- ▶ **Respect.** Demonstrating respect for each person, how the person thinks, the person's skills, and the perspective and expertise the person brings to the project team sets the stage for all project team members to adopt this behavior.

- ▶ **Positive discourse.** Throughout the project, diverse opinions, different ways of approaching situations, and misunderstandings will occur. These are a normal part of conducting projects. They present an opportunity to have a dialogue rather than a debate. A dialogue entails working with others to resolve divergent opinions. The goal is to arrive at a resolution that all parties can embrace. A debate, on the other hand, is a win-lose scenario where people are more interested in winning personally than they are in being open to alternative solutions to a problem.

- ▶ **Support.** Projects can be challenging from the perspectives of technical challenges, environmental influences, and interpersonal interactions. Supporting project team members through problem solving and removing impediments builds a supportive culture and leads to a trusting and collaborative environment. Support can also be demonstrated by providing encouragement, showing empathy, and engaging in active listening.

- ▶ **Courage.** Recommending a new approach to a problem or a way of working can be intimidating. Likewise, it can be challenging to disagree with a subject matter expert or someone with greater authority. However, demonstrating the courage that it takes to make a suggestion, disagree, or try something new enables a culture of experimentation and communicates to others that it is safe to be courageous and try new approaches.

- ▶ **Celebrating success.** Focusing on project goals, challenges, and issues often sidelines the fact that individual project team members and the project team as a whole are steadily progressing toward those goals. Because work takes priority, project team members may defer recognizing demonstrations of innovation, adaptation, service to others, and learning. However, recognizing such contributions in real time can keep the project team and individuals motivated.

2.2.3 HIGH-PERFORMING PROJECT TEAMS

One goal of effective leadership is to create a high-performing project team. There are a number of factors that contribute to high-performing project teams. The list below is not comprehensive, but it identifies some of the factors associated with high-performing project teams.

- ▶ **Open communication.** An environment that fosters open and safe communication allows for productive meetings, problem solving, brainstorming, and so forth. It is also the cornerstone for other factors, such as shared understanding, trust, and collaboration.

- ▶ **Shared understanding.** The purpose for the project and the benefits it will provide are held in common.

- ▶ **Shared ownership.** The more ownership of the outcomes that project team members feel, the better they are likely to perform.

- ▶ **Trust.** A project team in which its members trust each other is willing to go the extra distance to deliver success. People are less likely to do the extra work it may take to succeed if they do not trust their project team members, project manager, or the organization.

- ▶ **Collaboration.** Project teams that collaborate and work with each other rather than work in silos or compete tend to generate more diverse ideas and end up with better outcomes.

- ▶ **Adaptability.** Project teams that are able to adapt the way they work to the environment and the situation are more effective.

- ▶ **Resilience.** When issues or failures occur, high-performing project teams recover quickly.

- ▶ **Empowerment.** Project team members who feel empowered to make decisions about the way they work perform better than those who are micromanaged.

- ▶ **Recognition.** Project teams who are recognized for the work they put in and the performance they achieve are more likely to continue to perform well. Even the simple act of showing appreciation reinforces positive team behavior.

2.2.4 LEADERSHIP SKILLS

Leadership skills are useful for all project team members whether the project team is operating in an environment with a centralized authority or a shared leadership environment. The following sections describe some of the traits and activities associated with leadership.

2.2.4.1 Establishing and Maintaining Vision

Every project has a purpose. Understanding that purpose is critical for people to commit their time and energy in the right direction toward achieving the project purpose. The project vision summarizes the project's purpose clearly and succinctly. It describes a realistic, attractive view of the future project outcomes.

In addition to briefly describing the desired future state, the vision is a powerful motivational tool. It is a way to create passion and meaning for a project's envisioned goal. A common vision helps keep people pulling in the same direction. When immersed in the details of everyday work, a clear understanding of the end goal can help guide local decisions toward the desired project outcome.

A vision developed collaboratively between project team members and key stakeholders should answer these questions:

▶ What is the project purpose?

▶ What defines successful project work?

▶ How will the future be better when the project outcomes are delivered?

▶ How will the project team know that it is drifting from the vision?

A good vision is clear, concise, and actionable. It does the following:

▶ Summarizes the project with a powerful phrase or short description,

▶ Describes the best achievable outcome,

▶ Creates a common, cohesive picture in project team members' minds, and

▶ Inspires passion for the outcome.

2.2.4.2 Critical Thinking

Throughout the various project performance domains, there is a need to recognize bias, identify the root cause of problems, and consider challenging issues, such as ambiguity, complexity, and so forth. Critical thinking helps to accomplish these activities. Critical thinking includes disciplined, rational, logical, evidence-based thinking. It requires an open mind and the ability to analyze objectively. Critical thinking, especially when applied to discovery, can include conceptual imagination, insight, and intuition. It can also include reflective thinking and metacognition (thinking about thinking and being aware of one's awareness).

Project team members apply critical thinking to:

▶ Research and gather unbiased, well-balanced information;

▶ Recognize, analyze, and resolve problems;

▶ Identify bias, unstated assumptions, and values;

▶ Discern the use of language and the influence on oneself and others;

▶ Analyze data and evidence to evaluate arguments and perspectives;

▶ Observe events to identify patterns and relationships;

▶ Apply inductive, deductive, and abductive reasoning appropriately; and

▶ Identify and articulate false premises, false analogy, emotional appeals, and other faulty logic.

2.2.4.3 Motivation

Motivating project team members has two aspects: the first is understanding what motivates project team members to perform, and the second is working with project team members in such a way that they remain committed to the project and its outcomes.

Motivation to perform can be intrinsic or extrinsic. Intrinsic motivation comes from inside the individual or is associated with the work. It is associated with finding pleasure in the work itself rather than focusing on rewards. Extrinsic motivation is performing work because of an external reward such as a bonus. Much of the work done on projects is aligned with intrinsic motivation.

Examples of intrinsic motivation factors include:

▶ Achievement,

▶ Challenge,

▶ Belief in the work,

▶ Making a difference,

▶ Self-direction and autonomy,

▶ Responsibility,

▶ Personal growth,

▶ Relatedness, and

▶ Being part of a project team.

People are not motivated by just one thing; however, most people have a dominant motivator. To effectively motivate project team members, it is helpful to know each member's dominant motivator. For example, a project team member who is motivated by challenge will respond well to stretch goals and problems to solve. A project team member who is motivated by relatedness will respond to being part of a dynamic working group. Project team members who thrive on autonomy will perform better if they can establish their own ways of working and even their own work hours and cadence. Therefore, tailoring motivation methods based on individual preferences helps to elicit the best individual and project team performance.

2.2.4.4 Interpersonal Skills

Interpersonal skills that are used frequently in projects include emotional intelligence, decision making, and conflict resolution among others.

▶ **Emotional intelligence.** Emotional intelligence is the ability to recognize our own emotions and those of others. This information is used to guide thinking and behavior. Recognition of personal feelings, empathy for the feelings of others, and the ability to act appropriately are the cornerstones for effective communication, collaboration, and leadership.

Since projects are undertaken by people and for people, emotional intelligence—the ability to understand one's self and effectively sustain working relationships with others—is critical in project team environments.

There are multiple models for defining and explaining emotional intelligence. They converge on four key areas:

▷ *Self-awareness.* Self-awareness is the ability to conduct a realistic self-assessment. It includes understanding our own emotions, goals, motivations, strengths, and weaknesses.

▷ *Self-management.* Self-management, also known as self-regulation, is the ability to control and redirect disruptive feelings and impulses. It is the ability to think before acting, suspending snap judgments and impulsive decisions.

▷ *Social awareness.* Social awareness is about empathy and understanding and considering other people's feelings. This includes the ability to read nonverbal cues and body language.

▷ *Social skill.* Social skill is the culmination of the other dimensions of emotional intelligence. It is concerned with managing groups of people, such as project teams, building social networks, finding common ground with various stakeholders, and building rapport.

Self-awareness and self-management are required to remain calm and productive during difficult project circumstances. Social awareness and social skills allow for better bonds with project team members and project stakeholders. Emotional intelligence is a basis of all forms of leadership.

Figure 2-5 shows the key points for each of the four aspects of emotional intelligence and how they relate. The aspects having to do with oneself are on the top, and the social aspects are on the bottom. Awareness is on the left side, and management and skill are on the right side.

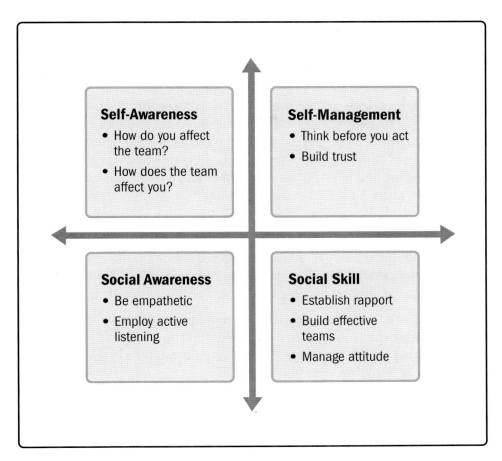

Self-Awareness
- How do you affect the team?
- How does the team affect you?

Self-Management
- Think before you act
- Build trust

Social Awareness
- Be empathetic
- Employ active listening

Social Skill
- Establish rapport
- Build effective teams
- Manage attitude

Figure 2-5. Components of Emotional Intelligence

Some models for emotional intelligence include a fifth area for motivation. Motivation in this context is about understanding what drives and inspires people.

▶ **Decision making.** Project managers and project teams make many decisions daily. Some decisions may be fairly inconsequential to the project outcome, such as where to go for a team lunch, and others will be very impactful, such as what development approach to use, which tool to use, or what vendor to select.

Decisions can be made unilaterally. This has the advantage of being fast but is prone to error when compared to engaging the wisdom of a diverse set of people. Unilateral decision making can also demotivate people who are impacted by the decision since they may feel their views and concerns were not considered.

Group-based decision making has the benefit of tapping into the broad knowledge base of a group. Engaging people in the decision-making process also increases buy-in to the outcome, even if the option selected may not have been everyone's first choice. Generally, inclusion increases commitment to the decision. The downside of group decision making is the time required and interruption to teamwork that can occur when taking people away from their work to be consulted in a decision.

Project team decision making often follows a diverge/converge pattern. This means stakeholders are first engaged to generate a broad set of solution alternatives or approaches. This is often done individually to avoid the effect of senior or charismatic stakeholders unduly influencing other stakeholders. Then, after a broad spectrum of decision alternatives have been generated, the project team converges on a preferred solution.

The goal is to make decisions quickly while engaging the diverse knowledge of a group in an inclusive and respectful manner. Some decisions may be made in a different direction than some people prefer, but everyone has an opportunity to explain their position. In the end, the deciding authority, whether an individual or a group, makes a decision based on the presented analysis and with consideration for stakeholder expectations.

Careful selection of which decisions should go for group discussion and voting limits the interruptions and task switching experienced by the project team. Many approaches such as Roman voting, wideband Delphi estimating, and fist of five voting use the diverge/converge pattern. They aim to engage individual input while voting at the same moment, which minimizes groupthink.

For those decisions that are beyond the authority of the project team to decide, the project team can investigate alternatives, consider impacts of each alternative, and escalate the decision to someone with the proper authority. This process aligns with the philosophy of "don't bring me problems, bring me solutions," while remaining aligned with organizational governance regarding decision-making authority.

▶ **Conflict management.** Conflict happens on all projects. Projects operate in dynamic environments and face many mutually exclusive constraints including budget, scope, schedule, and quality, which can lead to conflicts. It is not uncommon to want to avoid conflict, but not all conflict is negative. How conflict is handled can either lead to more conflict or to better decision making and stronger solutions.

Addressing conflict before it escalates beyond useful debate leads to better outcomes. The following approaches can help:

▷ *Keep communications open and respectful.* Because conflict can cause anxiety, it is important to keep a safe environment to explore the source of the conflict. Without a safe environment, people will stop communicating. Make sure words, tone of voice, and body language remain nonthreatening.

▷ *Focus on the issues, not the people.* Conflict is based on people perceiving situations differently. It should not be personal. The focus is on resolving the situation, not casting blame.

▷ *Focus on the present and future, not the past.* Stay focused on the current situation, not past situations. If something similar happened previously, bringing up the past will not resolve the current situation. In fact, it can serve to intensify the current situation even more.

▷ *Search for alternatives together.* Damage incurred from conflict can be repaired by looking for resolutions and alternatives together. It can also create more constructive relationships. This moves the conflict into more of a problem-solving space where people can work together to generate creative alternatives.

There are several models for addressing and resolving conflict. Some of them are discussed in Section 4.

2.2.5 TAILORING LEADERSHIP STYLES

As with all aspects of projects, leadership styles are also tailored to meet the needs of the project, the environment, and the stakeholders. Some of the variables that influence tailoring of leadership styles include:

▶ **Experience with the type of project.** Organizations and project teams with experience on a specific type of project may be more self-managing and require less leadership. When a project is new to an organization, the tendency is to provide more oversight and to use a more directive leadership style.

▶ **Maturity of the project team members.** Project team members who are mature in the technical field may need less oversight and direction than project team members who are new to the organization, the team, or the technical specialty.

▶ **Organizational governance structures.** Projects operate within a larger organizational system. There may be the expectation that the organizational leadership style of top management is recognized and reflected in the team's leadership. The organizational structure influences the degree to which authority and accountability are centralized or distributed.

▶ **Distributed project teams.** A global project workforce is more common today than in the past. In spite of the best efforts to connect people virtually, it can be challenging to create the same level of collaboration and relatedness that is achieved when working face to face. To minimize the pitfalls of distributed project teams, technology can be used to increase and improve communication. Examples include:

▷ Ensure there are collaboration sites for working together.

▷ Have a project team site to keep all relevant project and project team information available.

▷ Use audio and video capabilities for meetings.

▷ Use technology to maintain ongoing contact, such as messaging and texting.

▷ Build in time to get to know remote project team members.

▷ Have at least one face-to-face meeting to establish relationships.

2.2.6 INTERACTIONS WITH OTHER PERFORMANCE DOMAINS

The Team Performance Domain emphasizes the skills used by project managers and project team members throughout the project. These skills are woven into all other aspects of the project. Project team members are called on to demonstrate leadership qualities and skills throughout the project. Communicating the project vision and benefits to stakeholders while planning and throughout the life cycle is one example. Another example is employing critical thinking, problem solving, and decision making while engaging in project work. Accountability for outcomes is demonstrated throughout the Planning and Measurement Performance Domains.

2.2.7 CHECKING RESULTS

Table 2-3 identifies the outcomes from effective application of the Team Performance Domain on the left and ways of checking them on the right.

Table 2-3. Checking Outcomes—Team Performance Domain

Outcome	Check
Shared ownership	All project team members know the vision and objectives. The project team owns the deliverables and outcomes of the project.
A high-performing team	The project team trusts each other and collaborates. The project team adapts to changing situations and is resilient in the face of challenges. The project team feels empowered and empowers and recognizes members of the project team.
Applicable leadership and other interpersonal skills are demonstrated by all project team members	Project team members apply critical thinking and interpersonal skills. Project team member leadership styles are appropriate to the project context and environment.

2.3 DEVELOPMENT APPROACH AND LIFE CYCLE PERFORMANCE DOMAIN

<table>
<tr>
<td colspan="2">DEVELOPMENT APPROACH AND LIFE CYCLE PERFORMANCE DOMAIN</td>
</tr>
<tr>
<td>The Development Approach and Life Cycle Performance Domain addresses activities and functions associated with the development approach, cadence, and life cycle phases of the project.</td>
<td>Effective execution of this performance domain results in the following desired outcomes:

▶ Development approaches that are consistent with project deliverables.

▶ A project life cycle consisting of phases that connect the delivery of business and stakeholder value from the beginning to the end of the project.

▶ A project life cycle consisting of phases that facilitate the delivery cadence and development approach required to produce the project deliverables.</td>
</tr>
</table>

Figure 2-6. Development Approach and Life Cycle Performance Domain

This performance domain entails establishing the development approach, delivery cadence, and project life cycle needed to optimize project outcomes.

The following definitions are relevant to the Development Approach and Life Cycle Performance Domain:

Deliverable. Any unique and verifiable product, result, or capability to perform a service that is required to be produced to complete a process, phase, or project.

Development Approach. A method used to create and evolve the product, service, or result during the project life cycle, such as a predictive, iterative, incremental, adaptive, or hybrid method.

Cadence. A rhythm of activities conducted throughout the project.

Project Phase. A collection of logically related project activities that culminates in the completion of one or more deliverables.

Project Life Cycle. The series of phases that a project passes through from its start to its completion.

2.3.1 DEVELOPMENT, CADENCE, AND LIFE CYCLE RELATIONSHIP

The type of project deliverable(s) determines how it can be developed. The type of deliverable(s) and the development approach influence the number and cadence for project deliveries. The deliverable approach and the desired delivery cadence determine the project life cycle and its phases.

2.3.2 DELIVERY CADENCE

Delivery cadence refers to the timing and frequency of project deliverables. Projects can have a single delivery, multiple deliveries, or periodic deliveries.

- ▶ **Single delivery.** Projects that have a single delivery deliver at the end of the project. For example, a process reengineering project may not have any deliveries until near the end of the project when the new process is rolled out.

- ▶ **Multiple deliveries.** Some projects have multiple deliveries. A project may have multiple components that are delivered at different times throughout the project. A project to develop a new drug may have multiple deliveries, such as preclinical submissions, Phase 1 trial results, Phase 2 trial results, Phase 3 trial results, registration, and then launch. In this example, the deliveries are sequential. Some projects have deliveries that are developed separately rather than sequentially, such as a project to update building security. Deliveries may include physical barriers to entry, new badges, new key code pads, and so forth. Each of these is a separate delivery, but they do not need to come in a specific order. All of the deliveries are concluded before the project is considered to be completed.

- ▶ **Periodic deliveries.** Periodic deliveries are like multiple deliveries, but they are on a fixed delivery schedule, such as monthly or bimonthly. A new software application may have internal deliveries every two weeks, and then periodically release the deliveries into the market.

Another delivery option is called continuous delivery. Continuous delivery is the practice of delivering feature increments immediately to customers, often through the use of small batches of work and automation technology. Continuous delivery can be used for digital products. From the product management perspective, the emphasis is on delivering benefits and value throughout the product life cycle. Similar to a project, there are aspects that are development oriented. However, similar to a program, there can be many development cycles as well as maintenance activities. This type of undertaking works better with project teams that are stable and remain intact. Because the project teams are focused on one product, they can apply learning about the product, the stakeholders, and the market. This allows the team to respond to market trends and stay focused on value delivery. This practice is included in several approaches such as DevOps, #noprojects and Continuous Digital, for example.

2.3.3 DEVELOPMENT APPROACHES

A development approach is the means used to create and evolve the product, service, or result during the project life cycle. There are different development approaches, and different industries may use different terms to refer to development approaches. Three commonly used approaches are predictive, hybrid, and adaptive. As shown in Figure 2-7, these approaches are often viewed as a spectrum, from the predictive approach on one end of the spectrum, to the adaptive on the other end.

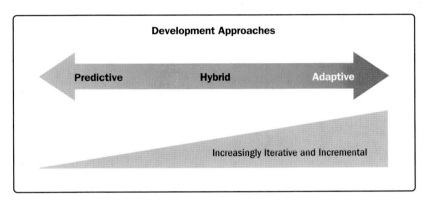

Figure 2-7. Development Approaches

▶ **Predictive approach.** A predictive approach is useful when the project and product requirements can be defined, collected, and analyzed at the start of the project. This may also be referred to as a waterfall approach. This approach may also be used when there is a significant investment involved and a high level of risk that may require frequent reviews, change control mechanisms, and replanning between development phases. The scope, schedule, cost, resource needs, and risks can be well defined in the early phases of the project life cycle, and they are relatively stable. This development approach allows the project team to reduce the level of uncertainty early in the project and do much of the planning up front. Predictive approaches may use proof-of-concept developments to explore options, but the majority of the project work follows the plans that were developed near the start of the project. Many times, projects that use this approach have templates from previous, similar projects.

A project to develop a new community center might use a predictive approach for the construction of the grounds and facilities. The scope, schedule, cost, and resources would be determined up front, and changes would likely be minimal. The construction process would follow the plans and blueprints.

▶ **Hybrid approach.** A hybrid development approach is a combination of adaptive and predictive approaches. This means that some elements from a predictive approach are used and some from an adaptive approach are used. This development approach is useful when there is uncertainty or risk around the requirements. Hybrid is also useful when deliverables can be modularized, or when there are deliverables that can be developed by different project teams. A hybrid approach is more adaptive than a predictive approach, but less so than a purely adaptive approach.

Hybrid approaches often use an iterative or incremental development approach. An iterative approach is useful for clarifying requirements and investigating various options. An iterative approach may produce sufficient capability to be considered acceptable prior to the final iteration. An incremental approach is used to produce a deliverable throughout a series of iterations. Each iteration adds functionality within a predetermined time frame (a timebox). The deliverable contains the capability to be considered as completed only after the final iteration.

The differences and interactions between iterative and incremental development are shown in Figure 2-8.

An example of a hybrid approach could be using an adaptive approach to develop a product that has significant uncertainty associated with the requirements. However, the deployment of the product can be done using a predictive approach. Another example is a project with two main deliverables where one deliverable is developed using an adaptive approach and the other using a predictive approach.

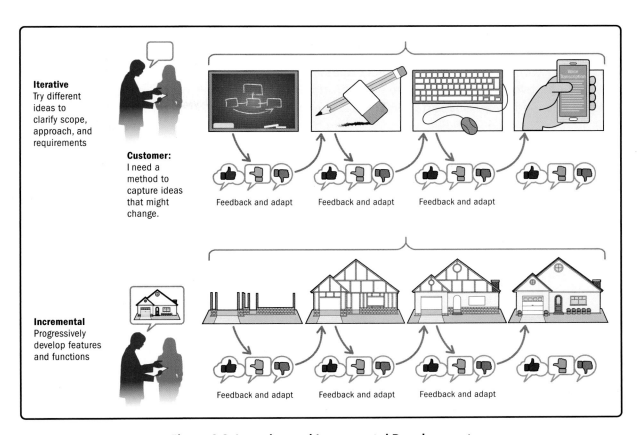

Figure 2-8. Iterative and Incremental Development

As part of the community center, a project to establish senior services could be developed and deployed iteratively. For example, the first iteration could be a Meals on Wheels program. This could be followed by a transportation service, then group outings and events, caregiver relief, adult day care, and so forth. Each service would be complete on its own and could be deployed when it was available. Each additional service would improve and increase the senior services for the community.

A project to establish training for community action patrol volunteers could use an incremental approach. The training, comprised of basic training, logistics training, and patrol training, can be developed by different people. It can be developed at the same time in modules, or one module can be developed, feedback gathered, and then subsequent modules can be developed. However, the community action patrol training program will only be complete after all the modules are developed, integrated, and deployed.

▶ **Adaptive approach.** Adaptive approaches are useful when requirements are subject to a high level of uncertainty and volatility and are likely to change throughout the project. A clear vision is established at the start of the project, and the initial known requirements are refined, detailed, changed, or replaced in accordance with user feedback, the environment, or unexpected events.

Adaptive approaches use iterative and incremental approaches. However, on the far side of the adaptive methods, the iterations tend to get shorter and the product is more likely to evolve based on stakeholder feedback.

While agility is a wide mindset that is broader than a development framework, agile approaches can be considered adaptive. Some agile approaches entail iterations that are 1 to 2 weeks in duration with a demonstration of the accomplishments at the end of each iteration. The project team is very engaged with the planning for each iteration. The project team will determine the scope they can achieve based on a prioritized backlog, estimate the work involved, and work collaboratively throughout the iteration to develop the scope.

The community center will need a website so community members can access information from their home computer, phone, or tablet. The high-level requirements, design, and page layouts can be defined up front. An initial set of information can be deployed on the website. User feedback, new services, and internal stakeholder needs would provide content for a backlog. The backlog information would be prioritized, and the web team would develop and deploy new content. As new requirements and new scope emerge, the estimates for the work would be developed, the work would be done, and once tested, it would be demonstrated for stakeholders. If approved, the work would be deployed to the website.

2.3.4 CONSIDERATIONS FOR SELECTING A DEVELOPMENT APPROACH

There are several factors that influence the selection of a development approach. They can be divided into categories of the product, service, or result; the project; and the organization. The following subsections describe the variables associated with each category.

2.3.4.1 Product, Service, or Result

There are many variables associated with the nature of the product, service, or result that influence the development approach. The following list outlines some of the variables to consider when selecting the development approach.

▶ **Degree of innovation.** Deliverables where the scope and requirements are well understood, that the project team has worked with before, and that allow for planning up front are well suited to a predictive approach. Deliverables that have a high degree of innovation or where the project team does not have experience are better suited to a more adaptive approach.

▶ **Requirements certainty.** When the requirements are well known and easy to define, a predictive approach fits well. When requirements are uncertain, volatile, or complex and are expected to evolve throughout the project, a more adaptive approach may be a better fit.

- ▶ **Scope stability.** If the scope of the deliverable is stable and not likely to change, a predictive approach is useful. If the scope is expected to have many changes, an approach that is closer to the adaptive side of the spectrum can be useful.

- ▶ **Ease of change.** Related to the requirements certainty and the scope stability, if the nature of the deliverable makes it difficult to manage and incorporate changes, then a predictive approach is best. Deliverables that can adapt easily to change can use an approach that is more adaptive.

- ▶ **Delivery options.** As described in Section 2.3.2 on Delivery Cadence, the nature of the deliverable and whether it can be delivered in components influences the development approach. Products, services, or results that can be developed and/or delivered in pieces are aligned with incremental, iterative, or adaptive approaches. Some large projects may be planned using a predictive approach, but there may be some pieces that can be developed and delivered incrementally.

- ▶ **Risk.** Products that are inherently high risk require analysis before choosing the development approach. Some high-risk products may require significant up-front planning and rigorous processes to reduce threats. Other products can reduce risk by building them modularly and adapting the design and development based on learning to take advantage of emerging opportunities or reduce the exposure to threats.

- ▶ **Safety requirements.** Products that have rigorous safety requirements often use a predictive approach as there is a need for significant up-front planning to ensure that all the safety requirements are identified, planned for, created, integrated, and tested.

- ▶ **Regulations.** Environments that have significant regulatory oversight may need to use a predictive approach due to the required process, documentation, and demonstration needs.

2.3.4.2 Project

Project variables that influence the development approach are centered around stakeholders, schedule constraints, and funding availability.

- ▶ **Stakeholders.** Projects that use adaptive methods require significant stakeholder involvement throughout the process. Certain stakeholders, such as the product owner, play a substantial role in establishing and prioritizing work.

- ▶ **Schedule constraints.** If there is a need to deliver something early, even if it is not a finished product, an iterative or adaptive approach is beneficial.

- ▶ **Funding availability.** Projects that work in an environment of funding uncertainty can benefit from an adaptive or iterative approach. A minimum viable product can be released with less investment than an elaborate product. This allows for market testing or market capture with minimum investment. Further investments can be made based on the market response to the product or service.

2.3.4.3 Organization

Organizational variables such as the structure, culture, capability, project team size, and location influence the development approach.

- ▶ **Organizational structure.** An organizational structure that has many levels, a rigid reporting structure, and substantial bureaucracy frequently uses a predictive approach. Projects that use adaptive methods tend to have a flat structure and may operate with self-organizing project teams.

- ▶ **Culture.** A predictive approach fits better in an organization with a culture of managing and directing, where the work is planned out and progress is measured against baselines. Adaptive approaches fit better within an organization that emphasizes project team self-management.

- ▶ **Organizational capability.** Transitioning from predictive development approaches to adaptive approaches and then to using agile methods is more than just stating that the organization will now be agile. It entails shifting the mindset starting at the executive level throughout the organization. Organizational policies, ways of working, reporting structure, and attitude should all be aligned in order to employ adaptive methods successfully.

- ▶ **Project team size and location.** Adaptive approaches, especially agile methods, often work better with project teams of 7 ± 2. Adaptive approaches also favor project teams that are located in the same physical space. Large project teams and project teams that are mostly virtual may do better by using an approach that is closer to the predictive side of the spectrum. However, there are approaches that seek to scale up the adaptive approaches to work with large and dispersed project teams.

2.3.5 LIFE CYCLE AND PHASE DEFINITIONS

The type and number of project phases in a project life cycle depend upon many variables, chief among them the delivery cadence and the development approach, as described previously. Examples of phases in a life cycle include:

▶ **Feasibility.** This phase determines if the business case is valid and if the organization has the capability to deliver the intended outcome.

▶ **Design.** Planning and analysis lead to the design of the project deliverable that will be developed.

▶ **Build.** Construction of the deliverable with integrated quality assurance activities is conducted.

▶ **Test.** Final quality review and inspection of deliverables are carried out before transition, go-live, or acceptance by the customer.

▶ **Deploy.** Project deliverables are put into use and transitional activities required for sustainment, benefits realization, and organizational change management are completed.

▶ **Close.** The project is closed, project knowledge and artifacts are archived, project team members are released, and contracts are closed.

Project phases often have a phase gate review (also known as stage gate) to check that the desired outcomes or exit criteria for the phase have been achieved before proceeding to the next phase. Exit criteria may tie to acceptance criteria for deliverables, contractual obligations, meeting specific performance targets, or other tangible measures.

Figure 2-9 shows a life cycle where one phase finishes before the next one begins. This type of life cycle would fit well with a predictive development approach since each phase is only performed once, and each phase focuses on a particular type of work. However, there are situations, such as adding scope, a change in requirements, or a change in the market that cause phases to be repeated.

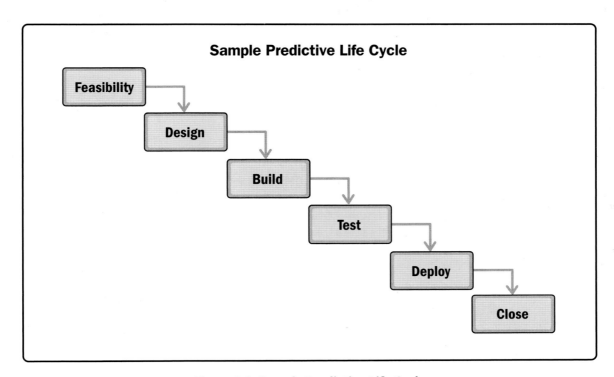

Figure 2-9. Sample Predictive Life Cycle

Figure 2-10 shows a life cycle with an incremental development approach. There are three iterations of plan, design, and build shown in this example. Each subsequent build would add functionality to the initial build.

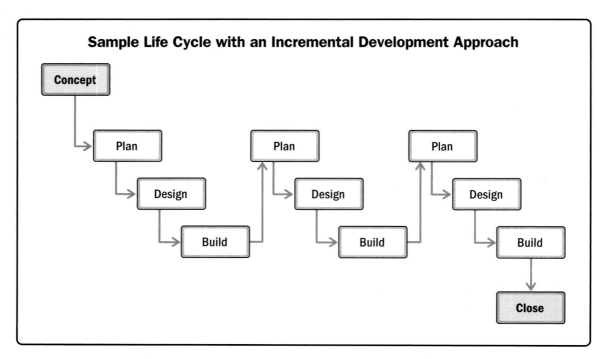

Figure 2-10. Life Cycle with an Incremental Development Approach

Figure 2-11 shows a life cycle using an adaptive development approach. At the end of each iteration (sometimes known as a *sprint*), the customer reviews a functional deliverable. At the review, the key stakeholders provide feedback, and the project team updates the project backlog of features and functions to prioritize for the next iteration.

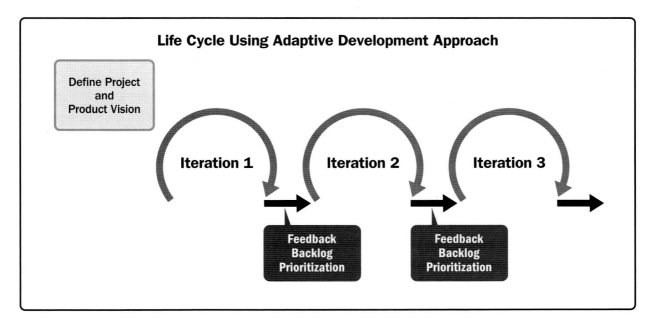

Figure 2-11. Life Cycle with Adaptive Development Approach

This approach can be modified for use in continuous delivery situations, as described in Section 2.3.2 on Delivery Cadence.

Several adaptive methodologies, including agile, use flow-based scheduling, which does not use a life cycle or phases. One goal is to optimize the flow of deliveries based on resource capacity, materials, and other inputs. Another goal is to minimize time and resource waste and optimize the efficiency of processes and the throughput of deliverables. Projects that use these practices and methods usually adopt them from the Kanban scheduling system used in lean and just-in-time scheduling approaches.

2.3.6 ALIGNING OF DELIVERY CADENCE, DEVELOPMENT APPROACH, AND LIFE CYCLE

The community center examples described in Section 2.3.3 will be revisited to demonstrate how the delivery cadence, development approach, and life cycle fit together. In this example, there are four products and services: the building, the community action patrol (CAP) training, the senior services, and the website. Table 2-4 describes the delivery cadence and the development approach.

Table 2-4. Delivery Cadence and Development Approach

Deliverable	Delivery Cadence	Development Approach
Building	Single delivery	Predictive
Senior services	Multiple deliveries	Iterative
Website	Periodic deliveries	Adaptive
Community action patrol training	Multiple deliveries	Incremental

Based on this information, a potential life cycle might be:

▶ **Start Up.** Entry criteria for this phase are that the business case has been approved and the project charter has been authorized. In this phase, the high-level roadmap is developed, initial funding requirements are established, project team and resource requirements are defined, a milestone schedule is created, and planning for a procurement strategy is defined. These deliverables should be complete prior to exiting the start-up phase. Exit criteria will be reviewed at an origination phase gate review.

▶ **Plan.** In this phase, the high-level information for the building is decomposed into detailed plans. A detailed design document for the CAP training is completed. An analysis of the senior services offering is completed along with a gap analysis. The initial wireframe for the website is created. These deliverables should be complete prior to exiting the planning phase. Exit criteria will be reviewed at a planning phase gate review.

▶ **Development.** This phase will overlap with the test and deploy phases since the deliverables have different delivery cadences and different approaches. The website will have early deliveries to inform the public of the progress for the community center. Some senior services and the CAP training may begin prior to the opening of the community center. Each deliverable may have a separate review prior to entering the testing phase.

▶ **Test.** This phase will overlap with the development and deploy phases. The type of test will depend on the deliverable. This phase includes inspections for the building, a beta delivery of the CAP courses, small-scale trials for the senior services, and operating in a test environment for each release for the website. Each deliverable will go through the applicable testing prior to moving to the deploy phase.

▶ **Deploy.** This phase will overlap with the development and test phases. The first deployment of the website may be somewhat early in the project. Activities in this phase will iterate as more deliverables become available. The final deployment for the project will be the opening of the community center. Ongoing updates to the website and the senior services will be part of operations once the community center is open.

▶ **Close.** This phase takes place periodically as deliverables are completed. When the initial website has been deployed, project personnel (including contractors) will be released and retrospectives or lessons learned for each deliverable will be completed. When the entire project is done, information from the various phase gate reviews and an overall evaluation of project performance compared to baselines will be conducted. Prior to final closeout, the project charter and the business case will be reviewed to determine if the deliverables achieved the intended benefits and value.

Figure 2-12 shows a possible life cycle for the community center project. The start-up and planning phases are sequential. The development, test, and deploy phases overlap because the different deliverables will be developed, tested, and deployed at different times, and some deliverables will have multiple deliveries. The development phase is shown in more detail to demonstrate different timing and delivery cadence. The test phase cadence would follow the development phase cadence. The deliveries are shown in the deploy phase.

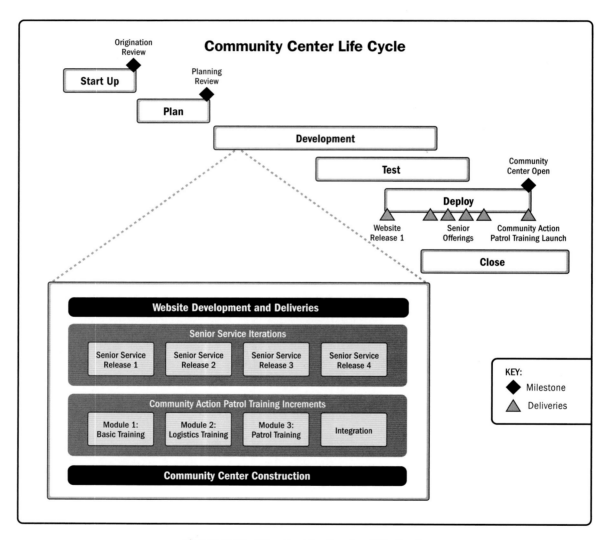

Figure 2-12. Community Center Life Cycle

What's in a Name? Not all project practitioners differentiate between the development approach and the life cycle. Some practitioners will say a project follows an agile life cycle when they are actually talking about the development approach. Some practitioners refer to predictive approaches as *waterfall.* Adaptive development approaches may also be known as evolutionary approaches.

Because project management is evolving, the language used continues to evolve. The best way to understand what a person is referring to is to determine how they are developing deliverables and ask them the names of the phases in the life cycle. This can help frame the project and understand how people are using terms.

2.3.7 INTERACTIONS WITH OTHER PERFORMANCE DOMAINS

The Development Approach and Life Cycle Performance Domain interacts with the Stakeholder, Planning, Uncertainty, Delivery, Project Work, and Team Performance Domains. The life cycle selected impacts the way in which planning is undertaken. Predictive life cycles undertake the bulk of the planning up front and then continue to replan by using rolling wave planning and progressive elaboration. Plans are also updated as threats and opportunities materialize.

The development approach and delivery cadence is one way to reduce uncertainty on projects. A deliverable that has a lot of risk associated with meeting regulatory requirements may choose a predictive approach to build in extra testing, documentation, and robust processes and procedures. A deliverable that has a lot of risk associated with stakeholder acceptance may choose an iterative approach and release a minimum viable product to the market to get feedback before developing additional features and functions.

The Development Approach and Life Cycle Performance Domain has significant overlap with the Delivery Performance Domain when considering delivery cadence and development approach. The delivery cadence is one of the main drivers of delivering value in alignment with the business case and the benefits realization plans. Eliciting the product requirements and meeting the quality requirements as described in the Delivery Performance Domain have a significant influence on the development approach.

The Team Performance Domain and the Development Approach and Life Cycle Performance Domain interact when it comes to project team capabilities and project team leadership skills. The project team's way of working and the project manager's style vary significantly depending on the development approach. A predictive approach usually entails more emphasis on up-front planning, measurement, and control. On the other end of the spectrum, an adaptive approach, especially when using agile methods, requires more of a servant leadership style and may have self-managing project teams.

2.3.8 MEASURING OUTCOMES

Table 2-5 identifies the outcomes on the left and ways of checking them on the right.

Table 2-5. Checking Outcomes—Development Approach and Life Cycle Performance Domain

Outcome	Check
Development approaches that are consistent with project deliverables	The development approach for deliverables (predictive, hybrid, or adaptive) reflects the product variables and is appropriate given the project and organizational variables.
A project life cycle consisting of phases that connect the delivery of business and stakeholder value from the beginning to the end of the project	Project work from launch to close is represented in the project phases. Phases include appropriate exit criteria.
Project life cycle phases that facilitate the delivery cadence and development approach required to produce the project deliverables	The cadence for development, testing, and deploying is represented in the life cycle phases. Projects with multiple deliverables that have different delivery cadences and development methods are represented by overlapping phases or phase repetitions, as necessary.

2.4 PLANNING PERFORMANCE DOMAIN

Planning organizes, elaborates, and coordinates project work throughout the project.

PLANNING PERFORMANCE DOMAIN

The Planning Performance Domain addresses activities and functions associated with the initial, ongoing, and evolving organization and coordination necessary for delivering project deliverables and outcomes.

Effective execution of this performance domain results in the following desired outcomes:

▶ The project progresses in an organized, coordinated, and deliberate manner.

▶ There is a holistic approach to delivering the project outcomes.

▶ Evolving information is elaborated to produce the deliverables and outcomes for which the project was undertaken.

▶ Time spent planning is appropriate for the situation.

▶ Planning information is sufficient to manage stakeholder expectations.

▶ There is a process for the adaptation of plans throughout the project based on emerging and changing needs or conditions.

Figure 2-13. Planning Performance Domain

The following definitions are relevant to the Planning Performance Domain:

Estimate. A quantitative assessment of the likely amount or outcome of a variable, such as project costs, resources, effort, or durations.

Accuracy. Within the quality management system, accuracy is an assessment of correctness.

Precision. Within the quality management system, precision is an assessment of exactness.

Crashing. A method used to shorten the schedule duration for the least incremental cost by adding resources.

Fast Tracking. A schedule compression method in which activities or phases normally done in sequence are performed in parallel for at least a portion of their duration.

Budget. The approved estimate for the project or any work breakdown structure (WBS) component or any schedule activity.

2.4.1 PLANNING OVERVIEW

The purpose of planning is to proactively develop an approach to create the project deliverables. The project deliverables drive the outcomes the project was undertaken to achieve. High-level planning may begin prior to project authorization. The project team progressively elaborates initial project documents, such as a vision statement, project charter, business case, or similar documents to identify or define a coordinated path to achieve the desired outcomes.

It is becoming more common for initial planning to consider social and environmental impacts in addition to the financial impacts (sometimes referred to as the triple bottom line). This may take the form of a product life cycle assessment which evaluates the potential environmental impacts of a product, process, or system. The product life cycle assessment informs the design of products and processes. It considers the impacts of materials and processes with regards to sustainability, toxicity, and the environment.

The amount of time spent planning, both up front and throughout the project, should be determined by the circumstances. It is inefficient to spend more time planning than is needed. Therefore, the information gained from planning should be sufficient to move forward in an appropriate manner but not more detailed than necessary. Project teams use planning artifacts to confirm stakeholder expectations and provide stakeholders with the information they need to make decisions, take action, and maintain alignment between the project and stakeholders.

2.4.2 PLANNING VARIABLES

Because each project is unique, the amount, timing, and frequency of planning varies. Variables that influence how project planning is conducted include, but are not limited to:

▶ **Development approach.** The development approach can influence how, how much, and when planning is conducted. Examples include:

▷ A specific phase for planning or organizing early in the life cycle. In these situations, much of the planning is performed up front. The initial plans are progressively elaborated with more detail throughout the project, but there is little change to the original scope.

▷ An approach with high-level planning up front, followed by a design phase where prototyping is used. After the project team and stakeholders agree to the design, the project team completes more detailed planning.

▷ Adaptive approaches where the project team conducts iterations. Some planning occurs up front to establish release plans and further planning occurs at the beginning of each iteration.

- ▶ **Project deliverables.** Often the project deliverables necessitate planning in a specific way. Construction projects require significant up-front planning to account for design, approvals, materials purchasing, logistics, and delivery. Product development or high-technology projects may use continuous and adaptive planning to allow for evolution and changes based on stakeholder feedback and technological advances.

- ▶ **Organizational requirements.** Organizational governance, policies, procedures, processes, and culture may require project managers to produce specific planning artifacts.

- ▶ **Market conditions.** Product development projects can take place in a highly competitive environment. In these situations, project teams can undertake a minimum amount of up-front planning as the emphasis is on speed to market. The cost of delay that extensive planning entails exceeds the risk of potential rework.

- ▶ **Legal or regulatory restrictions.** Regulatory agencies or statutes may require specific planning documents before granting an authorization to proceed or to secure approval to release the project deliverable into the market.

2.4.2.1 Delivery

Planning begins with understanding the business case, stakeholder requirements, and the project and product scope. *Product scope* is the features and functions that characterize a product, service, or result. *Project scope* is the work performed to deliver a product, service, or result with the specified features and functions.

Predictive planning approaches start with the high-level project deliverables up front and decompose them into more detail. This approach can employ a scope statement and/or a work breakdown structure (WBS) to decompose the scope into lower levels of detail.

Projects that use iterative or incremental approaches can have high-level themes or epics that are decomposed into features, which are then further decomposed into user stories and other backlog items. Work that is unique, significant, risky, or novel can be prioritized to reduce the uncertainty associated with project scope at the start of the project before significant investment has taken place. Project teams plan routine work based on the concept of last responsible moment. This approach defers a decision to allow the project team to consider multiple options until the cost of further delay would exceed the benefit. It reduces waste by not expending time in developing plans for work that may change or may not be needed.

2.4.2.2 Estimating

Planning entails developing estimates for work effort, duration, costs, people, and physical resources. Estimates are a quantitative assessment of the likely amount or outcome of a variable, such as project costs, resources, effort, or duration. As the project evolves, the estimates can change based on current information and circumstances. The project's phase in the life cycle impacts four aspects associated with estimating:

- ▶ **Range.** Estimates tend to have a broad range at the start of the project when there is not much information about the project and product scope, stakeholders, requirements, risks, and other information. Figure 2-14 shows a range of -25 to +75% at the start of exploring a project opportunity. Projects that are well along in their life cycle may have an estimating range of -5 to +10%.

- ▶ **Accuracy.** Accuracy refers to the correctness of an estimate. Accuracy is linked to range in that the lower the accuracy, the larger the potential range of values. An estimate at the start of the project will have less accuracy than one that is developed halfway through the project.

- ▶ **Precision.** Precision is different from accuracy (see Figure 2-15). Precision refers to the degree of exactness associated with the estimate. For example, an estimate of 2 days is more precise than "sometime this week." The precision of estimates should be compatible with the desired accuracy.

- ▶ **Confidence.** Confidence increases with experience. Experience working on a previous, similar project can help with the level of confidence required. For new and evolving technology components, the confidence in estimates is expected to be low.

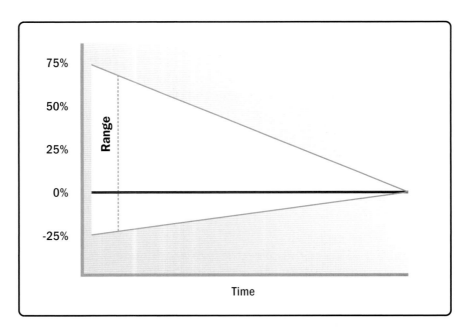

Figure 2-14. Estimate Range Decreases over Time

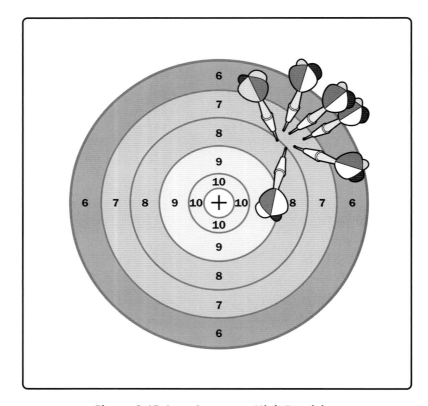

Figure 2-15. Low Accuracy, High Precision

There are different ways of presenting and/or adjusting estimates:

▶ **Deterministic and probabilistic estimating.** Deterministic estimates, also known as point estimates, present a single number or amount, such as 36 months.

Probabilistic estimates include a range of estimates along with the associated probabilities within the range. They can be developed manually by (a) developing a weighted average based on multiple likely outcomes, or (b) running a simulation to develop a probability analysis of a particular outcome, usually in terms of cost or schedule.

●●●●

A probabilistic estimate derived from a computer simulation has three associated factors:

1. A point estimate with a range such as 36 months +3 months/-1 month.

2. A statement of confidence such as a 95% confidence level.

3. A probability distribution describing the dispersion of the data within and around the given range.

Together these three items form a complete metric describing a probabilistic estimate.

●●●●

▶ **Absolute and relative estimating.** Absolute estimates are specific information and use actual numbers. An absolute estimate for effort might be shown as 120 hours of work. One person working full time could accomplish the work in 15 workdays, assuming 8 hours of productivity per workday.

While absolute estimates are specific, relative estimates are shown in comparison to other estimates. Relative estimates only have meaning within a given context.

One form of relative estimating is planning poker. In planning poker, the project team performing the work comes to a consensus on the effort that is necessary to deliver value. Using story points to estimate work could result in 64 story points being assigned for that work. New work is estimated using the amount of estimated work compared to points assigned to previous work. Therefore, new work effort is compared to previously known work effort.

▶ **Flow-based estimating.** Flow-based estimates are developed by determining the cycle time and throughput. Cycle time is the total elapsed time it takes one unit to get through a process. Throughput is the number of items that can complete a process in a given amount of time. These two numbers can provide an estimate to complete a specified quantity of work.

▶ **Adjusting estimates for uncertainty.** Estimates are inherently uncertain. Uncertainty by definition is associated with risk. Key deliverable dates or budget estimates may be adjusted, or contingency time or funds may be added, based on the outcomes of a simulation conducted to establish the range of uncertainty for these parameters.

2.4.2.3 Schedules

A schedule is a model for executing the project's activities, including durations, dependencies, and other planning information. Schedule planning can use predictive or adaptive approaches.

Predictive approaches follow a stepwise process as follows:

▶ **Step 1.** Decompose the project scope into specific activities.

▶ **Step 2.** Sequence related activities.

▶ **Step 3.** Estimate the effort, duration, people, and physical resources required to complete the activities.

▶ **Step 4.** Allocate people and resources to the activities based on availability.

▶ **Step 5.** Adjust the sequence, estimates, and resources until an agreed-upon schedule is achieved.

If the schedule model does not meet the initial desired end date, schedule compression methods are applied. Crashing is a schedule compression method that seeks to shorten the duration for the least incremental cost. Crashing can include adding people to activities, working overtime, or paying to expedite deliveries.

Fast tracking is a schedule compression method in which activities or tasks that are normally done in sequence are performed in parallel, at least for a portion of their duration. Fast tracking often entails applying leads and lags along a network path. A *lead* is where the work of a successor activity is accelerated, such as starting a successor activity before the predecessor has finished. In Figure 2-16, there is a lead between the finish of Task 2 and the start of Task 4.

A *lag* is a delay of a successor activity. An example of using a lag would be changing the type of relationship between activities, and then applying a lag. For example, rather than waiting for an activity to finish before the next one starts (a finish-to-start relationship), change the relationship to have the end of the successor activity finish a determined amount of time after the end of the predecessor (a finish-to-finish relationship). The network logic would show a lag between the finish of the predecessor and the finish of the successor activities. There is an example of a finish-to-finish relationship with a lag in Figure 2-16 between Task 8 and Task 7. A lag can also be applied between the start of one activity and the start of another activity (a start-to-start relationship).

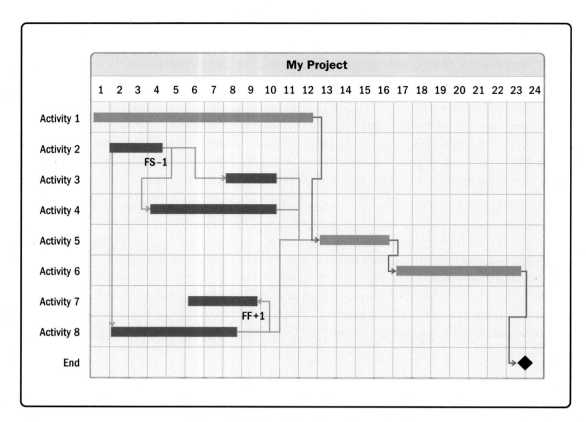

Figure 2-16. Fast Tracking Examples

When compressing the schedule, it is important to determine the nature of the dependencies between activities. Some activities cannot be fast tracked due to the nature of the work—others can. The four types of dependencies are:

▶ **Mandatory dependency.** A relationship that is contractually required or inherent in the nature of the work. This type of dependency usually cannot be modified.

▶ **Discretionary dependency.** A relationship that is based on best practices or project preferences. This type of dependency may be modifiable.

▶ **External dependency.** A relationship between project activities and non-project activities. This type of dependency usually cannot be modified.

▶ **Internal dependency.** A relationship between one or more project activities. This type of dependency may be modifiable.

Adaptive schedule planning uses incremental planning. One such scheduling approach is based on iterations and releases (see Figure 2-17). A high-level release plan is developed that indicates the basic features and functionality to be included in each release. Within each release, there will be two or more iterations. Each iteration adds business and/or stakeholder value. Value may include features, risk reduction, experimentation, or other ways of delivering or protecting value. The planning for the work in future releases is kept at a high level so the project team does not engage in planning that could change based on feedback from earlier releases.

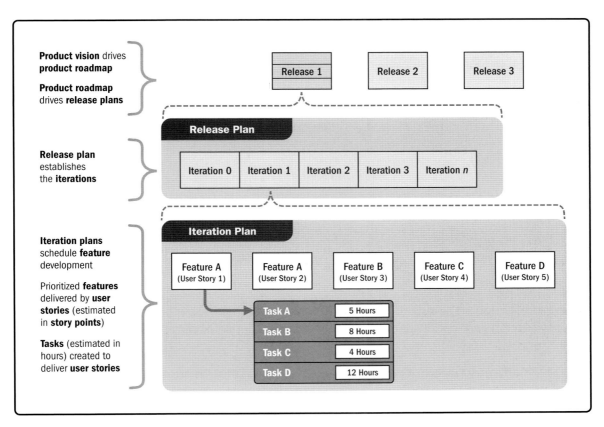

Figure 2-17. Release and Iteration Plan

Adaptive approaches often use timeboxes. The work in each timebox is based on a prioritized backlog. The project team determines the amount of work they can do in each timebox, estimates the work, and self-manages to accomplish the work. At the end of the timebox, the project team demonstrates the work completed. At that point, the backlog and estimates of work available to be done may be updated or reprioritized for the next timebox.

Determining the schedule involves using the information in the estimating section to determine overall duration and effort estimates. Regardless of the scheduling approach used, the relationship between effort and duration needs to be addressed. Some activities are effort driven, which means that the duration can be reduced by adding people. This approach can work up to a point, after which adding people might actually extend duration. Framing a building is effort driven. If more people are added, the duration can be reduced. Some activities are fixed duration, such as running a test or conducting employee training.

The nature of the work determines if and how much the duration can be reduced by adding people before increasing the time due to coordination, communication, conflict, and potential rework. There is no fixed formula to determine the reduction in duration due to the addition of people.

2.4.2.4 Budget

The project budget evolves from the agreed estimates for the project. The information in Section 2.4.2.2 on Estimating is applied to project costs to develop cost estimates. Cost estimates are then aggregated to develop the cost baseline. The cost baseline is often allocated across the project schedule to reflect when the costs will be incurred. This practice allows project managers to balance the funds approved in a specific budget period with the scheduled work. If there are funding limitations for a budget period, the work may need to be rescheduled to meet those limitations.

The project budget should include contingency reserve funds to allow for uncertainty. Contingency reserves are set aside to implement a risk response or to respond to risk events should they occur.

Management reserves are set aside for unexpected activities related to in-scope work. Depending on the organization's policies and organizational structure, management reserves may be managed by the project, the sponsor, product owner, or the PMO at the program and portfolio level. Figure 2-18 shows the budget build up.

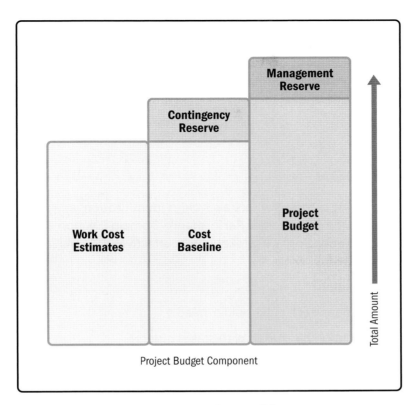

Total Amount

Project Budget Component

Figure 2-18. Budget Build Up

2.4.3 PROJECT TEAM COMPOSITION AND STRUCTURE

Planning for project team[2] composition begins with identifying the skill sets required to accomplish the project work. This entails evaluating not only the skills, but also the level of proficiency and years of experience in similar projects.

There are different cost structures associated with using internal project team members versus securing them from outside the organization. The benefit that outside skills bring to the project are weighed against the costs that will be incurred.

---

[2] This topic is about planning for the project team. Topics associated with project team leadership are addressed in the Team Performance Domain.

When planning for the project team, the project manager considers the ability and necessity for the project team to work in the same location. Small project teams that can work in the same room are able to take advantage of osmotic communication and can solve problems as they arise. Some project teams are physically dispersed. Project team members may be in different cities, time zones, or countries. On projects where project team members work virtually, more time is spent connecting people through technology.

2.4.4 COMMUNICATION

Communication planning overlaps with stakeholder identification, analysis, prioritization, and engagement as described in the Stakeholder Performance Domain (Section 2.1). Communication is the most important factor in engaging with stakeholders effectively. Planning communication for the project entails considering the following:

▶ Who needs information?

▶ What information does each stakeholder need?

▶ Why should information be shared with stakeholders?

▶ What is the best way to provide information?

▶ When and how often is information needed?

▶ Who has the information needed?

There may be different categories of information, such as internal and external, sensitive and public, or general and detailed. Analyzing the stakeholders, information needs, and categories of information provides the foundation for establishing the communications processes and plans for the project.

2.4.5 PHYSICAL RESOURCES

Physical resources apply to any resource that is not a person. It can include materials, equipment, software, testing environments, licenses, and so forth. Planning for physical resources entails estimating, as described in Section 2.4.2.2, as well as supply chain, logistics, and management. Projects with significant physical resources, such as engineering and construction projects, will need to plan for procurement activities to acquire the resources. This may be as simple as utilizing a basic ordering agreement or as complicated as managing, coordinating, and integrating several large procurement activities.

Planning for physical resources includes taking into account lead time for delivery, movement, storage, and disposition of materials, as well as a means to track material inventory from arrival on site to delivery of an integrated product. Project teams whose projects require significant physical materials think and plan strategically about the timing from order, to delivery, to usage. This can include evaluation of bulk ordering versus cost of storage, global logistics, sustainability, and integrating management of physical assets with the rest of the project.

2.4.6 PROCUREMENT

Procurements can happen at any time during a project. However, up-front planning helps to set expectations that ensure the procurement process is performed smoothly. Once the high-level scope is known, project teams conduct a make-or-buy analysis. This includes identifying those deliverables and services that will be developed in-house, and those that will be purchased from external sources. This information impacts the project team and the schedule. Contracting professionals need advance information on the type of goods needed, when they will be needed, and any technical specifications required for the procured goods or services.

2.4.7 CHANGES

There will be changes throughout the project. Some changes are a result of a risk event occurring or a project environment change, some are based on developing a deeper understanding of requirements, and others are due to customer requests or other reasons. Therefore, project teams should prepare a process for adapting plans throughout the project. This may take the form of a change control process, reprioritizing the backlog, or rebaselining the project. Projects that have a contractual element may need to follow a defined process for contract changes.

2.4.8 METRICS

There is a natural linkage between planning, delivering, and measuring work. That linkage is metrics. Establishing metrics includes setting the thresholds that indicate whether work performance is as expected, trending positively or negatively away from expected performance, or unacceptable. Deciding what to measure and how often is best informed by the phrase "only measure what matters."

Metrics associated with the product are specific to the deliverables being developed. Metrics associated with schedule and budget performance are often driven by organizational standards and are related to a baseline or an approved version of the schedule or budget against which actual results are compared.

As part of planning, the metrics, baselines, and thresholds for performance are established, as well as any test and evaluation processes and procedures that will be used to measure performance to the specification of the project deliverable. The metrics, baselines, and tests are used as the basis to evaluate variance of actual performance as part of the Measurement Performance Domain.

2.4.9 ALIGNMENT

Planning activities and artifacts need to remain integrated throughout the project. This means that planning for the performance in terms of scope and quality requirements aligns with delivery commitments, allocated funds, type and availability of resources, the uncertainty inherent in the project, and stakeholder needs. Project teams can require additional planning artifacts depending on the type of project. For example, logistics plans will need to integrate with material and delivery needs, testing plans will need to align with quality and delivery needs, and so forth.

Work on one project often occurs in parallel with other projects in a program or a release. The timing of the work of a single project should align with the needs of the work on related projects and the operations work of the organization.

Large projects may combine the planning artifacts into an integrated project management plan. For smaller projects, a detailed project management plan will be inefficient. Regardless of the timing, frequency, and degree of planning, the various aspects of the project need to remain aligned and integrated.

2.4.10 INTERACTIONS WITH OTHER PERFORMANCE DOMAINS

Planning occurs throughout the project and integrates with each performance domain. At the start of the project, the expected outcomes are identified and high-level plans to achieve them are developed. Depending on the selected development approach and life cycle, intensive planning may be conducted up front, and then plans may be adjusted to reflect the actual environment. Other life cycles encourage just enough planning at various points throughout the project with the expectation that plans will evolve.

Throughout the project, planning guides the project work, delivery of outcomes, and business value. Project teams and stakeholders establish measures of progress and success, and performance is compared to plans. Uncertainty and planning interact as project teams plan for how to address uncertainty and risks. Plans may need to be revised or new plans developed to account for events or conditions that emerge. The project team members, environment, and project details influence plans for working effectively with the project team and engaging proactively with stakeholders.

2.4.11 CHECKING RESULTS

Table 2-6 identifies the outcomes on the left and ways of checking them on the right.

Table 2-6. Checking Outcomes—Planning Performance Domain

Outcome	Check
The project progresses in an organized, coordinated, and deliberate manner.	A performance review of project results against the project baselines and other measurement metrics demonstrates that the project is progressing as planned. Performance variances are within thresholds.
There is a holistic approach to delivering the project outcomes.	The delivery schedule, funding, resource availability, procurements, etc., demonstrate that the project is planned in a holistic manner with no gaps or areas of misalignment.
Evolving information is elaborated to produce the deliverables and outcomes for which the project was undertaken.	Initial information about deliverables and requirements compared to current information demonstrates appropriate elaboration. Current information compared to the business case indicates the project will produce the deliverables and outcomes it was undertaken to deliver.
Time spent planning is appropriate for the situation.	Project plans and documents demonstrate that the level of planning is appropriate for the project.
Planning information is sufficient to manage stakeholder expectations.	The communications management plan and stakeholder information indicate that the communications are sufficient to manage stakeholder expectations.
There is a process for the adaptation of plans throughout the project, based on emerging and changing needs or conditions.	Projects using a backlog show the adaptation of plans throughout the project. Projects using a change control process have change logs and documentation from change control board meetings that demonstrate the change control process is being applied.

2.5 PROJECT WORK PERFORMANCE DOMAIN

PROJECT WORK PERFORMANCE DOMAIN

The Project Work Performance Domain addresses activities and functions associated with establishing project processes, managing physical resources, and fostering a learning environment.

Effective execution of this performance domain results in the following desired outcomes:

▶ Efficient and effective project performance.

▶ Project processes are appropriate for the project and the environment.

▶ Appropriate communication with stakeholders.

▶ Efficient management of physical resources.

▶ Effective management of procurements.

▶ Improved team capability due to continuous learning and process improvement.

Figure 2-19. Project Work Performance Domain

Project work is associated with establishing the processes and performing the work to enable the project team to deliver the expected deliverables and outcomes.

The following definitions are relevant to the Project Work Performance Domain:

Bid Documents. All documents used to solicit information, quotations, or proposals from prospective sellers.

Bidder Conference. The meetings with prospective sellers prior to the preparation of a bid or proposal to ensure all prospective vendors have a clear and common understanding of the procurement. Also known as contractor conferences, vendor conferences, or pre-bid conferences.

Explicit Knowledge. Knowledge that can be codified using symbols such as words, numbers, and pictures.

Tacit Knowledge. Personal knowledge that can be difficult to articulate and share such as beliefs, experience, and insights.

Project work keeps the project team focused and project activities running smoothly. This includes but is not limited to:

▶ Managing the flow of existing work, new work, and changes to work;

▶ Keeping the project team focused;

▶ Establishing efficient project systems and processes;

▶ Communicating with stakeholders;

▶ Managing material, equipment, supplies, and logistics;

▶ Working with contracting professionals and vendors to plan and manage procurements and contracts;

▶ Monitoring changes that can affect the project; and

▶ Enabling project learning and knowledge transfer.

2.5.1 PROJECT PROCESSES

The project manager and the project team establish and periodically review the processes the project team is using to conduct the work. This can take the form of reviewing task boards to determine if there are bottlenecks in the process, if work is flowing at the expected rate, and if there are any impediments that are blocking progress.

Process tailoring can be used to optimize the process for the needs of the project. In general, large projects have more process compared to small projects, and critical projects have more process than less significant projects. Tailoring takes into consideration the demands of the environment. Ways of optimizing the processes for the environment include:

▶ **Lean production methods.** Lean production uses techniques such as value stream mapping to measure the ratio of value-adding activities and non-value-adding activities. The metrics calculated form a basis and measurement system for identifying and removing waste from production systems.

▶ **Retrospectives or lessons learned.** These meetings provide an opportunity for the project team to review the way in which it works and to suggest changes to improve process and efficiency.

▶ **Where is the next best funding spent?** Asking this question can help project teams determine if they should continue with the current task or move onto the next activity to optimize value delivery.

Reviewing processes can entail determining if processes are efficient, or if there is waste in the process that can be eliminated. Time spent tracking conformance to process is time the project team cannot spend on delivering the outcomes for which the project was commissioned. Therefore, project teams utilize just enough time reviewing process conformance to maximize the benefits delivered from the review while still satisfying the governance needs of process.

Example of non-value-added work. A PMO wants to track the type of work project team members are doing. They ask the project team to record the type of work they are doing in specific categories on their time sheets. The time taken to categorize and record their time can be viewed as non-value-added work.

In addition to being efficient, processes should be effective. This means they need to comply with quality requirements, regulations, standards, and organizational policies in addition to producing the desired outcome. Process evaluation can include process audits and quality assurance activities to ensure processes are being followed and are accomplishing the intended outcomes.

2.5.2 BALANCING COMPETING CONSTRAINTS

Successfully leading a project includes understanding the constraints associated with the work. Constraints can take the form of fixed delivery dates, compliance to regulatory codes, a predetermined budget, quality policies, considerations of the triple bottom line, and so forth. The constraints may shift and change throughout the project. A new stakeholder requirement may entail expanding the schedule and budget. A reduction in budget may entail relaxing a quality requirement or reducing scope.

Balancing these shifting constraints, while maintaining stakeholder satisfaction, is an ongoing project activity. At times, it may include meeting with the customer, sponsor, or product owner to present alternatives and implications. Other times, the decisions and potential variances may be within the project team's authority to make trade-offs to deliver the end result. Either way, this balancing activity is ongoing throughout the project.

2.5.3 MAINTAINING PROJECT TEAM FOCUS

Project managers have a responsibility for assessing and balancing the project team focus and attention. This involves evaluating short- and long-term projections of progress toward delivery goals.

Leading the project team includes balancing the workload and assessing if project team members are satisfied with their work so they remain motivated. To maximize business and stakeholder value delivered throughout the project, project team attention needs to be kept in a healthy balance. Leading with a goal of maximizing overall delivered value involves focusing on production (delivering value) and protecting the project team's production capability (project team health and satisfaction). The goal is to keep the project team focused on delivering value and maintain awareness of when potential issues, delays, and cost overruns enter the project.

2.5.4 PROJECT COMMUNICATIONS AND ENGAGEMENT

Much of the project work is associated with communication and engagement, especially work associated with maintaining project team member and other stakeholder engagement. As described in the Stakeholder Performance Domain, communication entails formal and informal communication, in addition to verbal and written communication. Information can be collected in meetings, conversations, and by pulling information from electronic repositories. Once collected, it is distributed as indicated in the project management communications plan.

On a day-to-day basis, there are ad hoc requests for information, presentations, reports, and other forms of communication. An abundance of ad hoc communication requests may indicate that the communication planning was not sufficient to meet stakeholder needs. In this situation, further stakeholder engagement may be necessary to ensure stakeholder information requirements are met.

2.5.5 MANAGING PHYSICAL RESOURCES

Some projects require materials and supplies from third parties. Planning, ordering, transporting, storing, tracking, and controlling these physical resources can take a large amount of time and effort.

Large amounts of physical resources require an integrated logistics system. This is usually documented in company policies that are then implemented in projects. A logistics plan describes how the company policy will be implemented on the project. Supporting documentation includes estimates for the type of material, basis of estimates, expected usage over time, specifications for grade, and the time and location for deliveries.

The objectives from a physical resource perspective are to:

▶ Reduce or eliminate the material handling and storage on site,

▶ Eliminate wait times for materials,

▶ Minimize scrap and waste, and

▶ Facilitate a safe work environment.

All of this work is integrated with the master project schedule to provide clear expectations and communications for all parties involved.

2.5.6 WORKING WITH PROCUREMENTS

Many projects involve some form of contracting or procurement. Procurement can cover everything from material, capital equipment, and supplies to solutions, labor, and services. In most organizations, project managers do not have contracting authority. Rather, they work with contracting officers or other people with expertise in contracts, laws, and regulations. Organizations usually have rigorous policies and procedures associated with procurements. The policies identify who has authority to enter into a contract, the limits of authority, and the processes and procedures that should be followed.

Prior to conducting a procurement, the project manager and technically qualified project team members work with contracting professionals to develop the request for proposals (RFP), statement of work (SOW), terms and conditions, and other necessary documents to go out to bid.

2.5.6.1 The Bid Process

The bid process includes developing and publicizing bid documents, bidder conferences, and selecting a bidder.

Bid documents can include:

- ▶ **Request for information.** A request for information is used to gather more information from the market prior to sending out bid documents to a set of selected vendors.

- ▶ **Request for proposal.** This bid document is used for complex or complicated scope where the buyer is looking for the vendor to provide a solution.

- ▶ **Request for quote.** This bid document is used when price is the main deciding factor, and the proposed solution is readily available.

These three types cover the majority of bidding needs. There are other bid documents; however, they tend to be industry specific.

Once the bid documents are distributed, the buyer generally has a bidder conference to respond to bidder questions and provide clarifying information. Then the bidders develop their responses and deliver them to the buyer by the date specified in the bid documents.

Choosing the best vendor, sometimes known as source selection, is often based on a number of criteria, such as experience, references, price, and timely delivery. These variables may be weighted to reflect the relative importance of each. The buyer evaluates vendor bids against the criteria to select an appropriate vendor(s). The buyer and vendor negotiate terms and conditions. Most everything can be negotiated, from cost to delivery and payment dates, to location of work, ownership of intellectual property, and so forth.

2.5.6.2 Contracting

Eventually, the parties reach agreement and enter into a contract. The type of contracting vehicle depends on the size of the purchase, the stability of the scope of work, and the risk tolerances of the organizations.

For projects that use an adaptive approach for some deliverables and a predictive approach for others, a master agreement may be used for the overall contract. The adaptive work may be placed in an appendix or supplement. This allows the changes to occur on the adaptive scope without impacting the overall contract.

Once the vendor is selected, the project plans and documents are updated to incorporate vendor dates, resources, costs, quality requirements, risks, etc. From that point, the vendor becomes a project stakeholder. Information in the Stakeholders Performance Domain and Measurement Performance Domain will apply to the vendor(s) throughout the project.

Procurements can take place at any point during the project. All procurement activities are integrated into the project operations.

2.5.7 MONITORING NEW WORK AND CHANGES

In adaptive projects, there is an expectation that work will evolve and adapt. As a result, new work can be added to the product backlog, as needed. However, if more work is added than is being completed, or if the same amount of work is added that is being completed, the project will continue without end. The project manager works with the product owner to manage expectations around adding scope, the implications to the budget, and the availability of project team members. The product owner prioritizes the project backlog on an ongoing basis so that high-priority items are completed. If the schedule or budget is constrained, the product owner may consider the project done when the highest priority items are delivered.

In predictive projects, the project team actively manages changes to the work to ensure only approved changes are included in the scope baseline. Any changes to the scope are then accompanied by appropriate changes to the people, resources, schedule, and budget. Scope changes can add to uncertainty; therefore, any change requests should be accompanied by an evaluation of any new risks that are introduced due to the addition to or change in scope. The project manager works with the change control board and the change requestor to guide change requests through the change control process. Approved changes are integrated into the applicable project planning documents, product backlog, and project scope. The changes are also communicated to the appropriate stakeholders.

2.5.8 LEARNING THROUGHOUT THE PROJECT

Periodically, the project team may meet to determine what they can do better in the future (lessons learned) and how they can improve and challenge the process in upcoming iterations (retrospectives). Ways of working can evolve to produce better outcomes.

2.5.8.1 Knowledge Management

A lot of learning takes place during projects. Some of the learning is project specific, such as a faster way to accomplish specific work. Some learning can be shared with other project teams to improve outcomes, such as a quality assurance approach that results in fewer defects. Still other learning can be shared throughout the organization, such as training users how to work with a new software application.

2.5.8.2 Explicit and Tacit Knowledge

Throughout the project, project teams develop and share explicit knowledge. Explicit knowledge can be readily codified using words, pictures, or numbers. For example, the steps to a new process are explicit knowledge that can be documented. Explicit knowledge can be distributed using information management tools to connect people to information, such as manuals, registers, web searches, and databases.

Another type of knowledge is tacit knowledge. Tacit knowledge is challenging to express as it cannot be codified. Tacit knowledge is comprised of experience, insights, and practical knowledge or skill. Tacit knowledge is shared by connecting the people who need the knowledge with people who have the knowledge. This can be accomplished via networking, interviews, job shadowing, discussion forums, workshops, or other similar methods.

Because projects are temporary endeavors, much of the knowledge is lost once the project is completed. Being attentive to knowledge transfer serves the organization by not only delivering the value that the project was undertaken to achieve, it also allows the organization to gain knowledge from the experience of running projects.

2.5.9 INTERACTIONS WITH OTHER PERFORMANCE DOMAINS

The Project Work Performance Domain interacts and enables other performance domains on the project. Project work enables and supports efficient and effective planning, delivery, and measurement. It provides the environment for project team meetings, interactions, and stakeholder engagement to be effective. Project work supports navigating uncertainty, ambiguity, and complexity; and it balances their impacts with the other project constraints.

2.5.10 CHECKING RESULTS

Table 2-7 identifies the outcomes on the left and ways of checking them on the right.

Table 2-7. Checking Outcomes—Project Work Performance Domain

Outcome	Check
Efficient and effective project performance	Status reports show that project work is efficient and effective.
Project processes that are appropriate for the project and the environment	Evidence shows that the project processes have been tailored to meet the needs of the project and the environment. Process audits and quality assurance activities show that the processes are relevant and being used effectively.
Appropriate communication and engagement with stakeholders	The project communications management plan and communication artifacts demonstrate that the planned communications are being delivered to stakeholders. There are few ad hoc requests for information or misunderstandings that might indicate engagement and communication activities are not effective.
Efficient management of physical resources	The amount of material used, scrap discarded, and amount of rework indicate that resources are being used efficiently.
Effective management of procurements	A procurement audit demonstrates that appropriate processes utilized were sufficient for the procurement and that the contractor is performing to plan.
Effective handling of change	Projects using a predictive approach have a change log that demonstrates changes are being evaluated holistically with consideration for scope, schedule, budget, resource, stakeholder, and risk impacts. Projects using an adaptive approach have a backlog that shows the rate of accomplishing scope and the rate of adding new scope.
Improved capability due to continuous learning and process improvement	Team status reports show fewer errors and rework with an increase in velocity.

2.6 DELIVERY PERFORMANCE DOMAIN

DELIVERY PERFORMANCE DOMAIN

The Delivery Performance Domain addresses activities and functions associated with delivering the scope and quality that the project was undertaken to achieve.

Effective execution of this performance domain results in the following desired outcomes:

▶ Projects contribute to business objectives and advancement of strategy.

▶ Projects realize the outcomes they were initiated to deliver.

▶ Project benefits are realized in the time frame in which they were planned.

▶ The project team has a clear understanding of requirements.

▶ Stakeholders accept and are satisfied with project deliverables.

Figure 2-20. Delivery Performance Domain

Projects support strategy execution and the advancement of business objectives. Project delivery focuses on meeting requirements, scope, and quality expectations to produce the expected deliverables that will drive the intended outcomes.

The following definitions are relevant to the Delivery Performance Domain:

Requirement. A condition or capability that is necessary to be present in a product, service, or result to satisfy a business need.

Work Breakdown Structure (WBS). A hierarchical decomposition of the total scope of work to be carried out by the project team to accomplish the project objectives and create the required deliverables.

Definition of Done (DoD). A checklist of all the criteria required to be met so that a deliverable can be considered ready for customer use.

Quality. The degree to which a set of inherent characteristics fulfills requirements.

Cost of Quality (COQ). All costs incurred over the life of the product by investment in preventing nonconformance to requirements, appraisal of the product or service for conformance to requirements, and failure to meet requirements.

Projects provide business value by developing new products or services, solving problems, or fixing features that were defective or suboptimal. Projects often deliver multiple outcomes that stakeholders may value differently. For example, one group may value ease of use or the time-saving aspects of a deliverable while another group values its economic return or market differentiation.

2.6.1 DELIVERY OF VALUE

Projects that use a development approach that supports releasing deliverables throughout the project life cycle can start delivering value to the business, customer, or other stakeholders during the project. Projects that deliver the bulk of their deliverable at the end of the project life cycle generate value after the initial deployment.

Business value often continues to be captured long after the initial project has ended. Frequently, longer product and program life cycles are used to measure the benefits and value contributed by earlier projects.

A business case document often provides the business justification and a projection of anticipated business value from a project. The format of this business case varies based on the development approach and life cycle selected. Examples include business case documents with detailed estimates of return on investment or a lean, start-up canvas that describes high-level elements such as the problem, solution, revenue streams, and cost structures. These business documents demonstrate how the project outcomes align with the organization's business objectives.

Project-authorizing documents attempt to quantify the project's desired outcomes to allow for periodic measurement. These documents may range from detailed, baselined plans or high-level roadmaps that provide an overview of the project life cycle, major releases, key deliverables, reviews, and other top-level information.

2.6.2 DELIVERABLES

In this context, *deliverable* refers to the interim or final product, service, or results from a project. The deliverables enable the outcomes that the project was undertaken to create. Deliverables reflect the stakeholder requirements, scope, and quality, along with the long-term impacts to profit, people, and the planet.

2.6.2.1 Requirements

A requirement is a condition or capability that is necessary to be present in a product, service, or result to satisfy a business need. Requirements can be very high level, such as those found in a business case, or they can be very detailed, such as those found in acceptance criteria for a component of a system.

Projects that have a well-defined scope, which is relatively stable, generally work with project stakeholders to elicit and document the requirements during up-front planning. Projects that have a high-level understanding of the requirements at the start of a project may evolve those requirements over time. Some projects discover requirements during project work.

- **Requirements elicitation.** To elicit means to draw out, bring forth, or evoke. There is more to collecting requirements than interviewing or conducting focus groups. Sometimes requirements are drawn out by analyzing data, observing processes, reviewing defect logs, or other methods.

  Part of eliciting requirements is documenting them and gaining stakeholder agreement. Well-documented requirements meet the following criteria:

  ▷ *Clear.* There is only one way to interpret the requirement.

  ▷ *Concise.* The requirement is stated in as few words as possible.

  ▷ *Verifiable.* There is a way to verify that the requirement has been met.

  ▷ *Consistent.* There are no contradictory requirements.

  ▷ *Complete.* The set of requirements represents the entirety of the current project or product needs.

  ▷ *Traceable.* Each requirement can be recognized by a unique identifier.

- **Evolving and discovering requirements.** On projects that do not have clearly defined requirements up front, prototypes, demonstrations, storyboards, and mock-ups can be used to evolve the requirements. In these situations, stakeholders are more likely to take an "I'll know it when I see it" approach to developing requirements. Evolving requirements are common in projects using iterative, incremental, or adaptive development approaches. In some cases, new opportunities arise that change requirements.

- **Managing requirements.** Regardless of whether requirements are documented up front, evolved along the way, or discovered, there is a need to manage them. Ineffective requirements management can lead to rework, scope creep, customer dissatisfaction, budget overruns, schedule delay, and overall project failure. Therefore, many projects have one accountable person for requirements management. This person may serve as business analyst, product owner, value engineer, or other title. Those individuals managing requirements may use specialized software, backlogs, index cards, traceability matrices, or some other method to ensure there is an appropriate level of requirement flexibility versus stability, and that new and changing requirements are agreed to by all relevant stakeholders.

2.6.2.2 Scope Definition

As requirements are identified, the scope that will meet them is defined. Scope is the sum of the products, services, and results to be provided as a project. As scope is defined, it creates the need for more requirements identification. Therefore, like requirements, scope can be well defined up front, it can evolve over time, or it can be discovered.

▶ **Scope decomposition.** Scope can be elaborated using a scope statement to identify the major deliverables associated with the project and the acceptance criteria for each deliverable. Scope can also be elaborated by decomposing it into lower levels of detail using a work breakdown structure (WBS). A WBS is a hierarchical decomposition of the total scope of work to be carried out by the project team to accomplish the project objectives and create the required deliverables. Each level down in the hierarchy represents a greater level of detail of the deliverable and work required to produce it.

Another way to elaborate scope is by identifying the themes of the project in an agile charter, roadmap, or as part of the product hierarchy. Themes represent large groups of customer value reflected as user stories associated by a common factor, such as functionality, data source, or security level. To accomplish themes, the project team develops epics, which are logical containers for a large user story that is too big to complete within an iteration. Epics may be decomposed into features, a set of related requirements typically described as a short phrase or function, which represent specific behaviors of a product. Each feature will have multiple user stories. A user story is a brief description of an outcome for a specific user, which is a promise for a conversation to clarify details. The project team defines story details at the last responsible moment to avoid wasteful planning should the scope change. The story is a clear and concise representation of a requirement written from the end user's perspective.

▶ **Completion of deliverables.** Depending on the approach used, there are different ways to describe component or project completion:

▷ *Acceptance or completion criteria.* The criteria required to be met before the customer accepts the deliverable or before the project is considered complete are often documented in a scope statement.

▷ *Technical performance measures.* The technical specifications for a product may be documented in a separate specifications document, or they may be documented as an extension to the WBS. This extension, known as a WBS dictionary, elaborates the information for each deliverable (work package) in the WBS.

▷ *Definition of done.* The definition of done is used with adaptive approaches, particularly in software development projects. It is a checklist of all the criteria required to be met so that a deliverable can be considered ready for customer use.

2.6.2.3 Moving Targets of Completion

Projects that operate in uncertain and rapidly changing environments face the situation that a "good enough for release" or "done" goal may be subject to change. In markets where competitors are releasing new products frequently, the features planned for a new release may be updated. Likewise, new technology trends, such as mobile devices or wearable devices, might trigger a change in direction or introduce new requirements.

In these environments, the definition of the project goal being delivered or "done" is constantly moving. Project teams track the planned rate of project goal achievement relative to the rate of progress toward completion. The longer the project takes to complete, the further the project goal of "done" is likely to move. This is sometimes referred to as "done drift."

Figure 2-21 shows a scenario for developing a new smart watch. The initial schedule shows 12 months to develop the watch with the initial set of capabilities and features. As competitors launch similar products, the initial set of capabilities and features increases to stay relevant with the market. This pushes the launch date to Month 14. At 13 months, another competitor launches a product with even more capabilities. Adding these capabilities would delay the launch to Month 16. At some point, a decision will be made whether to release the product as is, even though it doesn't have the latest features, or continue to update the features prior to launch.

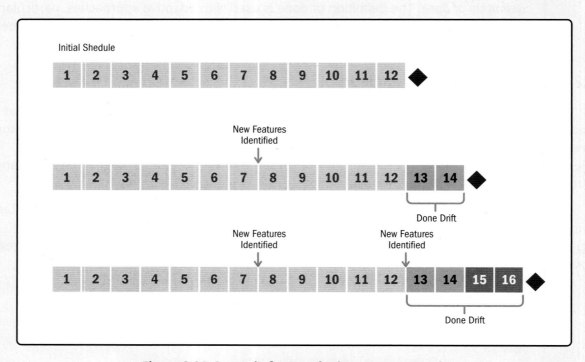

Figure 2-21. Scenario for Developing a Smart Watch

Projects that operate in a more stable environment often face "scope creep." This is when additional scope or requirements are accepted without adjusting the corresponding schedule, budget, or resource needs. To combat scope creep, project teams use a change control system where all changes are evaluated for the potential value they bring to the project and the potential resources, time, and budget needed to realize the potential value. The project team then presents the changes to the project governance body, product owner, or executive sponsor for formal approval.

2.6.3 QUALITY

Delivery is more than just scope and requirements. Scope and requirements focus on what needs to be delivered. Quality focuses on the performance levels that are required to be met. Quality requirements may be reflected in the completion criteria, definition of done, statement of work, or requirements documentation.

Much of the costs associated with quality are born by the sponsoring organization and are reflected in policies, procedures, and work processes. For example, organizational policies that govern how work is performed and procedures that prescribe work processes are often part of the organization's quality policy. The cost of overhead, training, and process audit are born by the organization, though they are employed by the project. Inherent in projects is balancing the quality needs of the processes and products with the costs associated with meeting those needs.

2.6.3.1 Cost of Quality

The cost of quality (COQ) methodology is used to find the appropriate balance for investing in quality prevention and appraisal to avoid defect or product failures. This model identifies four categories of costs associated with quality: prevention, appraisal, internal failure, and external failure. Prevention and appraisal costs are associated with the cost of compliance to quality requirements. Internal and external failure costs are associated with the cost of noncompliance.

▶ **Prevention.** Prevention costs are incurred to keep defects and failures out of a product. Prevention costs avoid quality problems. They are associated with the design, implementation, and maintenance of the quality management system. They are planned and incurred before actual operation. Examples include:

▷ *Product or service requirements,* such as the establishment of specifications for incoming materials, processes, finished products, and services;

▷ *Quality planning,* such as the creation of plans for quality, reliability, operations, production, and inspection;

▷ *Quality assurance,* such as the creation and maintenance of the quality system; and

▷ *Training,* such as the development, preparation, and maintenance of programs.

▶ **Appraisal.** Appraisal costs are incurred to determine the degree of conformance to quality requirements. Appraisal costs are associated with measuring and monitoring activities related to quality. These costs may be associated with evaluation of purchased materials, processes, products, and services to ensure that they conform to specifications. They could include:

▷ *Verification,* such as checking incoming material, process setup, and products against agreed specifications;

▷ *Quality audits,* such as confirmation that the quality system is functioning correctly; and

▷ *Supplier rating,* such as assessment and approval of suppliers of products and services.

- ► **Internal Failure.** Internal failure costs are associated with finding and correcting defects before the customer receives the product. These costs are incurred when the results of work fail to reach design quality standards. Examples include:

  - ▷ *Waste,* such as performance of unnecessary work or holding enough stock to account for errors, poor organization, or communication;

  - ▷ *Scrap,* such as defective product or material that cannot be repaired, used, or sold;

  - ▷ *Rework or rectification,* such as correction of defective material or errors; and

  - ▷ *Failure analysis,* such as activities required to establish the causes of internal product or service failure.

- ► **External Failure.** External failure costs are associated with defects found after the customer has the product and with remediation. Note that to consider these failures holistically requires thinking about the project's product while it is in operation after months or years, not just at the handover date. External failure costs occur when products or services that fail to reach design quality standards are not detected until after they have reached the customer. Examples include:

  - ▷ *Repairs and servicing,* for both returned products and those that are deployed;

  - ▷ *Warranty claims,* such as failed products that are replaced or services that are reperformed under a guarantee;

  - ▷ *Complaints,* for all work and costs associated with handling and servicing customers' complaints;

  - ▷ *Returns,* for handling and investigation of rejected or recalled products, including transport costs; and

  - ▷ *Reputation,* where reputation and public perception can be damaged depending on the type and severity of defects.

To optimize delivered value, early inspection and review work focused on finding quality issues as soon as possible are good investments. Attempts to "test-quality-in" late in the development life cycle are likely to fail because discovering quality issues late in development is time- and cost-prohibitive due to high rates of scrap and rework, along with the ripple effect to downstream outputs and stakeholders.

2.6.3.2 Cost of Change

The later a defect is found, the more expensive it is to correct. This is because design and development work have typically already occurred based on the flawed component. Also, activities are more costly to modify as the life cycle progresses since more stakeholders are impacted. This phenomenon is characterized by the cost of change curve (see Figure 2-22).

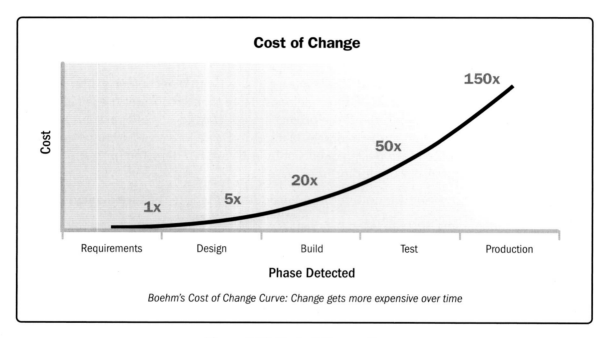

Figure 2-22. Cost of Change Curve

To counter the impacts of the cost of change curve, project teams design project processes to build in quality. This approach can include quality analysts working with designers and engineers to understand and determine how best to achieve quality during each step in the project life cycle. Being proactive about quality work helps avoid the high cost of change associated with fixing quality issues discovered later in the life cycle. It is quicker and more cost efficient to fix a design problem between two engineers than a component problem affecting hundreds of units or to recall a product impacting thousands of customers.

2.6.4 SUBOPTIMAL OUTCOMES

All projects attempt to deliver outcomes, though some may fail to do so or may produce suboptimal outcomes. The potential for suboptimal outcomes exists in every project. In the case of a fully experimental project, the organization is attempting to achieve a breakthrough, such as the creation of a completely new technology, for example. This requires deliberate investment in an uncertain outcome. Companies that produce new medicines or compounds may experience several failures before finding a successful formula. Some projects may fail to deliver outcomes because the market opportunity has passed or competitors were first to market with their offering. Effective project management can minimize negative outcomes, but such possibilities are part of the uncertainty of attempting to produce a unique deliverable.

2.6.5 INTERACTIONS WITH OTHER PERFORMANCE DOMAINS

The Delivery Performance Domain is the culmination of the work done in the Planning Performance Domain. The delivery cadence is based on the way work is structured in the Development Approach and Life Cycle Performance Domain. The Project Work Performance Domain enables the deliveries by establishing processes, managing physical resources, managing procurements, and so forth. Project team members perform the work in this performance domain for the relevant stakeholders. The nature of the work to create the deliveries will influence how the project team navigates uncertainty that impacts the project.

2.6.6 CHECKING RESULTS

Table 2-8 identifies the outcomes on the left and ways of checking them on the right.

Table 2-8. Checking Outcomes—Delivery Performance Domain

Outcome	Check
Projects contribute to business objectives and advancement of strategy	The business plan and the organization's strategic plan, along with the project authorizing documents, demonstrate that the project deliverables and business objectives are aligned.
Projects realize the outcomes they were initiated to deliver	The business case and underlying data indicate the project is still on track to realize the intended outcomes.
Project benefits are realized in the time frame in which they were planned	The benefits realization plan, business case, and/or schedule indicate that the financial metrics and scheduled deliveries are being achieved as planned.
The project team has a clear understanding of requirements	In predictive development, little change in the initial requirements reflects understanding. In projects where requirements are evolving, a clear understanding of requirements may not take place until well into the project.
Stakeholders accept and are satisfied with project deliverables	Interviews, observation, and end user feedback indicate stakeholder satisfaction with deliverables. Levels of complaints and returns can also be used to indicate satisfaction.

2.7 MEASUREMENT PERFORMANCE DOMAIN

MEASUREMENT PERFORMANCE DOMAIN

The **Measurement Performance Domain** addresses activities and functions associated with assessing project performance and taking appropriate actions to maintain acceptable performance.

Effective execution of this performance domain results in the following desired outcomes:

▶ A reliable understanding of the status of the project.

▶ Actionable data to facilitate decision making.

▶ Timely and appropriate actions to keep project performance on track.

▶ Achieving targets and generating business value by making informed and timely decisions based on reliable forecasts and evaluations.

Figure 2-23. Measurement Performance Domain

Measurement involves assessing project performance and implementing appropriate responses to maintain optimal performance.

The following definitions are relevant to the Measurement Performance Domain:

Metric. A description of a project or product attribute and how to measure it.

Baseline. The approved version of a work product used as a basis for comparison to actual results.

Dashboard. A set of charts and graphs showing progress or performance against important measures of the project.

The Measurement Performance Domain evaluates the degree to which the work done in the Delivery Performance Domain is meeting the metrics identified in the Planning Performance Domain. For example, performance can be measured and evaluated using baselines identified in the Planning Performance Domain. Having timely and accurate information about project work and performance allows the project team to learn and determine the appropriate action to take to address current or expected variances from the desired performance.

Measures are used for multiple reasons, including:

▶ Evaluating performance compared to plan;

▶ Tracking the utilization of resources, work completed, budget expended, etc.;

▶ Demonstrating accountability;

▶ Providing information to stakeholders;

▶ Assessing whether project deliverables are on track to deliver planned benefits;

▶ Focusing conversations about trade-offs, threats, opportunities, and options; and

▶ Ensuring the project deliverables will meet customer acceptance criteria.

The value of measurements is not in the collection and dissemination of the data, but rather in the conversations about how to use the data to take appropriate action. Therefore, while much of this performance domain addresses various types of measurements that can be captured, use of the measures occurs within the context of activities in other performance domains, such as project team and stakeholder discussions, coordinating project work, and so forth.

This performance domain focuses on measures for active projects. A portfolio leader may want to include measures that address the success of the project after it is completed, such as whether the project delivered the intended outcomes and benefits. Portfolio leaders may assess if the project outcome increased customer satisfaction, decreased cost per unit, or other measures that are not available until after the project has closed. Similarly, business managers may assess the project from the perspective of the value the outcome brings to the organization. Business measures might include the increase in market share, increase in profit, or decrease in cost per unit. The Measurement Performance Domain addresses measures and metrics that are used during the project.

2.7.1 ESTABLISHING EFFECTIVE MEASURES

Establishing effective measures helps to ensure the right things are measured and reported to stakeholders. Effective measures allow for tracking, evaluating, and reporting information that can communicate project status, help improve project performance, and reduce the likelihood of performance deterioration. These measures allow the project team to use information to make timely decisions and take effective actions.

2.7.1.1 Key Performance Indicators

Key performance indicators (KPIs) for projects are quantifiable measures used to evaluate the success of a project. There are two types of KPIs: leading indicators and lagging indicators.

▶ **Leading indicators.** Leading indicators predict changes or trends in the project. If the change or trend is unfavorable, the project team evaluates the root cause of the leading indicator measurement and takes actions to reverse the trend. Used in this way, leading indicators can reduce performance risk on a project by identifying potential performance variances before they cross the tolerance threshold.

Leading indicators may be quantifiable, such as the size of the project or the number of items that are in progress in the backlog. Other leading indicators are more difficult to quantify, but they provide early warning signs of potential problems. The lack of a risk management process, stakeholders who are not available or engaged, or poorly defined project success criteria are all examples of leading indicators that project performance may be at risk.

▶ **Lagging indicators.** Lagging indicators measure project deliverables or events. They provide information after the fact. Lagging indicators reflect past performance or conditions. Lagging indicators are easier to measure than leading indicators. Examples include the number of deliverables completed, the schedule or cost variance, and the amount of resources consumed.

Lagging indicators can also be used to find correlations between outcomes and environmental variables. For example, a lagging indicator that shows a schedule variance may show a correlation with project team member dissatisfaction. This correlation can assist the project team in addressing a root cause that may not have been obvious if the only measure was schedule status.

In and of themselves, KPIs are simply measures that have no real use unless and until they are used. Discussing leading and lagging indicators and identifying areas for improvement, as appropriate, can have a positive impact on performance.

2.7.1.2 Effective Metrics

Measuring takes time and effort, which could otherwise be spent on other productive work; therefore, project teams should only measure what is relevant and should ensure that the metrics are useful. Characteristics of effective metrics (or SMART criteria) include:

▶ **Specific.** Measurements are specific as to what to measure. Examples include the number of defects, the defects that have been fixed, or the average time it takes to fix defects.

▶ **Meaningful.** Measures should be tied to the business case, baselines, or requirements. It is not efficient to measure product attributes or project performance that do not lead to meeting objectives or improving performance.

▶ **Achievable.** The target is achievable given the people, technology, and environment.

▶ **Relevant.** Measures should be relevant. The information provided by the measure should provide value and allow for actionable information.

▶ **Timely.** Useful measurements are timely. Information that is old is not as useful as fresh information. Forward-looking information, such as emerging trends, can help project teams change direction and make better decisions.

● ● ● ●

The SMART acronym described previously can use alternative terms. For example, some people prefer "measurable" instead of *meaningful,* "agreed to" instead of *achievable,* "realistic" or "reasonable" instead of *relevant,* and "time bound" instead of *timely.*

● ● ● ●

2.7.2 WHAT TO MEASURE

What is measured, the parameters, and the measurement method depend on the project objectives, the intended outcomes, and the environment in which the project takes place. Common categories of metrics include:

▶ Deliverable metrics,

▶ Delivery,

▶ Baseline performance,

▶ Resources,

▶ Business value,

▶ Stakeholders, and

▶ Forecasts.

A balanced set of metrics helps to provide a holistic picture of the project, its performance, and its outcomes.

Sections 2.7.2.1 through 2.7.2.7 provide a brief description of these categories.

2.7.2.1 Deliverable Metrics

By necessity, the products, services, or results being delivered determine the useful measures. Customary measures include:

▶ **Information on errors or defects.** This measure includes the source of defects, number of defects identified, and number of defects resolved.

▶ **Measures of performance.** Measures of performance characterize physical or functional attributes relating to the system operation. Examples include size, weight, capacity, accuracy, reliability, efficiency, and similar performance measures.

▶ **Technical performance measures.** Quantifiable measures of technical performance are used to ensure system components meet technical requirements. They provide insights into progress in achieving the technical solution.

2.7.2.2 Delivery

Delivery measurements are associated with work in progress. These measures are frequently used in projects using adaptive approaches.

- ▶ **Work in progress.** This measure indicates the number of work items that are being worked on at any given time. It is used to help the project team limit the number of items in progress to a manageable size.

- ▶ **Lead time.** This measure indicates the amount of elapsed time from a story or chunk of work entering the backlog to the end of the iteration or the release. Lower lead time indicates a more effective process and a more productive project team.

- ▶ **Cycle time.** Related to lead time, cycle time indicates the amount of time it takes the project team to complete a task. Shorter times indicate a more productive project team. A consistent time helps predict the possible rate of work in the future.

- ▶ **Queue size.** This measure tracks the number of items in a queue. This metric can be compared to the work in progress limit. Little's Law states that queue size is proportional to both the rate of arrival in the queue and the rate of completion of items from the queue. One can gain insights into completion times by measuring work in progress and developing a forecast for future work completion.

- ▶ **Batch size.** Batch size measures the estimated amount of work (level of effort, story points, etc.) that is expected to be completed in an iteration.

- ▶ **Process efficiency.** Process efficiency is a ratio used in lean systems to optimize the flow of work. This measure calculates the ratio between value-adding time and non-value-adding activities. Tasks that are waiting increase the non-value-adding time. Tasks that are in development or in verification represent value-adding time. Higher ratios indicate a more efficient process.

2.7.2.3 Baseline Performance

The most common baselines are cost and schedule. Projects that track a scope or technical baseline can use information in the deliverable measures.

Most schedule measures track actual performance to planned performance related to:

▶ **Start and finish dates.** Comparing the actual start dates to the planned start dates and the actual finish dates to the planned finish dates can measure the extent to which work is accomplished as planned. Even if work is not on the longest path through the project (the critical path), late start and finish dates indicate that the project is not performing to plan.

▶ **Effort and duration.** Actual effort and duration compared to planned effort and duration indicates whether estimates for the amount of work and the time the work takes are valid.

▶ **Schedule variance (SV).** A simple schedule variance is determined by looking at performance on the critical path. When used with earned value management, it is the difference between the earned value and the planned value. Figure 2-24 shows an earned value graph illustrating the schedule variance.

▶ **Schedule performance index (SPI).** Schedule performance index is an earned value management measure that indicates how efficiently the scheduled work is being performed.

▶ **Feature completion rates.** Examining the rate of feature acceptance during frequent reviews can help assess progress and estimate completion dates and costs.

Common cost measures include:

▶ **Actual cost compared to planned cost.** This cost measure compares the actual cost for labor or resources to the estimated cost. This term may be referred to as the burn rate.

▶ **Cost variance (CV).** A simple cost variance is determined by comparing the actual cost of a deliverable to the estimated cost. When used with earned value management, it is the difference between the earned value and the actual cost. Figure 2-24 shows an earned value graph illustrating the cost variance.

▶ **Cost performance index (CPI).** An earned value management measure that indicates how efficiently the work is being performed with regard to the budgeted cost of the work.

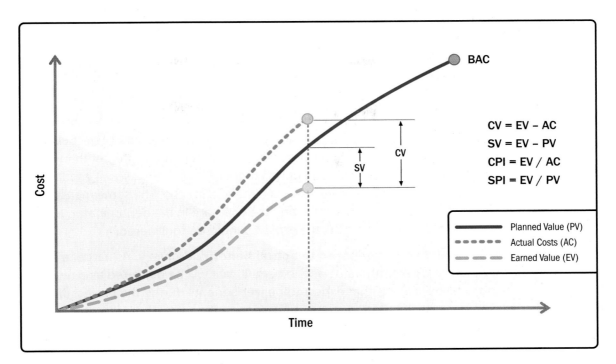

Figure 2-24. Earned Value Analysis Showing Schedule and Cost Variance

2.7.2.4 Resources

Resource measurements may be a subset of cost measurements since resource variances frequently lead to cost variances. The two measures evaluate price variance and usage variance. Measures include:

▶ **Planned resource utilization compared to actual resource utilization.** This measurement compares the actual usage of resources to the estimated usage. A usage variance is calculated by subtracting the planned usage from the actual usage.

▶ **Planned resource cost compared to actual resource cost.** This measurement compares the actual cost of resources to the estimated cost. Price variance is calculated by subtracting the estimated cost from the actual cost.

2.7.2.5 Business Value

Business value measurements are used to ensure the project deliverable stays aligned to the business case and the benefits realization plans. Business value has many aspects—both financial and nonfinancial. Metrics that measure financial business value include:

▶ **Cost-benefit ratio.** This is a measure of the expected present value of an investment with the initial cost. The cost-benefit ratio is used to determine if the costs of a project outweigh its benefits. If the costs are greater than the benefits, the result will be greater than 1.0. In this case, the project should not be considered unless there are regulatory, social good, or other reasons to do the project. A similar measure is a benefit-cost ratio. The same measures are used, but the benefits are in the numerator and the costs are in the denominator. For this measure, if the ratio is greater than 1.0, the project should be considered.

▶ **Planned benefits delivery compared to actual benefits delivery.** As part of a business case, organizations may identify value as the benefit that will be delivered as a result of doing the project. For projects that expect to deliver benefits during the project life cycle, measuring the benefits delivered and the value of those benefits, then comparing that information to the business case, provides information that can justify the continuation of the project, or in some cases, the cancellation of the project.

▶ **Return on investment (ROI).** A measure of the amount of financial return compared to the cost, ROI is generally developed as an input to the decision to undertake a project. There may be estimates of ROI at different points in time across the project life cycle. By measuring ROI throughout the project, the project team can determine if it makes sense to continue the investment of organizational resources.

▶ **Net present value (NPV).** The difference between the present value of inflows of capital and the present value of outflows of capital over a period of time, NPV is generally developed when deciding to undertake a project. By measuring the NPV throughout the project, the project team can determine if it makes sense to continue the investment of organizational resources.

2.7.2.6 Stakeholders

Stakeholder satisfaction can be measured with surveys or by inferring satisfaction, or lack thereof, and by looking at related metrics, such as:

▶ **Net Promoter Score® (NPS®).** A Net Promoter Score measures the degree to which a stakeholder (usually the customer) is willing to recommend a product or service to others. It measures a range from -100 to +100. A high Net Promoter Score not only measures satisfaction with a brand, product, or service, it is also an indicator of customer loyalty.

▶ **Mood chart.** A mood chart can track the mood or reactions of a group of very important stakeholders—the project team. At the end of each day, project team members can use colors, numbers, or emojis to indicate their frame of mind. Figure 2-25 shows a mood chart using emojis. Tracking the project team's mood or individual project team member's moods can help to identify potential issues and areas for improvement.

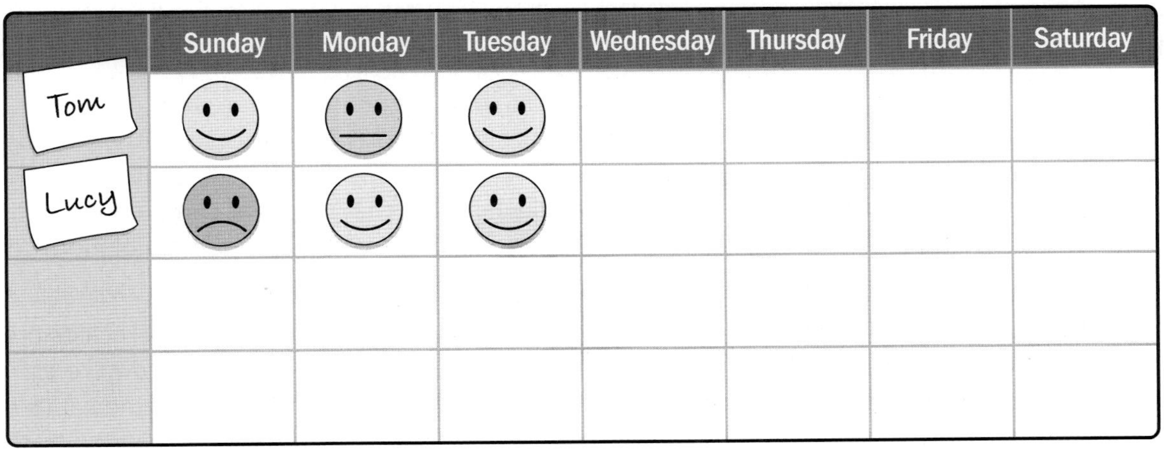

	Sunday	Monday	Tuesday	Wednesday	Thursday	Friday	Saturday
Tom	🙂	😐	🙂				
Lucy	🙁	🙂	🙂				

Figure 2-25. Mood Board

- **Morale.** Since mood boards can be subjective, another option is to measure project team morale. This can be done by surveys, asking project team members to rate their agreement on a scale of 1 to 5 to statements such as:

    ▷ I feel my work contributes to the overall outcomes.

    ▷ I feel appreciated.

    ▷ I am satisfied with the way my project team works together.

- **Turnover.** Another way to track morale is by looking at unplanned project team turnover. High rates of unplanned turnover may indicate low morale.

2.7.2.7 Forecasts

Project teams use forecasts to consider what might happen in the future so they can consider and discuss whether to adapt plans and project work accordingly. Forecasts can be qualitative, such as using expert judgment about what the future will hold. They can also be causal when seeking to understand the impact a specific event or condition will have on future events. Quantitative forecasts seek to use past information to estimate what will happen in the future. Quantitative forecasts include:

- **Estimate to complete (ETC).**[3] An earned value management measure that forecasts the expected cost to finish all the remaining project work. There are many different ways to calculate the estimate to complete. Assuming past performance is indicative of future performance, a common measurement is calculation of the budget at completion minus the earned value, then dividing by the cost performance index. For more calculations to determine the ETC, see *The Standard for Earned Value Management* [2].

- **Estimate at completion (EAC).** This earned value management measure forecasts the expected total cost of completing all work (see Figure 2-26). There are many different ways to calculate the estimate at completion. Assuming past performance is indicative of future performance, a common measurement is the budget at completion divided by the cost performance index. For more calculations to determine the EAC, see *The Standard for Earned Value Management* [2].

---

[3] Quantitative forecasts associated with earned value management are often used for very large projects. Some deliverables in those projects may use adaptive development methods. However, the forecasting metrics in earned value management are predominantly used in predictive environments.

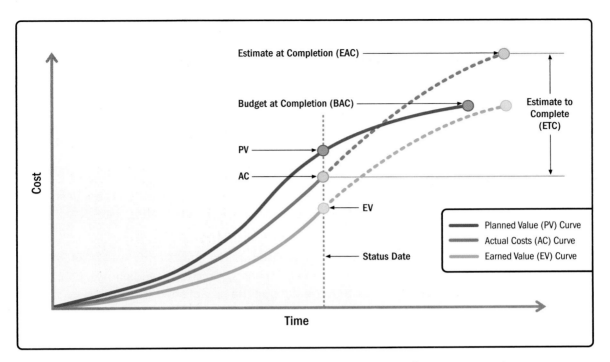

Figure 2-26. Forecast of Estimate at Completion and Estimate to Complete

▶ **Variance at completion (VAC).** An earned value management measure that forecasts the amount of budget deficit or surplus. It is expressed as the difference between the budget at completion (BAC) and the estimate at completion (EAC).

▶ **To-complete performance index (TCPI).** An earned value management measure that estimates the cost performance required to meet a specified management goal. TCPI is expressed as the ratio of the cost to finish the outstanding work to the remaining budget.

▶ **Regression analysis.** An analytical method where a series of input variables are examined in relation to their corresponding output results in order to develop a mathematical or statistical relationship. The relationship can be used to infer future performance.

▶ **Throughput analysis.** This analytical method assesses the number of items being completed in a fixed time frame. Project teams that use adaptive practices use throughput metrics such as features complete vs. features remaining, velocity, and story points to evaluate their progress and estimate likely completion dates. Using duration estimates and burn rates of stable project teams can help verify and update cost estimates.

2.7.3 PRESENTING INFORMATION

The measures being collected are important, but what is done with the measures is just as important. For information to be useful, it has to be timely, accessible, easy to absorb and digest, and presented so that it correctly conveys the degree of uncertainty associated with the information. Visual displays with graphics can help stakeholders absorb and make sense of information.

2.7.3.1 Dashboards

A common way of showing large quantities of information on metrics is a dashboard. Dashboards generally collect information electronically and generate charts that depict status. Often, dashboards offer high-level summaries of data and allow drill-down analysis into contributing data. Figure 2-27 provides an example of a dashboard.

Dashboards often include information displayed as stoplight charts (also known as RAG charts where RAG is an abbreviation for red-amber-green), bar charts, pie charts, and control charts. A text explanation can be used for any measures that are outside the established thresholds.

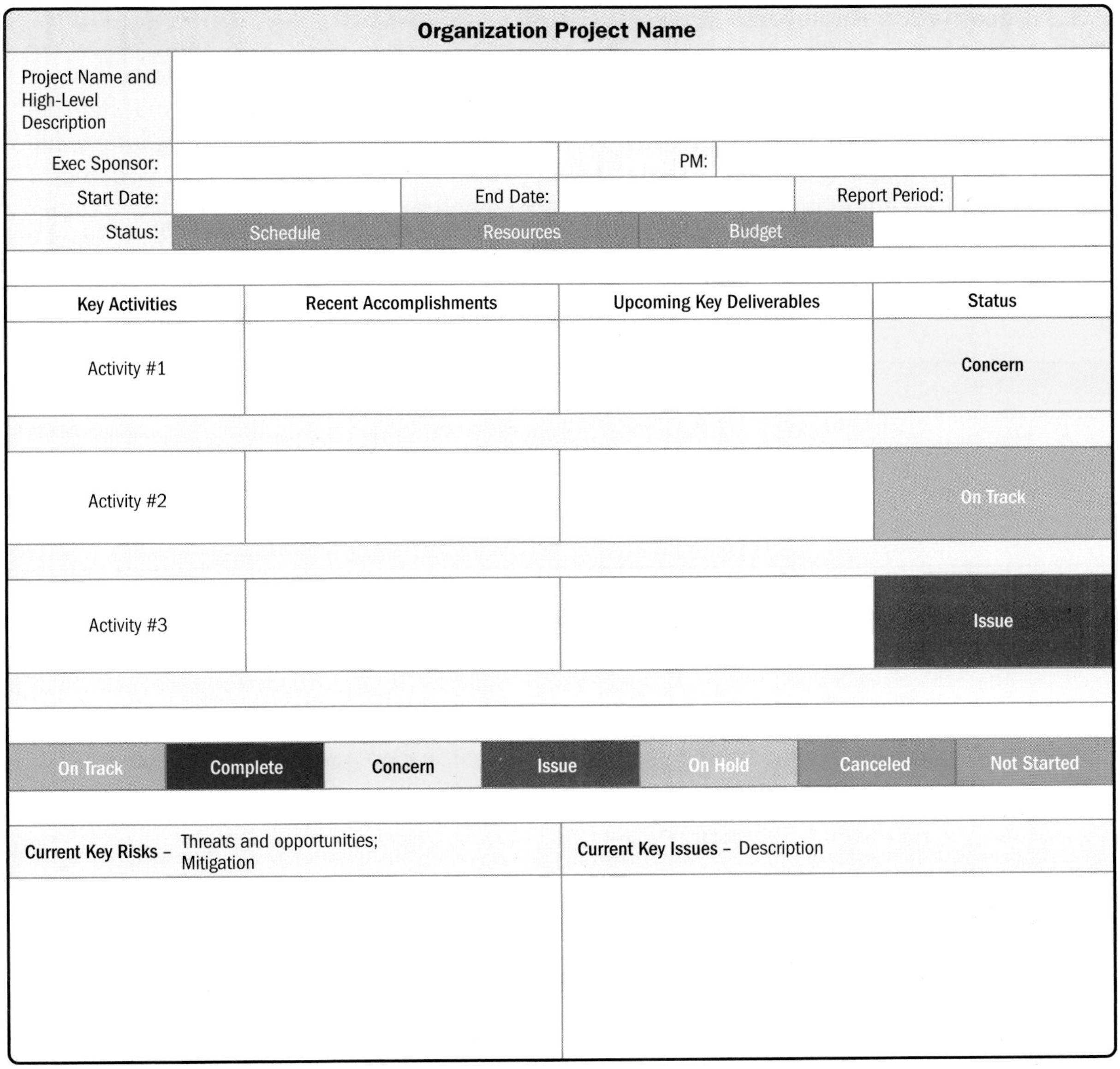

Organization Project Name			

Project Name and High-Level Description				
Exec Sponsor:			PM:	
Start Date:		End Date:		Report Period:
Status:	Schedule	Resources	Budget	

Key Activities	Recent Accomplishments	Upcoming Key Deliverables	Status
Activity #1			Concern
Activity #2			On Track
Activity #3			Issue

On Track	Complete	Concern	Issue	On Hold	Canceled	Not Started

Current Key Risks – Threats and opportunities; Mitigation	Current Key Issues – Description

Figure 2-27. Dashboard Example

2.7.3.2 Information Radiators

Information radiators, also known as big visible charts (BVCs), are visible, physical displays that provide information to the rest of the organization, enabling timely knowledge sharing. They are posted in a place where people can see the information easily, rather than having information in a scheduling or reporting tool. BVCs should be easy to update, and they should be updated frequently. They are often "low tech and high touch" in that they are manually maintained rather than electronically generated. Figure 2-28 shows an information radiator associated with work completed, work remaining, and risks.

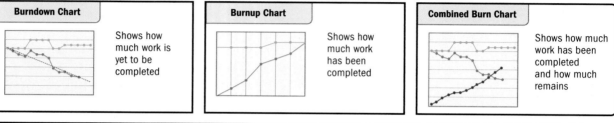

Burndown Chart — Shows how much work is yet to be completed

Burnup Chart — Shows how much work has been completed

Combined Burn Chart — Shows how much work has been completed and how much remains

Reference	Risk Description	Date	Likelihood	Impact	Risk Rating	Response	Owner
1	The main supplier cannot deliver on time because of other commercial commitments	03/21	Likely	High	High	Include financial penalties in contract; build contingency into the schedule; monitor contractor performance	Annie
2	The lead time for the leased line exceeds 90 days	03/21	Unlikely	Medium	Medium	Order leased line earlier than necessary; incur additional rental fees	Jim
3	Release of the new system is delayed because user acceptance testing commences after the planned start	03/21	Very likely	High	High	Employ temporary staff to free up resources for testing; revise project schedule	Mark
4	There is insufficient capacity to create additional database instances for data migration and testing	04/18	Very unlikely	Medium	Low	Prioritize projects; temporarily remove alternative development instance	Jim

Risk Log

Figure 2-28. Information Radiator

2.7.3.3 Visual Controls

In lean environments, information radiators are known as visual controls. Visual controls illustrate processes to easily compare actual against expected performance. Visual controls show a process using visual cues. Visual controls can be present for all levels of information from business value delivered to tasks that have started. They should be highly visible for anyone to see.

- **Task boards.** A task board is a visual representation of the planned work that allows everyone to see the status of the tasks. A task board can show work that is ready to be started (to do), work in progress, and work that is completed (see Figure 2-29).

  A task board allows anyone to see at a glance the status of a particular task or the number of tasks in each stage of work. Different color sticky notes can represent different types of work, and dots can be used to show how many days a task has been in its current position.

  Flow-based projects, such as those that use kanban boards, can use these charts to limit the amount of work in progress. If a column is approaching the work in progress limit, project team members can "swarm" around the current work to help those working on tasks that are slowing the flow.

- **Burn charts.** Burn charts, such as a burnup or burndown charts, can show project team velocity. Velocity measures the productivity rate at which the deliverables are produced, validated, and accepted within a predefined interval. A burnup chart can track the amount of work done compared to the expected work that should be done (see Figure 2-30). A burndown chart can show the number of story points remaining or the amount of risk exposure that has been reduced.

- **Other types of charts.** Visual charts can also include information such as an impediment list that shows a description of the impediment to getting work done, the severity, and the actions being taken to resolve the impediment.

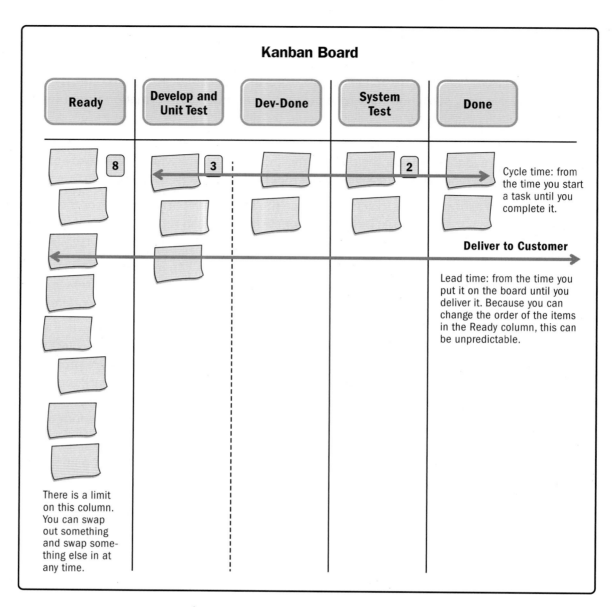

Figure 2-29. Task Board or Kanban Board

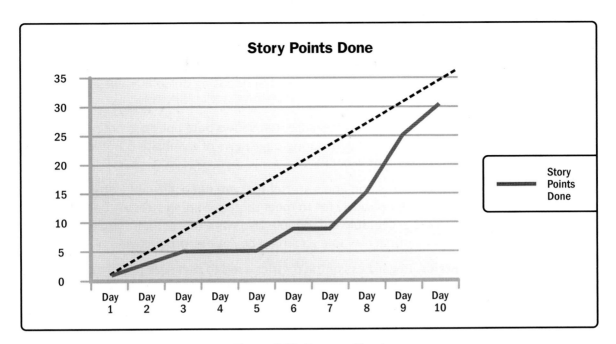

Figure 2-30. Burnup Chart

2.7.4 MEASUREMENT PITFALLS

Project measures help the project team meet the project objectives. However, there are some pitfalls associated with measurement. Awareness of these pitfalls can help minimize their negative effect.

- ▶ **Hawthorne effect.** The Hawthorne effect states that the very act of measuring something influences behavior. Therefore, take care in establishing metrics. For example, measuring only a project team's output of deliverables can encourage the project team to focus on creating a large volume of deliverables rather than focusing on deliverables that would provide higher customer satisfaction.

- ▶ **Vanity metric.** A vanity metric is a measure that shows data but does not provide useful information for making decisions. Measuring pageviews of a website is not as useful as measuring the number of new viewers.

- ▶ **Demoralization.** If measures and goals are set that are not achievable, project team morale may fall as they continuously fail to meet targets. Setting stretch goals and aspirational measures is acceptable, but people also want to see their hard work recognized. Unrealistic or unachievable goals can be counterproductive.

- ▶ **Misusing the metrics.** Regardless of the metrics used to measure performance, there is the opportunity for people to distort the measurements or focus on the wrong thing. Examples include:

  - ▷ Focusing on less important metrics rather than the metrics that matter most,

  - ▷ Focusing on performing well for the short-term measures at the expense of long-term metrics, and

  - ▷ Working on out-of-sequence activities that are easy to accomplish in order to improve performance indicators.

- ▶ **Confirmation bias.** As human beings, we tend to look for and see information that supports our preexisting point of view. This can lead us to false interpretations of data.

- ▶ **Correlation versus causation.** A common mistake in interpreting measurement data is confusing the correlation of two variables with the idea that one causes the other. For example, seeing projects that are behind schedule and over budget might infer that projects that are over budget cause schedule issues. This is not true, nor is it true that projects that are behind schedule cause budget overruns. Instead, there are likely other correlating factors that are not being considered, such as skill in estimating, the ability to manage change, and actively managing risk.

Being aware of the pitfalls associated with metrics can help with establishing effective metrics in addition to being vigilant regarding the dangers associated with inappropriate measures.

2.7.5 TROUBLESHOOTING PERFORMANCE

Part of measurement is having agreed to plans for measures that are outside the threshold ranges. Thresholds can be established for a variety of metrics such as schedule, budget, velocity, and other project-specific measures. The degree of variance will depend on stakeholder risk tolerances.

Figure 2-31 shows an example of a budget threshold set at +10% (orange) and -20% (green) of the predicted spend rate. The blue line is tracking the actual spend, and in January, it exceeded the +10% upper tolerance that would trigger the exception plan.

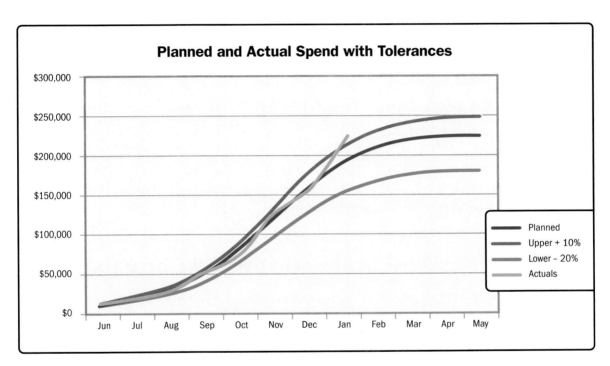

Figure 2-31. Planned and Actual Spend Rates

Ideally, project teams should not wait until a threshold has been breached before taking action. If a breach can be forecasted via a trend or new information, the project team can be proactive in addressing the expected variance.

An exception plan is an agreed-upon set of actions to be taken if a threshold is crossed or forecast. Exception plans do not have to be formal; they can be as simple as calling a stakeholder meeting to discuss the matter. The importance of the exception plan is to discuss the issue and develop a plan for what needs to be done. Then follow through to make sure the plan is implemented and determine if the plan is working.

2.7.6 GROWING AND IMPROVING

The intent in measuring and displaying data is to learn and improve. To optimize project performance and efficiency, only measure and report information that will:

▶ Allow the project team to learn,

▶ Facilitate a decision,

▶ Improve some aspect of the product or project performance,

▶ Help avoid an issue, and

▶ Prevent performance deterioration.

Applied appropriately, measurements facilitate the project team's ability to generate business value and achieve the project objectives and performance targets.

2.7.7 INTERACTIONS WITH OTHER PERFORMANCE DOMAINS

The Measurement Performance Domain interacts with the Planning, Project Work, and Delivery Performance Domains as plans form the basis for comparing the deliveries to plan. The Measurement Performance Domain can support the activities that are part of the Planning Performance Domain by presenting up-to-date information so that lessons learned can reflect favorable or unfavorable information for updating plans. The Team and Stakeholder Performance Domains interact as project team members develop the plans and create the deliverables and deliveries that are measured.

As unpredictable events occur, both positive and negative, they have an impact on the project performance and therefore on the project measurements and metrics. Responding to changes caused by uncertain events that have occurred includes updating measurements that have been impacted due to the change. Activities in the Uncertainty Performance Domain, such as identifying risks and opportunities, can be initiated based on performance measurements.

Part of the project work is working with the project team and other stakeholders to establish the metrics, gather the data, analyze the data, make decisions, and report on project status.

2.7.8 CHECKING RESULTS

Table 2-9 identifies the outcomes from effective application of the Measurement Performance Domain on the left and ways of checking them on the right.

Table 2-9. Checking Outcomes—Measurement Performance Domain

Outcome	Check
A reliable understanding of the status of the project	Audit measurements and reports demonstrate if data is reliable.
Actionable data to facilitate decision making	Measurements indicate whether the project is performing as expected or if there are variances.
Timely and appropriate actions to keep project performance on track	Measurements provide leading indicators and/or current status leads to timely decisions and actions.
Achieving targets and generating business value by making informed and timely decisions based on reliable forecasts and evaluations	Reviewing past forecasts and current performance demonstrates if previous forecasts reflect the present accurately. Comparing the actual performance to the planned performance and evaluating business documents will show the likelihood of achieving intended value from the project.

2.8 UNCERTAINTY PERFORMANCE DOMAIN

<table>
<tr><td colspan="2">

UNCERTAINTY PERFORMANCE DOMAIN

</td></tr>
<tr>
<td>

The Uncertainty Performance Domain addresses activities and functions associated with risk and uncertainty.

</td>
<td>

Effective execution of this performance domain results in the following desired outcomes:

▶ An awareness of the environment in which projects occur, including, but not limited to, the technical, social, political, market, and economic environments.

▶ Proactively exploring and responding to uncertainty.

▶ An awareness of the interdependence of multiple variables on the project.

▶ The capacity to anticipate threats and opportunities and understand the consequences of issues.

▶ Project delivery with little or no negative impact from unforeseen events or conditions.

▶ Opportunities are realized to improve project performance and outcomes.

▶ Cost and schedule reserves are utilized effectively to maintain alignment with project objectives.

</td>
</tr>
</table>

Figure 2-32. Uncertainty Performance Domain

Projects exist in environments with varying degrees of uncertainty. Uncertainty presents threats and opportunities that project teams explore, assess, and decide how to handle.

The following definitions are relevant to the Uncertainty Performance Domain:

Uncertainty. A lack of understanding and awareness of issues, events, paths to follow, or solutions to pursue.

Ambiguity. A state of being unclear, having difficulty in identifying the cause of events, or having multiple options from which to choose.

Complexity. A characteristic of a program or project or its environment that is difficult to manage due to human behavior, system behavior, and ambiguity.

Volatility. The possibility for rapid and unpredictable change.

Risk. An uncertain event or condition that, if it occurs, has a positive or negative effect on one or more project objectives.

Uncertainty in the broadest sense is a state of not knowing or unpredictability. There are many nuances to uncertainty, such as:

▶ Risk associated with not knowing future events,

▶ Ambiguity associated with not being aware of current or future conditions, and

▶ Complexity associated with dynamic systems having unpredictable outcomes.

Successfully navigating uncertainty begins with understanding the larger environment within which the project is operating. Aspects of the environment that contribute to project uncertainty include, but are not limited to:

▶ Economic factors such as volatility in prices, availability of resources, ability to borrow funds, and inflation/deflation;

▶ Technical considerations such as new or emerging technology, complexity associated with systems, and interfaces;

▶ Legal or legislative constraints or requirements;

▶ Physical environment as it pertains to safety, weather, and working conditions;

▶ Ambiguity associated with current or future conditions;

▶ Social and market influences shaped by opinion and media; and,

▶ Political influences, either external or internal to the organization.

This performance domain addresses the various aspects of uncertainty, implications of uncertainty, such as project risk, as well as options for navigating the various forms of uncertainty.

2.8.1 GENERAL UNCERTAINTY

Uncertainty is inherent in all projects. For this reason, the effects of any activity cannot be predicted precisely, and a range of outcomes can occur. Potential outcomes that benefit the project objectives are known as opportunities; potential outcomes that have a negative effect on objectives are called threats. Together, the set of opportunities and threats comprise the set of project risks. There are several options for responding to uncertainty:

- ▶ **Gather information.** Sometimes uncertainty can be reduced by finding out more information, such as conducting research, engaging experts, or performing a market analysis. It is also important to recognize when further information collection and analysis exceed the benefit of having the additional information.

- ▶ **Prepare for multiple outcomes.** In situations where there are only a few possible outcomes from an area of uncertainty, the project team can prepare for each of those outcomes. This entails having a primary solution available, as well as having backup or contingency plans in case the initial solution is not viable or effective. Where there is a large set of potential outcomes, the project team can categorize and assess the potential causes to estimate their likelihood of occurrence. This allows the project team to identify the most likely potential outcomes on which to focus.

- ▶ **Set-based design.** Multiple designs or alternatives can be investigated early in the project to reduce uncertainty. This allows the project team to look at trade-offs, such as time versus cost, quality versus cost, risk versus schedule, or schedule versus quality. The intention is to explore options so the project team can learn from working with the various alternatives. Ineffective or suboptimal alternatives are discarded throughout the process.

- ▶ **Build in resilience.** Resilience is the ability to adapt and respond quickly to unexpected changes. Resilience applies to both project team members and organizational processes. If the initial approach to product design or a prototype is not effective, the project team and the organization need to be able to learn, adapt, and respond quickly.

2.8.2 AMBIGUITY

There are two categories of ambiguity: conceptual ambiguity and situational ambiguity. Conceptual ambiguity—the lack of effective understanding—occurs when people use similar terms or arguments in different ways. For example, the statement, "The schedule was reported on track last week," is not clear. It isn't clear whether the schedule was on track last week or whether it was reported on last week. In addition, there could be some question as to what "on track" means. Ambiguity of this type can be reduced by formally establishing common rules and definitions of terms, such as what does "on track" mean.

Situational ambiguity surfaces when more than one outcome is possible. Having multiple options to solve a problem is a form of situational ambiguity. Solutions for exploration of ambiguity include progressive elaboration, experimentation, and the use of prototypes.

▶ **Progressive elaboration.** This is the iterative process of increasing the level of detail in a project management plan as greater amounts of information and more accurate estimates become available.

▶ **Experiments.** A well-designed series of experiments can help identify cause-and-effect relationships or, at least, can reduce the amount of ambiguity.

▶ **Prototypes.** Prototypes can help distinguish the relationships between different variables.

2.8.3 COMPLEXITY

Complexity is a characteristic of a program, project, or its environment, which is difficult to manage due to human behavior, system behavior, or ambiguity. Complexity exists when there are many interconnected influences that behave and interact in diverse ways. In complex environments, it is not uncommon to see an aggregation of individual elements leading to unforeseen or unintended outcomes. The effect of complexity is that there is no way of making accurate predictions about the likelihood of any potential outcome or even of knowing what outcomes might emerge. There are numerous ways to work with complexity; some of them are systems-based, some entail reframing, and others are based on process.

2.8.3.1 Systems-Based

Examples of working with complexity that is systems based include:

- **Decoupling.** Decoupling entails disconnecting parts of the system to both simplify the system and reduce the number of connected variables. Determining how a piece of a system works on its own reduces the overall size of the problem.

- **Simulation.** There may be similar though unrelated scenarios that can be used to simulate components of a system. A project to build a new airport that includes an area with shopping and restaurants can learn about consumer buying habits by seeking out analogous information on shopping malls and entertainment establishments.

2.8.3.2 Reframing

Examples of working with complexity that entail reframing are:

- **Diversity.** Complex systems require viewing the system from diverse perspectives. This can include brainstorming with the project team to open up divergent ways of seeing the system. It can also include Delphi-like processes to move from divergent to convergent thinking.

- **Balance.** Balancing the type of data used rather than only using forecasting data or data that report on the past or lagging indicators provides a broader perspective. This can include using elements whose variations are likely to counteract each other's potential negative effects.

2.8.3.3 Process-Based

Examples of working with complexity that is process based include:

- **Iterate.** Build iteratively or incrementally. Add features one at a time. After each iteration, identify what worked, what did not work, customer reaction, and what the project team learned.

- **Engage.** Build in opportunities to get stakeholder engagement. This reduces the number of assumptions and builds learning and engagement into the process.

- **Fail safe.** For elements of a system that are critical, build in redundancy or elements that can provide a graceful degradation of functionality in the event of a critical component failure.

2.8.4 VOLATILITY

Volatility exists in an environment that is subject to rapid and unpredictable change. Volatility can occur when there are ongoing fluctuations in available skill sets or materials. Volatility usually impacts cost and schedule. Alternatives analysis and use of cost or schedule reserve address volatility.

- ▶ **Alternatives analysis.** Finding and evaluating alternatives, such as looking at different ways to meet an objective, such as using a different mix of skills, resequencing work, or outsourcing work. Alternatives analysis may include identifying the variables to be considered in evaluating options, and the relative importance or weight of each variable.

- ▶ **Reserve.** Cost reserve can be used to cover budget overruns due to price volatility. In some circumstances, schedule reserve can be used to address delays due to volatility associated with resource availability.

Effectively navigating uncertainty, ambiguity, complexity, and volatility improves the ability to anticipate situations, make good decisions, plan, and solve problems.

2.8.5 RISK

Risks are an aspect of uncertainty. A risk is an uncertain event or condition that, if it occurs, has a positive or negative effect on one or more project objectives. Negative risks are called threats, and positive risks are called opportunities. All projects have risks since they are unique undertakings with varying degrees of uncertainty.

Project team members should proactively identify risks throughout the project to avoid or minimize the impacts of threats and trigger or maximize the impacts of opportunities. Both threats and opportunities have a set of possible response strategies that can be planned for implementation should the risk occur.

In order to navigate risk effectively, the project team needs to know what level of risk exposure is acceptable in pursuit of the project objectives. This is defined by measurable risk thresholds that reflect the risk appetite and attitude of the organization and project stakeholders. Risk thresholds express the acceptable variation around an objective that reflects the risk appetite of the organization and stakeholders. Thresholds are typically stated and communicated to the project team and reflected in the definitions of risk impact levels for the project.

Overall Project Risk

Overall project risk is the effect of uncertainty on the project as a whole, arising from all sources of uncertainty. This includes individual risks and the exposure to the implications of variation in project outcome, both positive and negative. Overall risk is often a function of complexity, ambiguity, and volatility. Responses to overall project risk are the same as for individual threats and opportunities, though responses are applied to the overall project rather than to a specific event. If the overall risk on the project is too high, the organization may choose to cancel the project.

2.8.5.1 Threats

A threat is an event or condition that, if it occurs, has a negative impact on one or more objectives. Five alternative strategies may be considered for dealing with threats, as follows:

- ▶ **Avoid.** Threat avoidance is when the project team acts to eliminate the threat or protect the project from its impact.

- ▶ **Escalate.** Escalation is appropriate when the project team or the project sponsor agrees that a threat is outside the scope of the project or that the proposed response would exceed the project manager's authority.

- ▶ **Transfer.** Transfer involves shifting ownership of a threat to a third party to manage the risk and to bear the impact if the threat occurs.

- ▶ **Mitigate.** In threat mitigation, action is taken to reduce the probability of occurrence and/ or impact of a threat. Early mitigation action is often more effective than trying to repair the damage after the threat has occurred.

- ▶ **Accept.** Threat acceptance acknowledges the existence of a threat, but no proactive action is planned. Actively accepting a risk can include developing a contingency plan that would be triggered if the event occurred; or it can include passive acceptance, which means doing nothing.

A response to a specific threat might include multiple strategies. For example, if the threat cannot be avoided, it may be mitigated to a level at which it becomes viable to transfer or to accept it.

The goal of implementing threat responses is to reduce the amount of negative risk. Risks that are accepted sometimes are reduced simply by the passage of time or because the risk event does not occur. Figure 2-33 shows how risks are tracked and reduced over time.

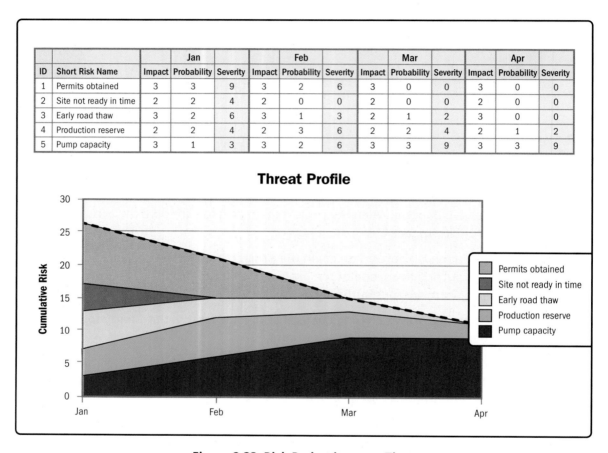

ID	Short Risk Name	Jan			Feb			Mar			Apr		
		Impact	Probability	Severity	Impact	Probability	Severity	Impact	Probability	Severity	Impact	Probability	Severity
1	Permits obtained	3	3	9	3	2	6	3	0	0	3	0	0
2	Site not ready in time	2	2	4	2	0	0	2	0	0	2	0	0
3	Early road thaw	3	2	6	3	1	3	2	1	2	3	0	0
4	Production reserve	2	2	4	2	3	6	2	2	4	2	1	2
5	Pump capacity	3	1	3	3	2	6	3	3	9	3	3	9

Figure 2-33. Risk Reduction over Time

PMBOK® Guide

2.8.5.2 Opportunities

An opportunity is an event or condition that, if it occurs, has a positive impact on one or more project objectives. An example of an opportunity could be a time and materials-based subcontractor who finishes work early, resulting in lower costs and schedule savings.

Five alternative strategies may be considered for dealing with opportunities, as follows:

- **Exploit.** A response strategy whereby the project team acts to ensure that an opportunity occurs.

- **Escalate.** As with threats, this opportunity response strategy is used when the project team or the project sponsor agrees that an opportunity is outside the scope of the project or that the proposed response would exceed the project manager's authority.

- **Share.** Opportunity sharing involves allocating ownership of an opportunity to a third party who is best able to capture the benefit of that opportunity.

- **Enhance.** In opportunity enhancement, the project team acts to increase the probability of occurrence or impact of an opportunity. Early enhancement action is often more effective than trying to improve the opportunity after it has occurred.

- **Accept.** As with threats, accepting an opportunity acknowledges its existence but no proactive action is planned.

Once a set of risk responses has been developed, it should be reviewed to see whether the planned responses have added any secondary risks. The review should also assess the residual risk that will remain once the response actions have been carried out. Response planning should be repeated until residual risk is compatible with the organization's risk appetite.

Taking an economic view of work prioritization allows the team to prioritize threat avoidance and reduction activities.

Comparing the expected monetary value (EMV) of a risk to the anticipated return on investment (ROI) of a deliverable or feature allows the project manager to have conversations with sponsors or product owners about where and when to incorporate risks responses into the planned work (see Figure 2-34).

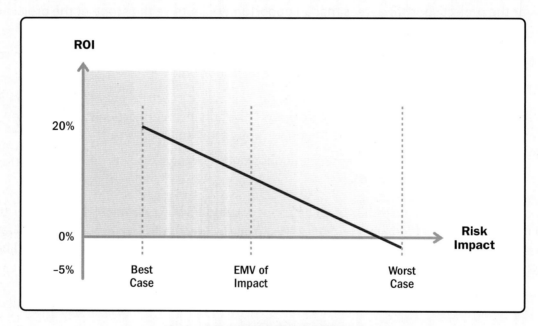

Figure 2-34. Risk-Adjusted ROI Curve

2.8.5.3 Management and Contingency Reserve

Reserve is an amount of time or budget set aside to account for handling risks. Contingency reserve is set aside to address identified risks should they occur. Management reserve is a budget category used for unknown events such as unplanned, in-scope work.

2.8.5.4 Risk Review

Establishing a frequent rhythm or cadence of review and feedback sessions from a broad selection of stakeholders is helpful for navigating project risk and being proactive with risk responses.

Daily standup meetings can be used in any project and are a source for identifying potential threats and opportunities. Reports of blockers or impediments could become threats if they continue to delay progress. Likewise, reports of progress and breakthroughs might point toward opportunities to be further leveraged and shared.

Frequent demonstrations of increments of the product or service, interim designs, or proof of concepts can surface threats and opportunities. Negative feedback from demonstrations or design reviews can be an early indicator of threats related to dissatisfaction from stakeholders if not corrected. Positive feedback helps inform the project team regarding the areas of development highly valued by the business representatives.

Addressing risk at weekly status meetings ensures that risk management remains relevant. These meetings can be used to identify new risks as well as identify changes to existing risks.

Retrospectives and lessons learned meetings can be used to identify threats to performance, project team cohesion, etc., and to seek improvements. They can also help identify practices to try different ways to exploit and enhance opportunities.

2.8.6 INTERACTIONS WITH OTHER PERFORMANCE DOMAINS

The Uncertainty Performance Domain interacts with the Planning, Project Work, Delivery, and Measurement Performance Domains from the product or deliverable perspective. As planning is conducted, activities to reduce uncertainty and risks can be built into the plans. These are carried out in the Delivery Performance Domain. Measurements can indicate if the risk level is changing over time.

Project team members and other stakeholders are the main sources of information regarding uncertainty. They can provide information, suggestions, and assistance in working with all the various forms of uncertainty.

The choice of life cycle and development approach impact how uncertainty will be addressed. On a predictive project where the scope is relatively stable, reserve in the schedule and budget can be used to respond to risks. On a project using an adaptive approach where the requirements are likely to evolve and where there may be ambiguity around how systems will interact or how stakeholders will react, the project team can adjust plans to reflect evolving understanding or use reserves to offset the impacts of realized risks.

2.8.7 CHECKING RESULTS

Table 2-10 identifies the outcomes on the left and ways of checking them on the right.

Table 2-10. Checking Outcomes—Uncertainty Performance Domain

Outcome	Check
An awareness of the environment in which projects occur, including, but not limited to, the technical, social, political, market, and economic environments	The team incorporates environmental considerations when evaluating uncertainty, risks, and responses.
Proactively exploring and responding to uncertainty	Risk responses are aligned with the prioritization of project constraints, such as budget, schedule, and performance.
An awareness of the interdependence of multiple variables on the project	Actions to address complexity, ambiguity, and volatility are appropriate for the project.
The capacity to anticipate threats and opportunities and understand the consequences of issues	Systems for identifying, capturing, and responding to risk are appropriately robust.
Project delivery with little or no negative impact from unforeseen events or conditions	Scheduled delivery dates are met, and the budget performance is within the variance threshold.
Realized opportunities to improve project performance and outcomes	Teams use established mechanisms to identify and leverage opportunities.
Cost and schedule reserves used effectively to maintain alignment with project objectives	Teams take steps to proactively prevent threats, thereby limiting use of cost or schedule reserve.

Tailoring

3.1 OVERVIEW

Tailoring is the deliberate adaptation of the project management approach, governance, and processes to make them more suitable for the given environment and the work at hand.

In a project environment, tailoring considers the development approach, processes, project life cycle, deliverables, and choice of people with whom to engage. The tailoring process is driven by the guiding project management principles in *The Standard for Project Management* [1], organizational values, and organizational culture. For instance, if a core organizational value is "customer centricity," then the activities selected for requirements elicitation and scope validation favor customer-centered approaches. This aligns with the principle of "Effectively engage with stakeholders." Likewise, an organization with a low appetite for risk may have many processes and procedures to guide projects throughout their life cycles. A similar company operating in the same market—but with a high tolerance for risk—may have fewer processes and procedures. In both of these examples, the organizations are aligned with the principle of "Optimize risk responses" even though their appetite, processes, and procedures are different.

Tailoring entails the mindful selection and adjustment of multiple project factors, regardless of whether the label of "tailoring" is used.

The alternative to tailoring is using an unmodified framework or methodology. There are many methodologies available that provide descriptions of processes, phases, methods, artifacts, and templates to be used in projects. These methodologies and their components are not customized to the organizational context.

Most of these methodologies have clear instructions stating they should not be applied rigorously but should be subject to a process of tailoring to determine which elements are most useful given the particular type, size, and complexity of the project. Some inexperienced practitioners try to apply the methodology verbatim without regard to project size, complexity, duration, or organizational context.

Tailoring involves understanding the project context, goals, and operating environment. Projects operate in complex environments that need to balance potentially competing demands that include, but are not limited to:

▶ Delivering as quickly as possible,

▶ Minimizing project costs,

▶ Optimizing the value delivered,

▶ Creating high-quality deliverables and outcomes,

▶ Providing compliance with regulatory standards,

▶ Satisfying diverse stakeholder expectations, and

▶ Adapting to change.

These factors need to be understood, evaluated, and balanced to create a practical operating environment for the project.

There may be situations that limit the degree to which project teams can tailor their approach, for example, when organizational policies mandate the use of a specific approach or a contract specifies a mandated approach.

3.2 WHY TAILOR?

Tailoring is performed to better suit the organization, operating environment, and project needs. Many variables factor into the tailoring process, including the criticality of the project and the number of stakeholders involved. Using these variables as an example, it is evident that the rigor, checks and balances, and reporting required for a critical project (e.g., building a nuclear reactor) are much greater than those for building a new office building.

Likewise, the communication and coordination of work necessary for a project team of 10 people is insufficient for a project team of 200 people. Too few processes can omit key activities that support effective project management, while employing more processes than required is costly and wasteful. Thus, tailoring facilitates appropriate management for the operating environment and the project needs.

The structure used to deliver projects can be extensive or minimal, rigorous or lightweight, robust or simple. There is no single approach that can be applied to all projects all of the time. Instead, tailoring should reflect the size, duration, and complexity of each individual project and should be adapted to the industry, organizational culture, and level of project management maturity of the organization.

Tailoring produces direct and indirect benefits to organizations. These include, but are not limited to:

▶ More commitment from project team members who helped to tailor the approach,

▶ Customer-oriented focus, as the needs of the customer are an important influencing factor in its development, and

▶ More efficient use of project resources.

3.3 WHAT TO TAILOR

Project aspects that can be tailored include:

▶ Life cycle and development approach selection,

▶ Processes,

▶ Engagement,

▶ Tools, and

▶ Methods and artifacts.

Sections 3.3.1 through 3.3.4 explore each of these in more detail.

3.3.1 LIFE CYCLE AND DEVELOPMENT APPROACH SELECTION

Deciding on a life cycle and the phases of the life cycle is an example of tailoring. Additional tailoring can be done when selecting the development and delivery approach for the project. Some large projects may use a combination of development and delivery approaches simultaneously. For instance, building a new data center could involve (a) the use of predictive approaches for the physical building construction and finishing and (b) an iterative approach for understanding and establishing the computing capabilities required. Viewed from a project level, this combination of approaches represents a hybrid approach, but the construction team and the computing team may only experience a predictive or iterative development approach.

3.3.2 PROCESSES

Process tailoring for the selected life cycle and development approach includes determining which portions or elements should be:

▶ *Added,* to bring required rigor, coverage, or address unique product or operating environment conditions, etc. (e.g., adding independent inspections for safety-critical projects);

▶ *Modified,* to better suit the project or project team requirements (e.g., modifying the format of project documents to accommodate project team members with vision limitations);

▶ *Removed,* to reduce cost or effort since it is no longer required or is not economical for the value it adds (e.g., removing the creation of meeting minutes for a small, colocated project team with good communications);

▶ *Blended,* to bring additional benefits or value by mixing or combining elements (e.g., adding appreciative inquiry methods from organizational management to the lessons learned meetings of predictive project management to help foster better collaboration); and

▶ *Aligned,* to harmonize elements so there is consistent definition, understanding, and application (e.g., many disciplines have standards and practices associated with risk management that are sufficiently different from each other that would need to be aligned). For example, on multidisciplinary project teams, different disciplines may have specific elements, such as their own language, tools, and practices related to the same area of focus.

3.3.3 ENGAGEMENT

Tailoring engagement for the people involved in the project includes:

▶ **People.** This entails evaluating the skills and capabilities of the project leadership and the project team; then selecting who should be involved and in what capacities based on the project type and operating conditions. For example, on a challenging or time-constrained project, assigning very experienced project team members is more logical than using inexperienced project team members.

▶ **Empowerment.** Empowerment involves choosing which responsibilities and forms of local decision making should be deferred to the project team. Some environments and team member capabilities support high levels of empowerment. In other situations, less empowerment with more supervision and direction might be preferable.

▶ **Integration.** Project teams can include contributors from contracted entities, channel partners, and other external entities in addition to staff from inside the sponsoring organization. Tailoring considers how to create one project team from a diverse collection of contributors to facilitate optimal project team performance and realization of project outcomes.

3.3.4 TOOLS

Selecting the tools (e.g., software or equipment) the project team will use for the project is a form of tailoring. Often, the project team has the best insight into the most suitable tools for the situation, but those choices might need tempering based on the associated costs. Additionally, organizational leaders can impose constraints that the project team cannot change.

3.3.5 METHODS AND ARTIFACTS

Tailoring the means that will be used to achieve the project outcomes is performed so that the methods are suited for the environment and the culture. Tailoring the documents, templates, and other artifacts that will be used on the project helps to make sure the artifacts are appropriate for the project and the organization. Section 4 contains numerous examples of methods and artifacts that can be considered when tailoring methods and artifacts.

3.4 THE TAILORING PROCESS

As noted in Section 2.5 of *The Standard for Project Management* [1], projects exist in environments that may have an influence on them. Prior to tailoring, the project environment needs to be analyzed and understood. Tailoring typically begins by selecting a development and delivery approach, tailoring it for the organization, tailoring it for the project, and then implementing its ongoing improvement. These steps in the process are shown in Figure 3-1 and described in more detail in Sections 3.4.1 through 3.4.4 of this guide.

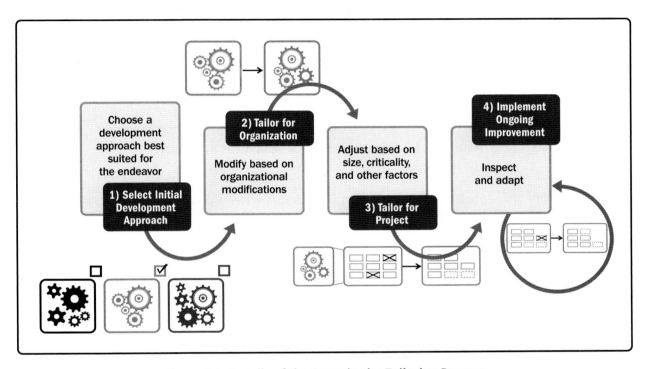

Figure 3-1. Details of the Steps in the Tailoring Process

3.4.1 SELECT INITIAL DEVELOPMENT APPROACH

This step determines the development approach that will be used for the project. Project teams apply their knowledge of the product, delivery cadence, and awareness of the available options to select the most appropriate development approach for the situation. Selecting the initial approach is depicted in Figure 3-2.

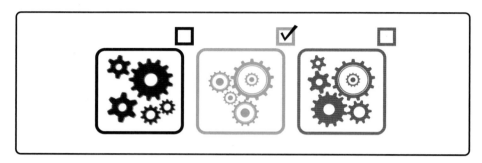

Figure 3-2. Selecting the Initial Development Approach

A suitability filter tool helps project teams consider whether a project has characteristics that lend themselves toward a predictive, hybrid, or adaptive approach. The suitability filter is an informational tool that combines its assessment with other data and decision-making activities so that the tailored approach is appropriate for each project. By evaluating criteria based on culture, project team, and project factors, a suitability filter generates a diagnostic visual that can be helpful in discussing and deciding on the initial approach.

3.4.2 TAILOR FOR THE ORGANIZATION

While project teams own and improve their processes, organizations often require some level of approval and oversight. Many organizations have a project methodology, general management approach, or general development approach that is used as a starting point for their projects. These guides are intended to support such things as repeatable processes, consistent measures of the organization's project capabilities, and continuous improvement of those capabilities. Organizations that have established process governance need to ensure tailoring is aligned to policy. To demonstrate that the project team's tailoring decisions do not threaten the organization's larger strategic or stewardship goals, project teams may need to justify using a tailored approach.

Additional constraints for tailoring for the organization include large, safety-critical projects and projects performed under contract. Large, safety-critical project tailoring suggestions may require additional oversight and approval to help prevent errors, loss, or subsequent issues. Projects that are performed under contract may have contract terms that specify the use of a particular life cycle, delivery approach, or methodology.

The tailoring process shown in Figure 3-3 uses factors such as project size, criticality, organizational maturity, and other considerations.

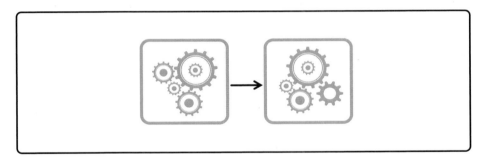

Figure 3-3. Tailoring the Approach for the Organization

Tailoring for the organization involves adding, removing, and reconfiguring elements of the approach to make it more suitable for the individual organization. This process is shown in Figure 3-4.

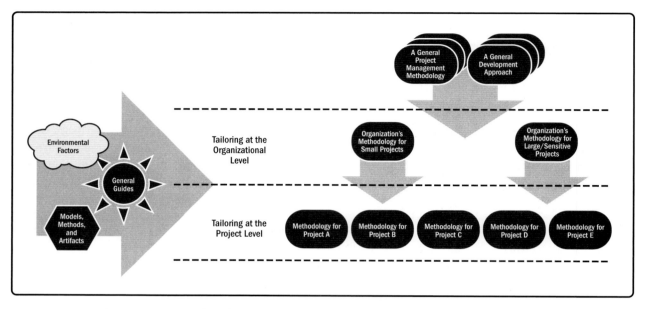

Figure 3-4. Assessing the Organizational and Project Factors When Tailoring

Organizations with a project management office (PMO) or value delivery office (VDO) may play a role in reviewing and approving tailored delivery approaches.

Tailoring that only impacts the project team (e.g., when they hold internal meetings, who works where, etc.) requires less oversight than tailoring that impacts external groups (e.g., how and when other departments are engaged, etc.). Therefore, internal project tailoring might be approved by the project manager while tailoring changes that impact external groups may require approval by the PMO or VDO. The PMO or VDO can assist project teams as they tailor their approaches by providing ideas and solutions from other project teams.

A VDO may be found in organizations that use more adaptive delivery approaches. The VDO serves an enabling role, rather than a management or oversight function. It focuses on coaching project teams; building adaptive skills and capabilities throughout the organization; and mentoring sponsors and product owners to be more effective in those roles.

3.4.3 TAILOR FOR THE PROJECT

Many attributes influence tailoring for the project. These include, but are not limited to:

▶ Product/deliverable,

▶ Project team, and

▶ Culture.

The project team should ask questions about each attribute to help guide them in the tailoring process. Answers to these questions can help identify the need to tailor processes, delivery approach, life cycle, tools, methods, and artifacts.

3.4.3.1 Product/Deliverable

Attributes associated with the product or deliverable include, but are not limited to:

▶ **Compliance/criticality.** How much process rigor and quality assurance is appropriate?

▶ **Type of product/deliverable.** Is the product well known and physical, for example, something easy to recognize and describe like a building? Or something intangible like software or the design of a new drug?

▶ **Industry market.** What market does the project, product, or deliverable serve? Is that market highly regulated, fast moving, or slow to evolve? What about competitors and incumbents?

▶ **Technology.** Is the technology stable and well established or rapidly evolving and at risk of obsolescence?

▶ **Time frame.** Is the project time frame short as in weeks or months, or long as in several years?

▶ **Stability of requirements.** How likely are there to be changes to core requirements?

▶ **Security.** Are elements of the product business confidential or classified?

▶ **Incremental delivery.** Is this something the project team can develop and get stakeholder feedback on incrementally, or something that is hard to evaluate until near completion?

3.4.3.2 Project Team

Project team considerations include:

▶ **Project team size.** How many full-time and part-time people will be working on the project?

▶ **Project team geography.** Where are the team members predominantly located geographically? Will some or all of the team be remote or colocated?

▶ **Organizational distribution.** Where are the team's supporting groups and other stakeholders located?

▶ **Project team experience.** Do the project team members have any experience in the industry, in the organization, or working with each other? Do they have the skills, tools, and technology required for the project under consideration?

▶ **Access to customer.** Is it practical to get frequent and timely feedback from customers or customer representatives?

3.4.3.3 Culture

Evaluating the culture includes considerations regarding:

▶ **Buy-in.** Is there acceptance, support, and enthusiasm for the proposed delivery approach?

▶ **Trust.** Are there high levels of trust that the project team is capable of and committed to delivering the project outcomes?

▶ **Empowerment.** Is the project team trusted, supported, and encouraged to own and develop its working environment, agreements, and decisions?

▶ **Organizational culture.** Do the organizational values and culture align with the project approach? This includes empowering versus specifying and checking, trusting local decision making versus requesting external decision making, etc.

Through the evaluation of these attributes, tailoring decisions around engagement, process, and tools can be made for the project. These removals and additions are depicted in Figure 3-5 with an "X" for removals and dotted boxes for the addition of trial processes

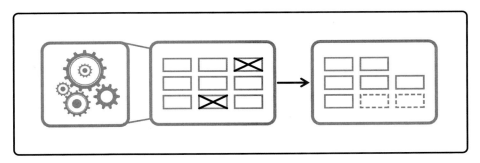

Figure 3-5. Tailoring the Approach for the Project

3.4.3.4 Implement Ongoing Improvement

The process of tailoring is not a single, one-time exercise. During progressive elaboration, issues with how the project team is working, how the product or deliverable is evolving, and other learnings will indicate where further tailoring could bring improvements. Review points, phase gates, and retrospectives all provide opportunities to inspect and adapt the process, development approach, and delivery frequency as necessary.

Keeping the project team engaged with improving its process can foster pride of ownership and demonstrate a commitment to implement ongoing improvements and quality. Engaging the project team to find and implement improvements also demonstrates trust in their skills and suggestions along with empowerment. Project team engagement with tailoring demonstrates a mindset of innovation and improvement rather than settling for the status quo.

The concept of adding, removing, and changing processes is shown in Figure 3-6.

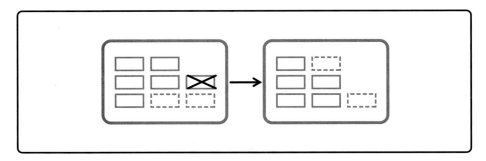

Figure 3-6. Implement Ongoing Improvement

How organizations tailor can itself be tailored. However, most organizations undertake some or all of the four steps described. They use elements of selecting an initial approach, tailoring for the organization, tailoring for the project, and implementing ongoing improvement as shown in Figure 3-7.

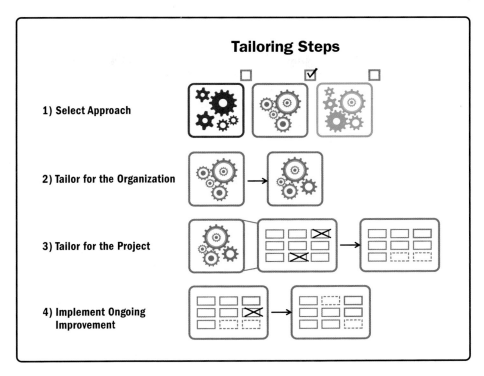

Figure 3-7. The Tailoring Process

3.5 TAILORING THE PERFORMANCE DOMAINS

The work associated with each performance domain can also be tailored, based on the uniqueness of the project. As shown in Figure 3-8, the principles for project management provide guidance for the behavior of project practitioners as they tailor the performance domains to meet the unique needs of the project context and the environment.

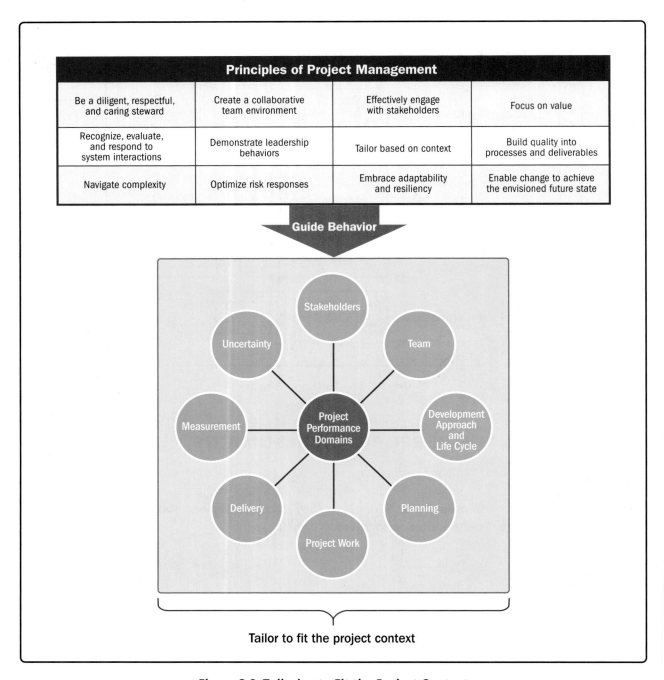

Figure 3-8. Tailoring to Fit the Project Context

Some tailoring considerations related to each of the performance domains include, but are not limited to:

3.5.1 STAKEHOLDERS

▶ Is there a collaborative environment for stakeholders and suppliers?

▶ Are the stakeholders internal or external to the organization, or both?

▶ What technologies are most appropriate and cost effective for communicating to stakeholders? What communication technology is available?

▶ Is one language used with stakeholders? Have allowances been made to adjust to stakeholders from diverse language groups?

▶ How many stakeholders are there? How diverse is the culture within the stakeholder community?

▶ What are the relationships within the stakeholder community? The more networks in which a stakeholder or stakeholder group participates, the more complex the networks of information and misinformation the stakeholder may receive.

3.5.2 PROJECT TEAM

▶ What is the physical location of project team members? Is the project team colocated? Is the project team in the same geographical area? Is the project team distributed across multiple time zones?

▶ Does the project team reflect diverse viewpoints and cultural perspectives?

▶ How will project team members be identified for the project? Are project team members full time or part time on the project? Are there available contractors capable of performing the work?

▶ Does the project team have an established culture? How will tailoring be influenced by the existing culture, and how will the existing culture be influenced by tailoring?

▶ How is project team development managed for the project? Are there organizational tools to manage project team development or will new ones need to be established?

▶ Are there project team members who have special needs? Will the project team need special training to manage diversity?

3.5.3 DEVELOPMENT APPROACH AND LIFE CYCLE

▶ Which development approach is appropriate for the product, service, or result? If adaptive, should the project be developed incrementally or iteratively? Is a hybrid approach best?

▶ What is an appropriate life cycle for this specific project? What phases should comprise the project life cycle?

▶ Does the organization have formal or informal audit and governance policies, procedures, and guidelines?

3.5.4 PLANNING

▶ How might internal and external environmental factors influence the project and its deliverable?

▶ What are the factors influencing durations (such as the correlation between available resources and their productivity)?

▶ Does the organization have formal or informal policies, procedures, and guidelines related to cost estimating and budgeting?

▶ How does the organization estimate cost when using adaptive approaches?

▶ Is there one main procurement or are there multiple procurements at different times with different sellers that add to the complexity of the procurement processes?

▶ Are local laws and regulations regarding procurement activities integrated with the organization's procurement policies? How does this affect contract auditing requirements?

3.5.5 PROJECT WORK

- ▶ What management processes are most effective based on the organizational culture, complexity, and other project factors?

- ▶ How will knowledge be managed in the project to foster a collaborative working environment?

- ▶ What information should be collected throughout and at the end of the project? How will the information be collected and managed? What technology is available to develop, record, transmit, retrieve, track, and store information and artifacts?

- ▶ Will historical information and lessons learned be made available to future projects?

- ▶ Does the organization have a formal knowledge management repository that a project team is required to use, and is it readily accessible?

3.5.6 DELIVERY

- ▶ Does the organization have formal or informal requirements management systems?

- ▶ Does the organization have existing formal or informal validation and control-related policies, procedures, and guidelines?

- ▶ What quality policies and procedures exist in the organization? What quality tools, techniques, and templates are used in the organization?

- ▶ Are there any specific quality standards in the industry that need to be applied? Are there any specific governmental, legal, or regulatory constraints that need to be taken into consideration?

- ▶ Are there areas of the project with unstable requirements? If so, what is the best approach for addressing the unstable requirements?

- ▶ How does sustainability factor into the elements of project management or product development?

3.5.7 UNCERTAINTY

▶ What is the risk appetite and risk tolerance for this endeavor?

▶ How are threats and opportunities best identified and addressed within the selected development approach?

▶ How will the presence of project complexity, technological uncertainty, product novelty, cadence, or progress tracking impact the project?

▶ Does the project's size in terms of budget, duration, scope, or project team size require a more detailed approach to risk management? Or is the project small enough to justify a simplified risk management process?

▶ Is a robust risk management approach demanded by high levels of innovation, new technology, commercial arrangements, interfaces, or other external dependencies? Or is the project simple enough that a reduced risk management process will suffice?

▶ How strategically important is the project? Is the level of risk increased for this project because it aims to produce breakthrough opportunities, addresses significant blocks to organizational performance, or involves major product innovation?

3.5.8 MEASUREMENT

▶ How is value measured?

▶ Are there measures for financial value and nonfinancial value?

▶ How will the project enable data capture and reporting related to benefits realization, both during the project and after the project is complete?

▶ What are the project status reporting requirements?

3.6 DIAGNOSTICS

Periodic reviews such as retrospectives or lessons learned are effective ways to determine if approaches are working well and if improvements can be made by tailoring. Project teams that do not use retrospectives can look to issues, threats, quality assurance statistics, and stakeholder feedback for signs that further tailoring or adaptation might be required or useful.

This section is intended as general guidance and does not address every possible situation that could surface within a project. Table 3-1 lists some common situations and suggested tailoring solutions for commonly encountered situations.

Table 3-1. Common Situations and Tailoring Suggestions

Situation	Tailoring Suggestion
Poor quality deliverables	Add more feedback verification loops and quality assurance steps.
Team members unsure of how to proceed or undertake their work	Add more guidance, training, and verification steps.
Long delays waiting for approvals	Try streamlining approval decisions through fewer people authorized to make decisions up to certain value thresholds.
Too much work in progress or high rates of scrap	Use techniques like value stream mapping and kanban boards to visualize the work, identify the issues, and propose solutions.
Stakeholders are not engaged or share negative feedback	Evaluate whether sufficient information is being shared with stakeholders; feedback loops are present and working; and deeper engagement may work better than simply communicating.
Lack of visibility and understanding of project progress	Check to ensure appropriate measures are being collected, analyzed, shared, and discussed during team and stakeholder meetings; validate agreement with the measures within the team and with stakeholders.
Issues and/or risks for which the team is unprepared continue to surface, requiring the team to react rather than progress work	Explore root causes to identify whether there are related gaps in project processes or activities.

3.7 SUMMARY

Tailoring involves the considered adaptation of approach, governance, and processes to make them more suitable for the given environment and the project at hand. It involves the analysis, design, and deliberate modification of the people elements, the processes employed, and the tools used. The tailoring process involves four steps:

- ▶ Select initial approach.
- ▶ Tailor for the organization.
- ▶ Tailor for the project.
- ▶ Implement ongoing improvement.

While the tailoring process is often undertaken by the project stakeholders, the bounds and approach to tailoring are usually governed by organizational guidelines. Organizational governance helps ensure the external interfaces between project teams mesh correctly and provides guidance in the form of tailoring considerations.

Models, Methods, and Artifacts

4

4.1 OVERVIEW

This section provides a high-level description of some commonly used models, methods, and artifacts that are useful in managing projects. The items listed in this section are not intended to be exhaustive or prescriptive, but rather to help project teams think about the options available to them.

In the context of this guide, terms are defined as follows:

▶ **Model.** A model is a thinking strategy to explain a process, framework, or phenomenon.

▶ **Method.** A method is the means for achieving an outcome, output, result, or project deliverable.

▶ **Artifact.** An artifact can be a template, document, output, or project deliverable.

As project teams consider the tailoring questions in Section 3.5 and decide on specific responses to those questions, they will start to build a framework for structuring their efforts to deliver the project outcomes. For example, project teams select specific methods to enable capturing and sharing the applicable information so they can track progress, improve project team performance in real time, and engage stakeholders.

Figure 4-1 shows how tailoring includes the models and methods used to perform work in the project performance domains. The deliverables and the artifacts are also tailored to the project, internal environment, and external environment.

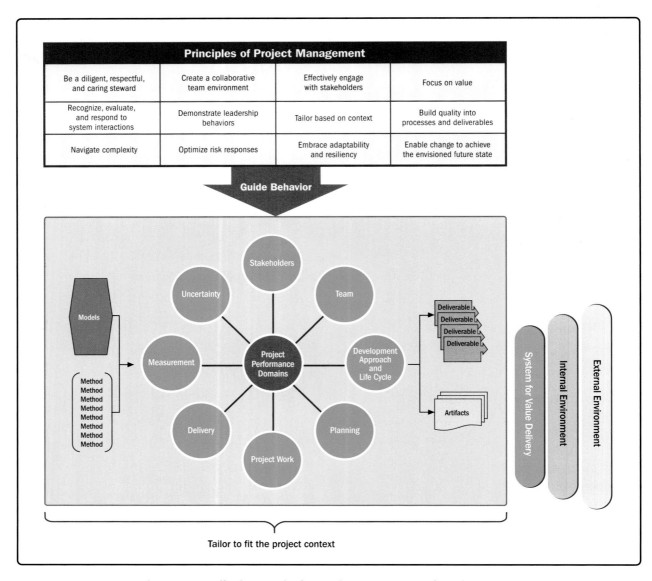

Figure 4-1. Tailoring to Fit the Project Context and Environment

As with any process, the use of models, methods, and artifacts has associated costs related to time, level of expertise/proficiency in use, impact on productivity, etc. Project teams should consider these implications when deciding which elements to use. As much as possible, project teams should avoid using anything that:

▶ Duplicates or adds unnecessary effort,

▶ Is not useful to the project team and its stakeholders,

▶ Produces incorrect or misleading information, or

▶ Caters to individual needs versus those of the project team.

4.2 COMMONLY USED MODELS

Models reflect small-scale, simplified views of reality and present scenarios, strategies, or approaches for optimizing work processes and efforts. A model helps to explain how something works in the real world. Models can shape behavior and point to approaches for solving problems or meeting needs. Some models were developed with projects and project teams in mind, others are more general in nature. Where feasible, models in this section are presented as they apply to projects. The content in this section does not describe how to develop or create new models.

The model descriptions presented provide a high-level view. Project team members and other stakeholders can refer to many sources (e.g., PMI's library of standards products and PMIstandards+™) for more-complete descriptions and explanations of the models.

4.2.1 SITUATIONAL LEADERSHIP MODELS

Situational leadership models are a subset of a vast array of leadership models. Just as project teams tailor the processes, methods, life cycles, and development approaches, leadership styles are also tailored. Situational leadership models describe ways to tailor one's leadership style to meet the needs of the individual and the project team. The following are examples of two situational leadership models.

4.2.1.1 Situational Leadership® II

Ken Blanchard's Situational Leadership® II measures project team member development using competence and commitment as the two main variables. Competence is the combination of ability, knowledge, and skill. Commitment speaks to the confidence and motivation an individual has. As an individual's competence and commitment evolve, leadership styles evolve from directing to coaching to supporting to delegating in order to meet the individual's needs.

4.2.1.2 OSCAR Model

The OSCAR coaching and mentoring model was developed by Karen Whittleworth and Andrew Gilbert. It helps individuals adapt their coaching or leadership styles to support individuals who have an action plan for personal development. The model refers to five contributing factors:

▶ **Outcome.** An outcome identifies the long-term goals of an individual and the desired result from each conversation session.

▶ **Situation.** A situation enables conversation about the current skills, abilities, and knowledge level of the project team member; why the person is at that level; and how that level impacts the individual's performance and peer relationships.

▶ **Choices/consequences.** Choice and/or consequences identify all the potential avenues for attaining the desired outcome and the consequences of each choice so an individual can choose viable avenues for reaching their long-term goals.

▶ **Actions.** An action commits to specific improvements by focusing on immediate and attainable targets that an individual can work toward within a specified time frame.

▶ **Review.** Holding regular meetings offers support and helps to ensure that individuals remain motivated and on track.

4.2.2 COMMUNICATION MODELS

Project success is dependent on effective communication. Communication models demonstrate concepts associated with how sender and receiver frames of reference impact the effectiveness of communication, how the communication medium influences the effectiveness of communication, and the types of disconnects between end-user expectations and reality. With the prevalence of multicultural project teams and dispersed stakeholders, these models provide a way of viewing communication styles and methods to enhance communication efficiency and effectiveness. There are many communication models that demonstrate different aspects of communication. Sections 4.2.2.1 through 4.2.2.3 provide a sampling of communication models.

4.2.2.1 Cross-Cultural Communication

A communication model developed by Browaeys and Price incorporates the idea that the message itself and how it is transmitted is influenced by the sender's current knowledge, experience, language, thinking, and communication styles, as well as stereotypes and relationship to the receiver. Similarly, the receiver's knowledge, experience, language, thinking, and communication styles, as well as stereotypes and relationship to the sender will influence how the message is interpreted.

4.2.2.2 Effectiveness of Communication Channels

Alistair Cockburn developed a model that describes the communication channels along the axes of effectiveness and richness. As defined by Richard Daft and Robert Lengel, richness relates to the amount of learning that can be transmitted through a medium. Media richness is a function of characteristics, including the ability to:

▶ Handle multiple information cues simultaneously,

▶ Facilitate rapid feedback,

▶ Establish a personal focus, and

▶ Utilize natural language.

Richness in communication allows a broad spectrum of information to be conveyed rapidly. Situations that entail complex, complicated, and personal information benefit from richer communication channels, such as face-to-face communication. Situations that impart simple, factual information can use less rich communication channels such as a note or a text message.

4.2.2.3 Gulf of Execution and Evaluation

Donald Norman described the gulf of execution as the degree to which an item corresponds with what a person expects it to do. Said another way, it is the difference between the intention of a user and what the item allows them to do or supports them in doing. A car that has the ability to parallel park itself would have a gulf of execution if the driver expected to push a button labeled "park" and have the car park itself, and the car did not park itself.

The gulf of evaluation is the degree to which an item supports the user in discovering how to interpret the item and interact with it effectively. The same parking example would show a gulf of evaluation if the controls were not designed in such a way that the driver could easily determine how to initiate the self-parking function.

4.2.3 MOTIVATION MODELS

People perform better when they are motivated, and people are motivated by different things. Understanding what motivates project team members and other stakeholders helps to tailor rewards to the individual, thereby eliciting more effective engagement. There are a significant number of models that illustrate how people are motivated. Four models are described in Sections 4.2.3.1 through 4.2.3.4, though these are a small representation of available models.

4.2.3.1 Hygiene and Motivational Factors

Frederick Herzberg conducted a study of motivational factors in working life. He believed that job satisfaction and dissatisfaction stem from conditions called motivational factors. Motivational factors include matters that relate to the content of the work, such as achievement, growth, and advancement. Insufficient motivational factors lead to dissatisfaction. Sufficient motivational factors lead to satisfaction.

Herzberg also identified hygiene factors related to the work, such as company policies, salary, and the physical environment. If hygiene factors are insufficient, they cause dissatisfaction. However, even if they are sufficient, they do not lead to satisfaction.

4.2.3.2 Intrinsic versus Extrinsic Motivation

Daniel Pink published several books about the intrinsic factors that motivate people. He stated that while extrinsic rewards, such as salary, are motivators to a certain extent, once a person is paid fairly for their work, the motivational power of extrinsic rewards ceases to exist. For complicated and challenging work, such as much of the work on projects, intrinsic motivators are far longer lasting and more effective. Pink identifies three types of intrinsic motivators: autonomy, mastery, and purpose:

▶ **Autonomy.** Autonomy is the desire to direct one's own life. This is aligned with being able to determine how, where, and when to accomplish work. Autonomy includes flexible work hours, working from home, and work on self-selecting and self-managing project teams.

▶ **Mastery.** Mastery is about being able to improve and excel. The desire to do excellent work, learn, and achieve goals are aspects of mastery.

▶ **Purpose.** Purpose speaks to the need to make a difference. Knowing the project vision and how work contributes to achieving that vision allows people to feel like they are making a difference.

4.2.3.3 Theory of Needs

David McClellan's model states that all people are driven by needs of achievement, power, and affiliation. The relative strength of each need depends on an individual's experiences and culture.

▶ **Achievement.** People who are motivated by achievement, such as reaching a goal, are motivated by activities and work that is challenging, but reasonable.

▶ **Power.** People who are motivated by power like to organize, motivate, and lead others. They are motivated by increased responsibility.

▶ **Affiliation.** People who are motivated by affiliation seek acceptance and belonging. They are motivated by being part of a team.

4.2.3.4 Theory X, Theory Y, and Theory Z

Douglas McGregor devised the Theory X and Theory Y models, which represent a spectrum of employee motivation and corresponding management styles. This was later expanded to include Theory Z.

▶ **Theory X.** The X side of the spectrum assumes individuals work for the sole purpose of income. They are not ambitious or goal oriented. The corresponding management style to motivate these individuals is a hands-on and top-down approach. This management style is often seen in a production or labor-intensive environment, or one with many layers of management.

▶ **Theory Y.** The Y side of the spectrum assumes that individuals are intrinsically motivated to do good work. The corresponding management style has a more personal coaching feel. The manager encourages creativity and discussion. This management style is often seen in creative and knowledge worker environments.

▶ **Theory Z.** Abraham Maslow saw Theory Z as a transcendent dimension to work where individuals are motivated by self-realization, values, and a higher calling. The optimal management style in this situation is one that cultivates insight and meaning.

William Ouchi's version of Theory Z focuses on motivating employees by creating a job for life where the focus is on the well-being of employees and their families. This style of management seeks to promote high productivity, morale, and satisfaction.

4.2.4 CHANGE MODELS

Many projects contain an aspect of changing systems, behaviors, activities, and sometimes, cultures. Managing this type of change requires thinking about how to transition from the current to the future desired state. There are many models that describe the activities necessary for successful change management. Sections 4.2.4.1 through 4.2.4.5 provide a sampling of the change models.

4.2.4.1 Managing Change in Organizations

Managing Change in Organizations: A Practice Guide [3] is an iterative model that is based on common elements across a range of change management models. The framework has five associated elements interconnected through a series of feedback loops:

- ▶ **Formulate change.** This element focuses on building the rationale to help people understand why change is needed and how the future state will be better.

- ▶ **Plan change.** The identification of activities helps people prepare for the transition from the current to the future state.

- ▶ **Implement change.** This iterative element focuses on demonstrating the future state capabilities, checking to ensure the capabilities are having the intended impact, and making necessary improvements or adaptations in response.

- ▶ **Manage transition.** This element considers how to address needs related to the change that may surface once the future state is achieved.

- ▶ **Sustain change.** This element seeks to ensure that the new capabilities continue and previous processes or behaviors cease.

4.2.4.2 ADKAR® Model

Jeff Hiatt developed the ADKAR® Model which focuses on five sequential steps that individuals undergo when adapting to change:

- ▶ **Step 1: Awareness.** This step identifies why the change is necessary.

- ▶ **Step 2: Desire.** Once people know why the change is necessary, there needs to be a desire to be part of and support the change.

- ▶ **Step 3: Knowledge.** People need to understand how to change. This includes understanding new processes and systems in addition to new roles and responsibilities. Knowledge can be imparted through training and education.

- ▶ **Step 4: Ability.** In this step, knowledge is supported with hands-on practice and access to expertise and help as needed.

- ▶ **Step 5: Reinforcement.** Reinforcement supports the sustainment of the change. This can include rewards, recognition, feedback, and measurement.

4.2.4.3 The 8-Step Process for Leading Change

John Kotter introduced the 8-Step Process for Leading Change for transforming organizations. It is a top-down approach where the need for and approach to change originates at the top levels of the organization, and then is promoted down through the organization's layers of management to the change recipients. The eight steps are:

▶ **Step 1: Create urgency.** Identify potential threats and opportunities that drive the need for change.

▶ **Step 2: Form a powerful coalition.** Identify the change leaders. Change leaders are not necessarily based on hierarchy. The change leaders should be influential people from a variety of roles, expertise, social, and political importance.

▶ **Step 3: Create a vision for change.** Identify the values that are central to the change. Then create a brief vision statement that summarizes the change. Next, identify a strategy to realize the vision.

▶ **Step 4: Communicate the vision.** Communicate the vision throughout the change process. Apply the vision throughout all aspects of the organization. Senior management and the change coalition should consistently communicate the vision and demonstrate the urgency and benefits of the change.

▶ **Step 5: Remove obstacles.** All change comes with obstacles. Sometimes the obstacles are outdated processes, sometimes they are based on the organizational structure, and sometimes they are people resistant to change. Regardless, all obstacles need to be addressed.

▶ **Step 6: Create short-term wins.** Identify quick and easy wins to build momentum and support for the change.

▶ **Step 7: Build on the change.** Once the short-term wins are complete, the organization needs to set goals for continued improvement.

▶ **Step 8: Anchor the changes in corporate culture.** Ensure the change becomes ingrained into the culture: continue to communicate the vision, tell success stories, recognize people in the organization who embody and empower the change, and continue to support the change coalition.

4.2.4.4 Virginia Satir Change Model

Virginia Satir developed a model of how people experience and cope with change. Its purpose is to help project team members understand what they are feeling and enable them to move through change more efficiently.

▶ **Late status quo.** This initial stage is when everything feels familiar and can be characterized as "business as usual." For some people, business as usual may be good because they know what to expect. For others, this status may feel a bit stale or boring.

▶ **The foreign element.** Something happens that shifts the status quo in this stage. This may include initiating a project that introduces change to people's usual way of working. There is often a period of resistance and reduction in performance after the change is introduced. People may ignore the change or dismiss its relevance.

▶ **Chaos.** People are in unfamiliar territory. They are no longer comfortable, and performance drops to its lowest level. Feelings, actions, and behaviors are unpredictable. Some people feel anxious, others may shut down, and some individuals may feel excited. Chaos can make people very creative as they try to find ways to make sense of the situation. They try various ideas and behaviors to see which of these has a positive outcome.

▶ **The transforming idea.** People come to a point where they come up with an idea that helps them make sense of the situation. They begin to see how they can find a way out of the chaos and cope with the new reality. Work performance begins to increase.

▶ **Practice and integration.** People try to implement their new ideas or behaviors. There may be setbacks and a period of trial and error, but eventually they learn what works and what doesn't. This leads to improved performance. Often performance is at a higher level than it was before the foreign element was introduced.

▶ **New status quo.** People get used to the new environment, and their performance stabilizes. Eventually, the new status quo becomes the normal way of working.

4.2.4.5 Transition Model

William Bridges' Transition Model provides an understanding of what occurs to individuals psychologically when an organizational change takes place. This model differentiates between change and transition. Change is situational and happens whether or not people transition through it. Transition is a psychological process where people gradually accept the details of the new situation and the changes that come with it.

The model identifies three stages of transition associated with change:

▶ **Ending, losing, and letting go.** The change is introduced in this stage. It is often associated with fear, anger, upset, uncertainty, denial, and resistance to the change.

▶ **The neutral zone.** The change is happening in this stage. In some instances, people may feel frustration, resentment, confusion, and anxiety about the change. Productivity may drop as people learn new ways of doing work. In other instances, people may become very creative, innovative, and passionate about trying new ways of working.

▶ **The new beginning.** At this point, people accept and even embrace the change. They are becoming more adept at the new skills and the new ways of working. People are often open to learning and are energized by the change.

4.2.5 COMPLEXITY MODELS

Projects exist in a state of ambiguity and require interactions among multiple systems, often with uncertain outcomes. Complexity is a challenge to work with. The two models described in Sections 4.2.5.1 and 4.2.5.2 provide a framework to understand complexity and determine how to make decisions in a complex environment.

4.2.5.1 Cynefin Framework

The Cynefin framework, created by Dave Snowden, is a conceptual framework used to diagnose cause-and-effect relationships as a decision-making aid. The framework offers five problem and decision-making contexts:

- Where there is an obvious cause-and-effect relationship, best practices are used to make decisions.

- Complicated relationships exist when there is a set of known unknowns or a range of correct answers. In these situations, it is best to assess the facts, analyze the situation, and apply good practices.

- Complex relationships include unknown unknowns. There is no apparent cause and effect, and there are no obvious right answers. In complex environments, one should probe the environment, sense the situation, and respond with action. This style uses emergent practices that allow for repeated cycles of probe-sense-respond as complex environments change in reaction to multiple stimuli, and what worked once may not be effective the next time.

- In chaotic environments, the cause and effects are unclear. There is too much confusion to wait to understand the situation. In these situations, the first step is to take action to try and stabilize the situation, then sense where there is some stability, and respond by taking steps to get the chaotic situation to a complex situation.

- Disordered relationships lack clarity and may require breaking them into smaller parts whose context links with one of the other four contexts.

The Cynefin framework helps identify behaviors, such as probing, sensing, responding, acting, and categorizing, which can help impact the relationships between variables and guide actions.

4.2.5.2 Stacey Matrix

Ralph Stacey developed the Stacey matrix which is similar to the Cynefin framework, but it looks at two dimensions to determine the relative complexity of a project: (a) the relative uncertainty of the requirements for the deliverable, and (b) the relative uncertainty of the technology that will be used to create the deliverable. Based on the relative uncertainty of these dimensions, a project is considered simple, complicated, complex, or chaotic. The degree of complexity is one factor that influences tailoring methods and practices for the project.

4.2.6 PROJECT TEAM DEVELOPMENT MODELS

Project teams move through different stages of development. Understanding the stage of the team in its development helps project managers support the project team and its growth. The two models presented in Sections 4.2.6.1 and 4.2.6.2 illustrate how project teams move through different stages to become high-performing project teams.

4.2.6.1 Tuckman Ladder

Bruce Tuckman articulated the stages of team development as forming, storming, norming, and performing. Many people add a fifth stage, adjourning.

- ▶ **Forming.** The project team first comes together. Members get to know each other's name, position on the project team, skill sets, and other pertinent background information. This might occur in the kickoff meeting.

- ▶ **Storming.** Project team members jockey for position on the team. This phase is where people's personalities, strengths, and weaknesses start to come out. There might be some conflict or struggle as people figure out how to work together. Storming might go on for some time or pass relatively quickly.

- ▶ **Norming.** The project team starts to function as a collective body. At this point, project team members know their places on the team and how they relate to and interface with all the other members. They are starting to work together. There might be some challenges as work progresses, but these issues are resolved quickly, and the project team moves into action.

- ▶ **Performing.** The project team becomes operationally efficient. This is the mature project team stage. Project teams that have been together for a while are able to develop a synergy. By working together, project team members accomplish more and produce a high-quality product.

- ▶ **Adjourning.** The project team completes the work and disperses to work on other things. If the project team has formed good relationships, some project team members might be sad about leaving the project team.

The project team culture in this model starts in the forming stage and evolves throughout the rest of the development stages. While this model shows a linear progression, project teams can move back and forth between theses stages. In addition, not all project teams achieve the performing or even the norming stages.

4.2.6.2 Drexler/Sibbet Team Performance Model

Allan Drexler and David Sibbet developed a team performance model with seven steps. Steps 1 through 4 describe the stages in creating a project team, and steps 5 through 7 cover project team sustainability and performance.

- ▶ **Step 1: Orientation.** Orientation answers the question of *why*. In this stage, the project team learns the purpose and mission for the project. This usually occurs at a kickoff meeting, or is documented in a business case, project charter, or lean start-up canvas.

- ▶ **Step 2: Trust building.** Trust building answers the question of *who*. This stage sheds light on who is on the project team and the skills and abilities each person brings. It can also include information about key stakeholders who may not be part of the project team but can influence the project team.

- ▶ **Step 3: Goal clarification.** Goal clarification answers *what*. In this stage, the project team elaborates the high-level project information. This may include finding out more about stakeholder expectations, requirements, assumptions, and deliverable acceptance criteria.

- ▶ **Step 4: Commitment.** Commitment addresses the question of *how*. In this stage, the project team starts to define plans to achieve the goals. This can include milestone schedules, release plans, high-level budgets, resource needs, and so forth.

- ▶ **Step 5: Implementation.** High-level plans are decomposed into greater levels of detail, such as a detailed schedule or backlog. The project team starts working together to produce deliverables.

- ▶ **Step 6: High performance.** After the project team has worked together for some time, project team members reach a high level of performance. They work well together, don't need much oversight, and experience synergies within the project team.

- ▶ **Step 7: Renewal.** Renewal is the stage of working through changes on the project team or the project. The deliverables, stakeholders, environment, project team leadership, or team membership may change. This causes the project team to consider if the past behavior and actions are still sufficient, or if the project team needs to go back to a previous stage to reset the expectations and ways of working together.

4.2.7 OTHER MODELS

The models described in Sections 4.2.7.1 through 4.2.7.5 cover a wide range of topics, including conflict management, negotiation, planning, Process Groups, and salience.

4.2.7.1 Conflict Model

Conflict is common on projects. Conflict can be healthy and productive when handled well. It can result in greater trust among project team members and a deeper commitment to the outcomes. Fear of conflict can restrict communication and creativity. However, conflict can be unhealthy as well. Addressing conflict inappropriately can lead to dissatisfaction, lack of trust, and reduced morale and motivation. The model based on work by Ken Thomas and Ralph Kilmann describes six ways of addressing conflict by focusing on the relative power between the individuals and the desire to maintain a good relationship as follows:

▶ **Confronting/problem solving.** Confronting a conflict treats the conflict as a problem to be solved. This style of conflict resolution is used when the relationship between parties is important, and when each person has confidence in the other party's ability to problem-solve.

▶ **Collaborating.** Collaborating involves incorporating multiple views about the conflict. The objective is to learn about the various views and see things from multiple perspectives. This is an effective method when there is trust among the participants and when there is time to come to consensus. A project manager may facilitate this type of conflict resolution between project team members.

▶ **Compromising.** There are some conflicts in which all parties will not be fully satisfied. In those instances, finding a way to compromise is the best approach. Compromise entails a willingness to give and take. This allows all parties to get something they want, and it avoids escalating the conflict. This style is often used when the parties involved have equal "power." A project manager may compromise with a technical manager regarding the availability of a project team member to work on the project.

- ▶ **Smoothing/accommodating.** Smoothing and accommodating are useful when reaching the overarching goal is more important than the disagreement. This approach maintains harmony in the relationship and can create good will between the parties. This approach is also used when there is a difference in the relative authority or power of the individuals. For example, this approach may be appropriate when there is a disagreement with the sponsor. Since the sponsor outranks the project manager or project team member, and there is a desire to maintain a good relationship with the sponsor, adopting an accommodating posture may be appropriate.

- ▶ **Forcing.** Forcing is used when there is not enough time to collaborate or problem-solve. In this scenario, one party forces their will on the other. The party forcing has more power than the other party. A forcing style may be used if there is a health and safety conflict that needs to be resolved immediately.

- ▶ **Withdrawal/avoiding.** Sometimes a problem will go away on its own, or sometimes discussions get heated and people need a cooling-off period. In both scenarios, withdrawing from the situation is appropriate. Withdrawal is also used in a no-win scenario, such as complying with a requirement imposed by a regulatory agency instead of challenging the requirement.

4.2.7.2 Negotiation

There are many models for negotiation. One model is Steven Covey's principle of "Think Win-Win." This principle applies to all interactions, not just negotiations, but it is described here in the context of negotiation. In negotiations, there are different possible outcomes:

- ▶ **Win-win.** This is the optimal outcome, where each person is satisfied with the outcome.

- ▶ **Win-lose/lose-win.** This describes a competition perspective where in order to win, someone else loses. It may also come from a martyr perspective where someone chooses to lose so that others can win.

- ▶ **Lose-lose.** This outcome can occur when win-win outcomes may have been possible, but competition overwhelms collaboration. In this scenario, everyone ends up worse off.

A win-win perspective is generally found when the following aspects are present:

▶ **Character.** The parties involved are mature, demonstrate integrity, and share the perspective that there is enough value for everybody.

▶ **Trust.** The parties trust each other, establish agreements on how to operate, and are accountable.

▶ **Approach.** Each party is willing to look at the situation from the other's point of view. The parties work together to identify key issues and concerns. They identify what an acceptable solution looks like and identify options to achieve an acceptable solution.

4.2.7.3 Planning

Barry Boehm developed a model that compares the time and effort invested in developing plans to reduce risk, including the delay and other costs associated with overplanning. By taking more time to plan up front, many projects can reduce uncertainty, oversights, and rework. However, the longer the time spent planning, the longer it takes to get a return on investment, the more market share could be lost, and the more circumstances can change by the time the output is delivered. The intent of this model is to help identify the optimum amount of planning, sometimes called the sweet spot. The sweet spot is different for every project; therefore, there is no correct answer for the right amount of planning overall. This model demonstrates that there is a point where additional planning becomes counterproductive.

4.2.7.4 Process Groups

Project management processes can be organized into logical groupings of project management inputs, tools and techniques, and outputs that are tailored to meet the needs of the organization, stakeholders, and the project.

Groups of processes are *not* project phases. The Process Groups interact within each phase of a project life cycle. It is possible that all of these processes could occur within a single phase. Processes may be iterated within a phase or life cycle. The number of iterations and interactions between processes varies based on the needs of the project.

Projects that follow a process-based approach may use the following five process groupings as an organizing structure:

- **Initiating.** Those processes performed to define a new project or a new phase of an existing project by obtaining authorization to start the project or phase.

- **Planning.** Those processes required to establish the scope of the project, refine the objectives, and define the course of action required to attain the objectives that the project was undertaken to achieve.

- **Executing.** Those processes performed to complete the work defined in the project management plan to satisfy the project requirements.

- **Monitoring and Controlling.** Those processes required to track, review, and regulate the progress and performance of the project; identify any areas in which changes to the plan are required; and initiate the corresponding changes.

- **Closing.** Those processes performed to formally complete or close a project, phase, or contract.

These Process Groups are independent of the delivery approach, application areas (such as marketing, information services, and accounting), or industry (such as construction, aerospace, and telecommunications). In a process-based approach, the output of one process generally becomes an input to another process or is a deliverable of the project or project phase. For example, a project management plan and project documents, such as the risk register, assumption log, etc., which are produced in the planning process grouping, are inputs to the executing process grouping where updates are made to associated artifacts.

4.2.7.5 Salience Model

The Salience Model is about stakeholders. Salience means prominent, noticeable, or perceived as important. This model was proposed by Ronald K. Mitchell, Bradley R. Agle, and Donna J. Wood. The authors denoted a stakeholder identification based on three variables: power to influence, legitimacy of the stakeholders' relationships with the project, and the urgency of the stakeholders' claim on the project for stakeholder engagement.

4.3 MODELS APPLIED ACROSS PERFORMANCE DOMAINS

Different models are more likely to be useful in different project performance domains. While the needs of the project, stakeholders, and organizational environment will determine which models are most applicable for a specific project, there are some performance domains that are more likely to make use of each model. Table 4-1 suggests the performance domain(s) where each model is most likely to be of use; however, the project manager and project team have the ultimate responsibility for selecting the right models for their project.

Table 4-1. Mapping of Models Likely to Be Used in Each Performance Domain

Model	Performance Domain							
	Team	Stakeholders	Dev Approach and Life Cycle	Planning	Project Work	Delivery	Measurement	Uncertainly
Situational Leadership Models:								
Situational Leadership® II	X				X			
OSCAR	X				X			
Communication Models:								
Cross-cultural communication	X	X		X	X			
Effectiveness of communication channels	X	X		X	X			
Gulf of execution and evaluation		X				X		
Motivation Models:								
Hygiene and motivation factors	X			X	X			
Intrinsic versus extrinsic motivation	X			X	X			
Theory of needs	X			X	X			
Theory X, Theory Y, and Theory Z	X			X	X			
Change Models:								
Managing Change in Organizations		X		X	X			
ADKAR®		X		X	X			
8-Step Process for Leading Change		X		X	X			
Transition		X		X	X			
Complexity Models:								
Cynefin framework			X	X	X	X		X
Stacey matrix			X	X	X	X		X
Project Team Development Models:								
Tuckman Ladder	X				X			
Drexler/Sibbet Team Performance	X				X			
Other Models:								
Conflict	X	X			X			
Negotiation		X		X	X	X		
Planning			X	X	X			
Process Groups				X	X	X	X	
Salience		X		X	X			

4.4 COMMONLY USED METHODS

A method is a means for achieving an outcome, output, result, or project deliverable. The methods described here are a sampling of those commonly used to support project work. There are many methods that are not described here, either because they are used in project management the same way they are in other disciplines, such as interviewing, focus groups, checklists, and so forth, or because they are not frequently used across a broad spectrum of projects (i.e., the methods are industry specific).

Many of the methods are related by the purpose they serve, such as estimating or data gathering, and therefore, are presented in a group. Others are related by the type of activity involved, such as those in the meetings and analysis groups.

The content in this section is not meant to describe how a method is performed. The descriptions are presented at a high level with more detailed information available from many sources, including PMIstandards+.

4.4.1 DATA GATHERING AND ANALYSIS

Data gathering and analysis methods are used to collect, assess, and evaluate data and information to gain a deeper understanding of a situation. The outputs of data analysis may be organized and presented as one of the artifacts shown in Section 4.6.6. The data gathering and analysis methods described here, coupled with the artifacts described in Section 4.6.6, are often used to inform decisions.

▶ **Alternatives analysis.** Alternatives analysis is used to evaluate identified options in order to select the options or approaches to perform the work of the project.

▶ **Assumption and constraint analysis.** An assumption is a factor that is considered to be true, real, or certain, without proof or demonstration. A constraint is a limiting factor that affects the execution of a project, program, portfolio, or process. This form of analysis ensures that assumptions and constraints are integrated into the project plans and documents, and that there is consistency among them.

- **Benchmarking.** Benchmarking is the comparison of actual or planned products, processes, and practices to those of comparable organizations, which identifies best practices, generates ideas for improvement, and provides a basis for measuring performance.

- **Business justification analysis methods.** This group of analysis methods is associated with authorizing or justifying a project or a decision. The outcomes of the following analyses are often used in a business case that justifies undertaking a project:

  - ▷ *Payback period.* The payback period is the time needed to recover an investment, usually in months or years.

  - ▷ *Internal rate of return (IRR).* The internal rate of return is the projected annual yield of a project investment, incorporating both initial and ongoing costs into an estimated percentage growth rate a given project is expected to have.

  - ▷ *Return on investment (ROI).* Return on investment is the percent return on an initial investment, calculated by taking the projected average of all net benefits and dividing them by the initial cost.

  - ▷ *Net present value (NPV).* Net present value is the future value of expected benefits, expressed in the value those benefits have at the time of investment. NPV considers current and future costs and benefits and inflation.

  - ▷ *Cost-benefit analysis.* A cost-benefit analysis is a financial analysis tool used to determine the benefits provided by a project against its costs.

- **Check sheet.** A check sheet is a tally sheet that can be used as a checklist when gathering data. Check sheets can be used to collect and segregate data into categories. Check sheets can also be used to create histograms and matrices as described in Section 4.6.6.

- **Cost of quality.** The cost of quality includes all costs incurred over the life of the product by investment in preventing nonconformance to requirements, appraisal of the product or service for conformance to requirements, and failure to meet requirements.

- **Decision tree analysis.** A decision tree analysis is a diagramming and calculation method for evaluating the implications of a chain of multiple options in the presence of uncertainty. Decision trees can use the information generated from an expected monetary value analysis to populate the branches of the decision tree.

- **Earned value analysis.** Earned value analysis is a method that utilizes a set of measures associated with scope, schedule, and cost to determine the cost and schedule performance of a project.

- **Expected monetary value (EMV).** The expected monetary value is the estimated value of an outcome expressed in monetary terms. It is used to quantify the value of uncertainty, such as a risk, or compare the value of alternatives that are not necessarily equivalent. The EMV is calculated by multiplying the probability that an event will occur and the economic impact the event would have should it occur.

- **Forecast.** A forecast is an estimate or prediction of conditions and events in the project's future, based on information and knowledge available at the time of the forecast. Qualitative forecasting methods use the opinions and judgments of subject matter experts. Quantitative forecasting uses models where past information is used to predict future performance. Causal or econometric forecasting, such as regression analysis, identifies variables that can have significant impact on future outcomes.

- **Influence diagram.** This diagram is a graphical representation of situations showing causal influences, time ordering of events, and other relationships among variables and outcomes.

- **Life cycle assessment.** This assessment is a tool used to evaluate the total environmental impact of a product, process, or system. It includes all aspects of producing a project deliverable, from the origin of materials used in the deliverable to its distribution and ultimate disposal.

- **Make-or-buy analysis.** A make-or-buy analysis is the process of gathering and organizing data about product requirements and analyzing them against available alternatives such as the purchase versus internal manufacture of the product.

- **Probability and impact matrix.** A probability and impact matrix is a grid for mapping the probability of occurrence of each risk and its impact on project objectives if that risk occurs.

- **Process analysis.** This analysis is a systematic review of the steps and procedures to perform an activity.

- **Regression analysis.** A regression analysis is an analytical technique where a series of input variables are examined in relation to their corresponding output results in order to develop a mathematical or statistical relationship.

- ▶ **Reserve analysis.** This analytical technique is used to evaluate the amount of risk on the project and the amount of schedule and budget reserve to determine whether the reserve is sufficient for the remaining risk. The reserve contributes to reducing risk to an acceptable level.

- ▶ **Root cause analysis.** This analytical technique is used to determine the basic underlying cause of a variance, defect, or a risk. A root cause may underlie more than one variance, defect, or risk.

- ▶ **Sensitivity analysis.** This analytical technique is used to determine which individual project risks or other sources of uncertainty have the most potential impact on project outcomes by correlating variations in project outcomes with variations in elements of a quantitative risk analysis model.

- ▶ **Simulations.** This analytical technique uses models to show the combined effect of uncertainties in order to evaluate their potential impact on objectives. A Monte Carlo simulation is a method of identifying the potential impacts of risk and uncertainty using multiple iterations of a computer model to develop a probability distribution of a range of outcomes that could result from a decision or course of action.

- ▶ **Stakeholder analysis.** This technique involves systematically gathering and analyzing quantitative and qualitative information about stakeholders to determine whose interests should be taken into account throughout the project.

- ▶ **SWOT analysis.** A SWOT analysis assesses the strengths, weaknesses, opportunities, and threats of an organization, project, or option.

- ▶ **Trend analysis.** A trend analysis uses mathematical models to forecast future outcomes based on historical results.

- ▶ **Value stream mapping.** Value stream mapping is a lean enterprise method used to document, analyze, and improve the flow of information or materials required to produce a product or service for a customer.

- ▶ **Variance analysis.** Variance analysis is used to determine the cause and degree of difference between the baseline and actual performance.

- ▶ **What-if scenario analysis.** This analytical technique evaluates scenarios in order to predict their effect on project objectives.

4.4.2 ESTIMATING

Estimating methods are used to develop an approximation of work, time, or cost on a project.

▶ **Affinity grouping.** Affinity grouping involves classifying items into similar categories or collections on the basis of their likeness. Common affinity groupings include T-shirt sizing and Fibonacci numbers.

▶ **Analogous estimating.** Analogous estimating assesses the duration or cost of an activity or a project using historical data from a similar activity or project.

▶ **Function point.** A function point is an estimate of the amount of business functionality in an information system. Function points are used to calculate a functional size measurement (FSM) of a software system.

▶ **Multipoint estimating.** Multipoint estimating assesses cost or duration by applying an average or weighted average of optimistic, pessimistic, and most likely estimates when there is uncertainty with the individual activity estimates.

▶ **Parametric estimating.** Parametric estimating uses an algorithm to calculate cost or duration based on historical data and project parameters.

▶ **Relative estimating.** Relative estimating is used to create estimates that are derived from performing a comparison against a similar body of work, taking effort, complexity, and uncertainty into consideration. Relative estimating is not necessarily based on absolute units of cost or time. Story points are a common unitless measure used in relative estimating.

▶ **Single-point estimating.** Single-point estimating involves using data to calculate a single value that reflects a best-guess estimate. A single-point estimate is opposed to a range estimate, which includes the best- and worst-case scenario.

▶ **Story point estimating.** Story point estimating involves project team members assigning abstract, but relative, points of effort required to implement a user story. It tells the project team about the difficulty of the story considering the complexity, risks, and effort involved.

▶ **Wideband Delphi.** Wideband Delphi is a variation of the Delphi estimating method where subject matter experts complete multiple rounds of producing estimates individually, with a project team discussion after each round, until a consensus is achieved. For Wideband Delphi, those who created the highest and lowest estimates explain their rationale, following which everyone reestimates. The process repeats until convergence is achieved. Planning poker is a variation of Wideband Delphi.

4.4.3 MEETINGS AND EVENTS

Meetings are an important means for engaging the project team and other stakeholders. They are a primary means of communication throughout the project.

▶ **Backlog refinement.** At a backlog refinement meeting, the backlog is progressively elaborated and (re)prioritized to identify the work that can be accomplished in an upcoming iteration.

▶ **Bidder conference.** Meetings with prospective sellers prior to the preparation of a bid or proposal to ensure all prospective vendors have a clear and common understanding of the procurement. This meeting may also be known as contractor conferences, vendor conferences, or pre-bid conferences.

▶ **Change control board.** A change control board meeting includes the group of people who are accountable for reviewing, evaluating, approving, delaying, or rejecting changes to the project. The decisions made at this meeting are recorded and communicated to the appropriate stakeholders. This meeting may also be referred to as a change control meeting.

▶ **Daily standup.** A standup is a brief collaboration meeting during which the project team reviews its progress from the previous day, declares intentions for the current day, and highlights any obstacles encountered or anticipated. This meeting may also be referred to as a daily scrum.

▶ **Iteration planning.** An iteration planning meeting is used to clarify the details of the backlog items, acceptance criteria, and work effort required to meet an upcoming iteration commitment. This meeting may also be referred to as a sprint planning meeting.

▶ **Iteration review.** An iteration review is held at the end of an iteration to demonstrate the work that was accomplished during the iteration. This meeting may also be referred to as a sprint review.

▶ **Kickoff.** A kickoff meeting is a gathering of project team members and other key stakeholders at the outset of a project to formally set expectations, gain a common understanding, and commence work. It establishes the start of a project, phase, or iteration.

- ▶ **Lessons learned meeting.** A lessons learned meeting is used to identify and share the knowledge gained during a project, phase, or iteration with a focus on improving project team performance. This meeting can address situations that could have been handled better in addition to good practices and situations that produced very favorable outcomes.

- ▶ **Planning meeting.** A planning meeting is used to create, elaborate, or review a plan or plans and secure commitment for the plan(s).

- ▶ **Project closeout.** A project closeout meeting is used to obtain final acceptance of the delivered scope from the sponsor, product owner, or client. This meeting indicates that the product delivery is complete.

- ▶ **Project review.** A project review meeting is an event at the end of a phase or a project to assess the status, evaluate the value delivered, and determine if the project is ready to move to the next phase, or transition to operations.

- ▶ **Release planning.** Release planning meetings identify a high-level plan for releasing or transitioning a product, deliverable, or increment of value.

- ▶ **Retrospective.** A retrospective is a regularly occurring workshop in which participants explore their work and results in order to improve both process and product. Retrospectives are a form of lessons learned meeting.

- ▶ **Risk review.** A meeting to analyze the status of existing risks and identify new risks. This includes determining if the risk is still active and if there have been changes to the risk attributes (such as probability, impact, urgency, etc.). Risk responses are evaluated to determine if they are effective or should be updated. New risks may be identified and analyzed and risks that are no longer active may be closed. Risk reassessment is an example of a risk-review meeting.

- ▶ **Status meeting.** A status meeting is a regularly scheduled event to exchange and analyze information about the current progress of the project and its performance.

- ▶ **Steering committee.** A meeting where senior stakeholders provide direction and support to the project team and make decisions outside of the project team's authority.

4.4.4 OTHER METHODS

The methods described in this section don't fit into a specific category; however, they are common methods that are used for a variety of purposes on projects.

▶ **Impact mapping.** Impact mapping is a strategic planning method that serves as a visual roadmap for the organization during product development.

▶ **Modeling.** Modeling is the process of creating simplified representations of systems, solutions, or deliverables such as prototypes, diagrams, or storyboards. Modeling can facilitate further analysis by identifying gaps in information, areas of miscommunication, or additional requirements.

▶ **Net Promoter Score (NPS®).** An index that measures the willingness of customers to recommend an organization's products or services to others. The score is used as a proxy for gauging the customer's overall satisfaction with an organization's product or service and the customer's loyalty to the brand.

▶ **Prioritization schema.** Prioritization schema are methods used to prioritize portfolio, program, or project components, as well as requirements, risks, features, or other product information. Examples include a multicriteria weighted analysis and the MoSCoW (must have, should have, could have, and won't have) method.

▶ **Timebox.** A timebox is a short, fixed period of time in which work is to be completed, such as 1 week, 2 weeks, or 1 month.

4.5 METHODS APPLIED ACROSS PERFORMANCE DOMAINS

Different methods are more likely to be useful in each of the performance domains. While the needs of the delivery approach, product, and organizational environment will determine which methods are most applicable for a specific project, there are some performance domains that are more likely to make use of specific methods. Table 4-2 suggests the performance domain(s) where each method is most likely to be of use; however, the project manager and/or project team have the ultimate responsibility for selecting the right methods for their project.

Table 4-2. Mapping of Methods Likely to Be Used in Each Performance Domain

Method	Team	Stakeholders	Dev Approach and Life Cycle	Planning	Project Work	Delivery	Measurement	Uncertainly
Data Gathering and Analysis Methods:								
Alternatives analysis				X	X	X		X
Assumptions and constraints analysis				X		X		X
Benchmarking						X	X	
Business justification analysis				X			X	
Payback period			X	X			X	
Internal rate of return				X			X	
Return on investment				X			X	
Net present value			X	X		X	X	
Cost-benefit ratio				X			X	
Check sheet						X	X	
Cost of quality				X		X	X	
Decision tree analysis				X				
Earned value analysis				X			X	
Expected monetary value				X				
Forecasting							X	
Influence diagram				X				
Life cycle assessment				X				
Make-or-buy analysis				X	X			
Probability and impact matrix				X				X
Process analysis				X	X	X	X	
Regression analysis				X			X	
Root cause analysis					X	X		
Sensitivity analysis				X	X	X		
Simulation				X			X	
Stakeholder analysis		X		X	X			
SWOT analysis				X				X
Trend analysis							X	
Value stream mapping				X	X	X		
Variance analysis							X	
What-if scenario analysis				X				X

Table 4-2. Mapping of Methods Likely to Be Used in Each Performance Domain (cont.)

Method	Team	Stakeholders	Dev Approach and Life Cycle	Planning	Project Work	Delivery	Measurement	Uncertainty
Estimating Methods:								
Affinity grouping				X				
Analogous estimating				X				
Function points				X				
Multipoint estimating				X				
Parametric estimating				X				
Relative estimating				X				
Single-point estimating				X				
Story point estimation				X				
Wideband Delphi				X				
Meeting and Event Methods:								
Backlog refinement		X		X	X	X		
Bidder conference		X		X	X			
Change control board					X	X		
Daily standup				X	X			
Iteration review		X			X	X		
Iteration planning		X		X	X	X		
Kickoff	X	X			X			
Lessons learned		X		X	X	X		
Planning					X			
Project closeout	X	X			X			
Project review		X			X	X	X	
Release planning		X		X				
Retrospective	X			X				
Risk review					X			X
Status					X		X	
Steering committee		X			X			
Other Methods:								
Impact mapping	X	X		X		X	X	
Modeling						X		
Net Promoter Score®		X					X	
Prioritization schema		X			X			
Timebox			X	X	X	X	X	

4.6 COMMONLY USED ARTIFACTS

An artifact is a template, document, output, or project deliverable. There are many documents or deliverables that are not described here, either because (a) they are somewhat generic, such as updates; (b) they are industry specific; or (c) they are a result of a specific method that was used to create it, for example, while cost estimates are an important artifact, they are the result of various estimating methods.

The content in this section is not meant to describe how to develop or create an artifact. The descriptions are presented at a high level as project managers and/or project team members are expected to tailor the use of these artifacts to meet the needs of their particular project. There is more detailed information on these and other artifacts from many sources, including PMIstandards+.

4.6.1 STRATEGY ARTIFACTS

Documents that are created prior to or at the start of the project that address strategic, business, or high-level information about the project. Strategy artifacts are developed at the start of a project and do not normally change, though they may be reviewed throughout the project.

▶ **Business case.** A business case is a value proposition for a proposed project that may include financial and nonfinancial benefits.

▶ **Business model canvas.** This artifact is a one-page visual summary that describes the value proposition, infrastructure, customers, and finances. These are often used in lean start-up situations.

▶ **Project brief.** A project brief provides a high-level overview of the goals, deliverables, and processes for the project.

▶ **Project charter.** A project charter is a document issued by the project initiator or sponsor that formally authorizes the existence of a project and provides the project manager with the authority to apply organizational resources to project activities.

▶ **Project vision statement.** This document is a concise, high-level description of the project that states the purpose, and inspires the project team to contribute to the project.

▶ **Roadmap.** This document provides a high-level time line that depicts milestones, significant events, reviews, and decision points.

4.6.2 LOGS AND REGISTERS

Logs and registers are used to record continuously evolving aspects of the project. They are updated throughout the project. The terms log and register are sometimes used interchangeably. It is not uncommon to see the term *risk register* or *risk log* referring to the same artifact.

▶ **Assumption log.** An assumption is a factor that is considered to be true, real, or certain, without proof or demonstration. A constraint is a factor that limits the options for managing a project, program, portfolio, or process. An assumption log records all assumptions and constraints throughout the project.

▶ **Backlog.** A backlog is an ordered list of work to be done. Projects may have a product backlog, a requirements backlog, impediments backlog, and so forth. Items in a backlog are prioritized. The prioritized work is then scheduled for upcoming iterations.

▶ **Change log.** A change log is a comprehensive list of changes submitted during the project and their current status. A change can be a modification to any formally controlled deliverable, project management plan component, or project document.

▶ **Issue log.** An issue is a current condition or situation that may have an impact on the project objectives. An issue log is used to record and monitor information on active issues. Issues are assigned to a responsible party for follow up and resolution.

▶ **Lessons learned register.** A lessons learned register is used to record knowledge gained during a project, phase, or iteration so that it can be used to improve future performance for the project team and/or the organization.

▶ **Risk-adjusted backlog.** A risk-adjusted backlog is a backlog that includes work and actions to address threats and opportunities.

▶ **Risk register.** A risk register is a repository in which outputs of risk management processes are recorded. Information in a risk register can include the person responsible for managing the risk, probability, impact, risk score, planned risk responses, and other information used to get a high-level understanding of individual risks.

▶ **Stakeholder register.** A stakeholder register records information about project stakeholders, which includes an assessment and classification of project stakeholders.

4.6.3 PLANS

A plan is a proposed means of accomplishing something. Project teams develop plans for individual aspects of a project and/or combine all of that information into an overarching project management plan. Plans generally are written documents but may also be reflected on visual/virtual whiteboards.

- **Change control plan.** A change control plan is a component of the project management plan that establishes the change control board, documents the extent of its authority, and describes how the change control system will be implemented.

- **Communications management plan.** This plan is a component of the project, program, or portfolio management plan that describes how, when, and by whom information about the project will be administered and disseminated.

- **Cost management plan.** This plan is a component of a project or program management plan that describes how costs will be planned, structured, and controlled.

- **Iteration plan.** This plan is a detailed plan for the current iteration.

- **Procurement management plan.** This plan is a component of the project or program management plan that describes how a project team will acquire goods and services from outside of the performing organization.

- **Project management plan.** The project management plan is a document that describes how the project will be executed, monitored and controlled, and closed.

- **Quality management plan.** This plan is a component of the project or program management plan that describes how applicable policies, procedures, and guidelines will be implemented to achieve the quality objectives.

- **Release plan.** This plan sets expectations for the dates, features, and/or outcomes expected to be delivered over the course of multiple iterations.

- **Requirements management plan.** This plan is a component of the project or program management plan that describes how requirements will be analyzed, documented, and managed.

- **Resource management plan.** This plan is a component of the project management plan that describes how project resources are acquired, allocated, monitored, and controlled.

- **Risk management plan.** This plan is a component of the project, program, or portfolio management plan that describes how risk management activities will be structured and performed.

- **Scope management plan.** This plan is a component of the project or program management plan that describes how the scope will be defined, developed, monitored, controlled, and validated.

- **Schedule management plan.** This plan is a component of the project or program management plan that establishes the criteria and the activities for developing, monitoring, and controlling the schedule.

- **Stakeholder engagement plan.** This plan is a component of the project management plan that identifies the strategies and actions required to promote productive involvement of stakeholders in project or program decision making and execution.

- **Test plan.** This document describes deliverables that will be tested, tests that will be conducted, and the processes that will be used in testing. It forms the basis for formally testing the components and deliverables.

4.6.4 HIERARCHY CHARTS

Hierarchy charts begin with high-level information that is progressively decomposed into greater levels of detail. The information at the upper levels encompasses all the information at the lower or subsidiary levels. Hierarchy charts are often progressively elaborated into greater levels of detail as more information is known about the project.

- **Organizational breakdown structure.** This chart is a hierarchical representation of the project organization, which illustrates the relationship between project activities and the organizational units that will perform those activities.

- **Product breakdown structure.** This chart is a hierarchical structure reflecting a product's components and deliverables.

- **Resource breakdown structure.** This chart is a hierarchical representation of resources by category and type.

- **Risk breakdown structure.** This chart is a hierarchical representation of potential sources of risks.

- **Work breakdown structure.** This chart is a hierarchical decomposition of the total scope of work to be carried out by the project team to accomplish the project objectives and create the required deliverables.

4.6.5 BASELINES

A baseline is the approved version of a work product or plan. Actual performance is compared to baselines to identify variances.

▶ **Budget.** A budget is the approved estimate for the project or any work breakdown structure (WBS) component or any schedule activity.

▶ **Milestone schedule.** This type of schedule presents milestones with planned dates.

▶ **Performance measurement baseline.** Integrated scope, schedule, and cost baselines are used for comparison to manage, measure, and control project execution.

▶ **Project schedule.** A project schedule is an output of a schedule model that presents linked activities with planned dates, durations, milestones, and resources.

▶ **Scope baseline.** This baseline is the approved version of a scope statement, work breakdown structure (WBS), and its associated WBS dictionary that can be changed using formal change control procedures and is used as the basis for comparison to actual results.

4.6.6 VISUAL DATA AND INFORMATION

Visual data and information are artifacts that organize and present data and information in a visual format, such as charts, graphs, matrices, and diagrams. Visualizing data makes it easier to absorb data and turn it into information. Visualization artifacts are often produced after data have been collected and analyzed. These artifacts can aid in decision making and prioritization.

▶ **Affinity diagram.** This diagram shows large numbers of ideas classified into groups for review and analysis.

▶ **Burndown/burnup chart.** This chart is a graphical representation of the work remaining in a timebox or the work completed toward the release of a product or project deliverable.

▶ **Cause-and-effect diagram.** This diagram is a visual representation that helps trace an undesirable effect back to its root cause.

▶ **Cumulative flow diagram (CFD).** This chart indicates features completed over time, features in development, and those in the backlog. It may also include features at intermediate states, such as features designed but not yet constructed, those in quality assurance, or those in testing.

- ▶ **Cycle time chart.** This diagram shows the average cycle time of the work items completed over time. A cycle time chart may be shown as a scatter diagram or a bar chart.

- ▶ **Dashboards.** This set of charts and graphs shows progress or performance against important measures of the project.

- ▶ **Flowchart.** This diagram depicts the inputs, process actions, and outputs of one or more processes within a system.

- ▶ **Gantt chart.** This bar chart provides schedule information where activities are listed on the vertical axis, dates are shown on the horizontal axis, and activity durations are shown as horizontal bars placed according to start and finish dates.

- ▶ **Histogram.** This bar chart shows the graphical representation of numerical data.

- ▶ **Information radiator.** This artifact is a visible, physical display that provides information to the rest of the organization, enabling timely knowledge sharing.

- ▶ **Lead time chart.** This diagram shows the trend over time of the average lead time of the items completed in work. A lead time chart may be shown as a scatter diagram or a bar chart.

- ▶ **Prioritization matrix.** This matrix is a scatter diagram where effort is shown on the horizontal axis and value on the vertical axis, divided into four quadrants to classify items by priority.

- ▶ **Project schedule network diagram.** This graphical representation shows the logical relationships among the project schedule activities.

- ▶ **Requirements traceability matrix.** This matrix links product requirements from their origin to the deliverables that satisfy them.

- ▶ **Responsibility assignment matrix (RAM).** This matrix is a grid that shows the project resources assigned to each work package. A RACI chart is a common way of showing stakeholders who are responsible, accountable, consulted, or informed and are associated with project activities, decisions, and deliverables.

- ▶ **Scatter diagram.** This graph shows the relationship between two variables.

- ▶ **S-curve.** This graph displays cumulative costs over a specified period of time.

- ▶ **Stakeholder engagement assessment matrix.** This matrix compares current and desired stakeholder engagement levels.

- ▶ **Story map.** A story map is a visual model of all the features and functionality desired for a given product, created to give the project team a holistic view of what they are building and why.

- ▶ **Throughput chart.** This chart shows the accepted deliverables over time. A throughput chart may be shown as a scatter diagram or a bar chart.

- ▶ **Use case.** This artifact describes and explores how a user interacts with a system to achieve a specific goal.

- ▶ **Value stream map.** This is a lean enterprise method used to document, analyze, and improve the flow of information or materials required to produce a product or service for a customer. Value stream maps can be used to identify waste.

- ▶ **Velocity chart.** This chart tracks the rate at which the deliverables are produced, validated, and accepted within a predefined interval.

4.6.7 REPORTS

Reports are formal records or summaries of information. Reports communicate relevant (usually summary level) information to stakeholders. Often reports are given to stakeholders who are interested in the project status, such as sponsors, business owners, or PMOs.

- ▶ **Quality report.** This project document includes quality management issues, recommendations for corrective actions, and a summary of findings from quality control activities. It may include recommendations for process, project, and product improvements.

- ▶ **Risk report.** This project document is developed progressively throughout the risk management processes and summarizes information on individual project risks and the level of overall project risk.

- ▶ **Status report.** This document provides a report on the current status of the project. It may include information on progress since the last report and forecasts for cost and schedule performance.

4.6.8 AGREEMENTS AND CONTRACTS

An agreement is any document or communication that defines the intentions of the parties. In projects, agreements take the form of contracts or other defined understandings. A contract is a mutually binding agreement that obligates the seller to provide the specified product, service, or result and obligates the buyer to pay for it. There are different types of contracts, some of which fall within a category of fixed-price or cost-reimbursable contracts.

▶ **Fixed-price contracts.** This category of contract involves setting a fixed price for a well-defined product, service, or result. Fixed-price contracts include firm fixed price (FFP), fixed-price incentive fee (FPIF), and fixed price with economic price adjustment (FP-EPA), among others.

▶ **Cost-reimbursable contracts.** This category of contracts involves payments to the seller for actual costs incurred for completing the work plus a fee representing seller profit. These contracts are often used when the project scope is not well defined or is subject to frequent change. Cost-reimbursable contracts include cost plus award fee (CPAF), cost plus fixed fee (CPFF), and cost plus incentive fee (CPIF).

▶ **Time and materials (T&M).** This contract establishes a fixed rate, but not a precise statement of work. It can be used for staff augmentation, subject matter expertise, or other outside support.

▶ **Indefinite delivery indefinite quantity (IDIQ).** This contract provides for an indefinite quantity of goods or services, with a stated lower and upper limit, and within a fixed time period. These contracts can be used for architectural, engineering, or information technology engagements.

▶ **Other agreements.** Other types of agreements include memorandum of understanding (MOU), memorandum of agreement (MOA), service level agreement (SLA), basic ordering agreement (BOA), among others.

4.6.9 OTHER ARTIFACTS

The documents and deliverables described here do not fit into a specific category; however, they are important artifacts that are used for a variety of purposes.

- ▶ **Activity list.** This document provides a tabulation of schedule activities that shows the activity description, activity identifier, and a sufficiently detailed scope of work description so project team members understand what work is to be performed.

- ▶ **Bid documents.** Bid documents are used to request proposals from prospective sellers. Depending on the goods or services needed, bid documents can include, among others:

    - ▷ Request for information (RFI),

    - ▷ Request for quotation (RFQ), and

    - ▷ Request for proposal (RFP).

- ▶ **Metrics.** Metrics describe an attribute and how to measure it.

- ▶ **Project calendar.** This calendar identifies working days and shifts that are available for scheduled activities.

- ▶ **Requirements documentation.** This document is a record of product requirements and relevant information needed to manage the requirements, which includes the associated category, priority, and acceptance criteria.

- ▶ **Project team charter.** This document records the project team values, agreements, and operating guidelines, and establishes clear expectations regarding acceptable behavior by project team members.

- ▶ **User story.** A user story is a brief description of an outcome for a specific user, which is a promise of a conversation to clarify details.

4.7 ARTIFACTS APPLIED ACROSS PERFORMANCE DOMAINS

Different artifacts are more likely to be useful in different performance domains. While the delivery approach, product, and organizational environment will determine which artifacts are most applicable for a specific project, there are some performance domains that are more likely to make use of specific artifacts. Table 4-3 suggests the performance domain(s) where each artifact is more likely to be of use; however, the project manager and/or project team has the ultimate responsibility for selecting and tailoring the artifacts for their project.

Table 4-3. Mapping of Artifacts Likely to Be Used in Each Performance Domain

Artifact	Performance Domain							
	Team	Stakeholders	Dev Approach and Life Cycle	Planning	Project Work	Delivery	Measurement	Uncertainty
Strategy Artifacts:								
Business case		X		X				
Project brief		X		X				
Project charter		X		X				
Project vision statement		X		X				
Roadmap		X	X	X				
Log and Register Artifacts:								
Assumption log				X	X	X		X
Backlog				X	X	X		
Change log					X	X		
Issue log					X			
Lessons learned register					X			
Risk-adjusted backlog				X				X
Risk register				X	X	X		X
Stakeholder register		X		X				
Plan Artifacts:								
Change control plan				X	X	X		
Communications management plan		X		X	X			
Cost management plan				X				
Iteration plan				X				
Procurement management plan				X	X			
Project management plan		X		X	X			
Quality management plan				X	X	X		
Release plan				X		X		
Requirements management plan				X		X		
Resource management plan				X	X			
Risk management plan				X	X			X
Scope management plan				X		X		

Table 4-3. Mapping of Artifacts Likely to Be Used in Each Performance Domain (cont.)

Artifact	Team	Stakeholders	Dev Approach and Life Cycle	Planning	Project Work	Delivery	Measurement	Uncertainty
Schedule management plan				X	X	X		
Stakeholder engagement plan		X		X				
Test plan				X	X	X	X	
Hierarchy Chart Artifacts:								
Organizational breakdown structure	X	X		X				
Product breakdown structure				X		X		
Resource breakdown structure	X			X	X		X	
Risk breakdown structure					X			X
Work breakdown structure				X		X	X	
Baseline Artifacts:								
Budget				X	X		X	
Milestone schedule			X	X	X		X	
Performance measurement baseline				X	X	X	X	
Project schedule				X	X		X	
Scope baseline				X	X	X	X	
Visual Data and Information Artifacts:								
Affinity diagram				X	X			
Burn chart				X		X	X	
Cause-and-effect diagram					X	X		X
Cycle time chart						X	X	
Cumulative flow diagram						X	X	
Dashboard					X		X	
Flow chart				X	X	X		
Gantt chart				X	X		X	
Histogram							X	
Information radiator					X		X	
Lead time chart						X	X	
Prioritization matrix		X			X	X		

Table 4-3. Mapping of Artifacts Likely to Be Used in Each Performance Domain (cont.)

Artifact	Team	Stakeholders	Dev Approach and Life Cycle	Planning	Project Work	Delivery	Measurement	Uncertainty
Project schedule network diagram				X	X			
Requirements traceability matrix				X		X	X	
Responsibility assignment matrix				X	X			
Scatter diagram					X	X	X	
S-curve				X			X	
Stakeholder engagement assessment matrix		X		X	X			
Story map				X		X		
Throughput chart						X	X	
Use case				X		X		
Value stream map					X	X	X	
Velocity chart						X	X	
Report Artifacts:								
Quality report					X	X	X	
Risk report					X			X
Status report					X			
Agreements and Contracts:								
Fixed-price		X		X	X	X	X	X
Cost-reimbursable		X		X	X	X	X	X
Time and materials		X		X	X	X	X	X
Indefinite time indefinite quantity (IDIQ)		X		X	X	X	X	X
Other agreements		X		X	X	X	X	X
Other Artifacts:								
Activity list	X	X		X	X			
Bid documents		X		X	X			
Metrics				X		X	X	
Project calendars	X			X	X			
Requirements documentation		X		X		X	X	
Project team charter	X				X			
User story		X		X		X		

REFERENCES

[1] Project Management Institute. 2020. *The Standard for Project Management.* Newtown Square, PA: Author.

[2] Project Management Institute. 2019. *The Standard for Earned Value Management.* Newtown Square, PA: Author.

Appendix X1
Contributors and Reviewers of
The Standard for Project Management and
A Guide to the Project Management Body
of Knowledge – Seventh Edition

The Project Management Institute is grateful to all of the contributors for their support and acknowledges their outstanding contributions to the project management profession.

X1.1 CONTRIBUTORS

The following list of contributors had input into shaping the content of the standard and/or the guide. Individuals listed in bold served on the *PMBOK® Guide* – Seventh Edition Development Team. Inclusion of an individual's name in the list does not represent his or her approval or endorsement of the final content in all its parts.

Cynthia Snyder Dionisio, Chair,
　MBA, PMI-ACP, PMP
Michael Griffiths, Cochair, PMI-ACP, PMP
Nicholas Clemens, PMI-ACP, PMP
Jean Luc Favrot, PMI-ACP, PMP, SPC5
Jesse Fewell, CST, PMI-ACP, PMP
Emily Jingjing Hu, MPM, PRINCE2, PMP
Betsy Kauffman, PMI-ACP, PMP, ICP-ACC
Nader K. Rad, PMP
Giampaolo Marucci, PhD, PMI-ACP,
　PMP, CSM
Klaus Nielsen, MBA, PMI-ACP, PMP
Maria Specht, MSc, PMP, NLP
Maricarmen Suarez, MBA, PMP, PgMP
Laurent Thomas, PhD, SPC, PMI-ACP, PMP
Jorge Federico Vargas Uzaga, PMP
Mike Cooley, CSM, SCPM, PMP
Diana E. A.García Sánchez
Carlos Gonzalez Bejarano
Venkatram Vasi Mohanvasi

Marwan Abdalla, MBA, PMI-RMP, PMP
Abdalla Yassin Abdalla Mohammed,
　Eng, MBA, PMI-RMP, PMP
Majed Abdeen, MSc, PMP, TOGAF
Habeeb Abdulla, MS, CSM, PMP
Tetsuhide Abe, PMP
Ali Abedi, PhD, CSM, PMI-ACP, PMP
Carlos Acuña, PMP, PgMP, PfMP
Renee Adair, PMP
Albert Agbemenu, MSc, PMP
Kevin Aguanno, CMC, PMI-ACP, PMP
Fawad Ahmad Khan, PMI-PBA, PMP
Prescort Leslie Ahumuza, Agile SM, CAPM, PMP
Ali Akbar Forouzesh Nejad
Phil Akinwale
Emi Akiode, PMP
Tarik Al Hraki, MBA, PMI-RMP, PMP
Ahmed Alageed, PhD, PMI-ACP, PMP
Ruqaya Al Badi, PMP
Francesco Albergo, PMP

Amer Albuttma, PMI-SP, PMP

Mohamed Aldoubasi, Eng, MBA, PMI-RMP, PMP

Emad Al Ghamdi, Eng, EMBA, PMP

Ahmed Ali Eziza, Eng, PMP, IPMO-E

Mehdi Alibakhshi, PMI-PBA, PMP

Hammam Alkouz, MBA, PMI-RMP, PMP

Michel Allan, MBA, PMI-RMP, PMP

Sonja Almlie, CCBA, PMI-ACP, PMP

Ahmad Al-Musallami, PMI-ACP, PMI-SP, PMP

Moajeb Almutairi, PMP

Husain Al-Omani, PMP, PgMP, PfMP

Ahmed Alsenosy, PHD, PMP, PgMP, PfMP

Mohand Alsikhan, PMP, CISM

Abdulrahman Alulaiyan, MBA, CCMP, PMP

Carlos Alvarez G., PMP

Jaime Andres Alvarez Ospina,
     MBA, PMI-RMP, PMP

Nahlah Alyamani, PMI-ACP, PMP, PgMP

Angelo Amaral, PSM, PMI-ACP, PMP

Shahin Amiri, MBA, PMP

Serge Amon, MBA, PMP

Anabella Amoresano, PMP

Ashwani Anant, PMI-RMP, PMI-SP, PMP

Filipy Henrique Bonfim Andrade, Eng, GPjr, PMP

David Anyacho

Charalampos Apostolopoulos, PhD, PgMP, PfMP

Alejandro Gabriel Aramburu, PMP

Christine Aras

Kenichiro Aratake, PMP

Viviane Arazi, PMP, PgMP

Eileen Arnold

Reza Atashfaraz, MSc, PMP

Sivaram Athmakuri, PMP, PMI-ACP, PMI-PBA

Sharaf Attas, PMI-RMP, PMP

Carlos Augusto Freitas, CAPM, PMP

Shahin Avak, PMP

Zaheer Ahmad Awan, CSM, PMI-ACP, PMP

Khaled Azab, ITIL4, PMP

Vahid Azadmanesh, DBA, PMP, PfMP

Emad E. Aziz, PMP, PgMP, PfMP

Akbar Azwir, PMO-CP, PMI-SP, PMP

Osama Azzam, HBDP, ICYB, PMP

Nabeel Babeker

Amgad Badewi, PhD, MSP, AP, PMP

Amir Bahadorestani, RA, TA

Kenneth Bainey, MBA, CCP, PMP

Jardel Baldo

Kristi Baldwin, RYT, PMP

Pablo Bálsamo, PMI-RMP, PMI-SP, PMP

Zhang Baozhong, MSc, PMP, PgMP

Manuel F. Baquero V., PhD, MSc, PMP

Haytham Baraka, PMI-RMP, PMP, CCP

Mohammad Moneer Barazi, MBA, PMP

Maria Cristina Barbero, MBA, PMI-ACP, PMP

Andre Barcaui, PhD, PMI-ACP, PMP

Amalia Barthel, PMP

Saeed Baselm

Eduardo Bazo Safra, Mg, PMP

Pierre Beaudry, Jr., MGP, CSM, PMP

Gregory Becker, PMP

Martial Bellec, PMI-ACP, PMP, PgMP

Peter Berndt de Souza Mello, PgC, PMI-SP, PMP

Rafael Beteli Silva Zanon, MBA, PMI-PBA, PMP

Jeff Beverage, CSP-SM, PMI-ACP, PMP

Shantanu Bhamare, CSM, LIMC, PMP

Ajay Bhargove, BE, PGDBA, PMP

Sanjoy Bhattacharjee, MSBIA, PMI-ACP, PMP

Deepa Bhide, PhD, PMP

Şafak Bilgi Akdemir

Mohammed Bin Askar, PMP, PgMP, PfMP

Nigel Blampied, PhD, PE, PMP

Greta Blash, CDAI, PgMP, PMI-PBA

Stephen Blash

Gisela Bolbrügge, PhD, PSM1, PMP

Kiron Bondale, PMI-ACP, PMI-RMP, PMP

Simona Bonghez, PhD, PMP

Mariana Borga, MBA, LSSBB, PMP

Raul Borges, PMP

David Borja Padilla, MSc, PMI-RMP, PMP

Boshoff, PMP, PRINCE2, AgilePM

Miguel A. Botana Cobas, MBA, PMP

Pieter Botman, Eng

Rodolphe Boudet, PMP

Farid Bouges

Betty Boushey, PMP

Younes Bousnah, MBA, PMP

Andrea Boxsley

Blaine Boxwell, MBA, PMP

Joan Boyadjman

Padmakar Boyapati, PMP

Didier Brackx, PhD, EMS, P3O, PMP

Leslie Bradshaw

Damiano Bragantini, PMP
Fabio Braggio, MBA, PMP
Ellie Braham, AOP, PMP
Fernando Brandão, PMP
Jim Branden, MBA, PMP
Wayne R. Brantley, MSEd, PMI-ACP, PMP
Myrna Bravo, PMP
Bernd Brier
Ana Briseño, MTIA, PMP
Syed Asad Hasnain Bukhari, MBA, MIS, PMP
Syed Qamar Abbas Bukhari, MBA, MSPM, PMP
Gizem Bulu
Rev. Andy Burns, CDAI, PMI-ACP, PMP
Robert Buttrick, BEng, CEng, FAPM Hon
Dieter Butz, PhD, PMP
Karl Buxton, PMP
Andrea Caccamese, PRINCE2, PMP
Roberto A. Cadena Legaspi, MCI, PMP
Feren Calderwood, MSc, PMP
Saverio Calvano, MSc, PMP
Diego Calvetti, MSc, PMP
Luis Alberto Cordero-Calvo, MPM, PMP
Adrien Camp, MEng, PMI-ACP, PMP
Bryan Campbell, PMI-ACP, PMP, PgMP
Charles Campbell, PhD, PMP
Heberth Campos, PMI-ACP, PMI-RMP, PMP
Ricardo P. Cantú, MBA, MSc, PMP
Alexandre Caramelo Pinto, MSc, TOGAF, PMP
Andrea Carbert, PMP, PMI-ACP
Cheryl Carstens, CAPM, PMP
Chris Cartwright, MPM
Laura Solano De Carvalho
Pietro Casanova, PMP
Shoshanna Caster
Larry Cebuano, PMP
Manu Chandrashekhar, PMP
Paul C. Charlesraj, MS, MRICS, AMASCE
Panos Chatzipanos, PhD, FASCE, D.WRE
Nguyen Si Trieu Chau, PMP, PgMP, PfMP
Jing Chen
Lily Chen, PMP
Karl Cheney, PMP, MPM, MPA
Ramesh Chepur, CSQA, PRINCE2, PMP
Mona Chevis
Oussama Chriss, PMP
Jorge Clemente, CPA, PMP

Xavier Clerfeuille, MSc, NLP
Ashley Cometto, MBA
Sergio Luis Conte, PhD, PMI-PBA, PMI-ACP, PMP
Carlos Contreras G., CSM, CSPO, PMP
Helio Costa
Pathica Coulat
Thaigo Cristo
Joshua Cunio, CPD, LSSBB, PMP
Joseph Czarnecki, SCPM, PMP
Alexandre Venâncio da Silva
Long Dam, PMP, PgMP, PfMP
Graziella D'Amico, CBAP, PMI-PBA, PMP
Farshid Damirchilo, MSc, PMP
Teodor Darabaneanu, PMP
Russell Darnall, DM, MPM, PMP
Yazmine Darcy, MBA, PMI-ACP, PMP
Kaustav Das, MCP, PMP
Gina Davidovic, PMP, PgMP
Curtis Davis
José de Franca, PMP
Viviane de Paula, PMP
Michael DeCicco, CSM, PMP
Mustafa Degerli, PhD, PSM, PMI-RMP, PMP
Murat Dengiz
Valerie Denney, DBA, PMP
Saju Devassy, MBA, POPM, PMP
Yaso Dhatry Kala, LSSMBB
Philip Diab
Michelle Gois Gadelha Dias
Danil Dintsis
Gilberto Francisco Do Vale, MBA PM
Roland Doerr, MBA, CSM, PMP
Mustafa Donmez, PMP
Bala Doppalapudi, MBA, B.Tech, PMP
Jorge A. Dueñas Lozano, VMA, PMP
Josée Dufour, PMP
Darya Duma
Eunice Duran, PMP, PgMP, PfMP
Arijit Dutt, PMP
Valecia Dyett, PhD, PMP
Nicolas Egiaian, PMP
Bechir El Hosni
Salwa El Mesbahi, PMP
Claude El Nakhel Khalil,
    PharmD, MBA, PMP
Abdulrahman Eldabak, PMP

Rafik Eldaly
Sameh Eldeeb Thabet Wahba,
    Eng, CPMC, PMC, PMP
Ahmed Eldeep, PMI-RMP, PMP
Walla Siddig Elhadey Mohamed,
    PMI-ACP, PMI-RMP, PMP
Ahmed Elhakim, PMI-RMP, PMP
Osman Elhassan, MBA, PMI-RMP, PMP
Aileen Ellis, CSM, PMP, PgMP
Wael Elmetwaly, PMI-ACP, PMP
Khaled El-Nakib, MSc, PMI-RMP, PMP
Basel El-Saady, PMP
Constance Emerson
Algin Erozan, MSc, PMP
Fernando Escobar, MSc, PMP
Behnam Faizabadi
Delphine Falcoz, PMP
Saurater (Sam) Faraday,
    MBA, PMI-ACP, PMI-RMP
Jamil Faraj
Fereydoun Fardad, PMI-PBA, PMI-RMP, PMP
Jason Farley
John Farlik, DBA, PMI-ACP, PMP
Scott, Fass, MPA, PMP
Edoardo Favari, PhD, PMP
Amr Fayez Moustafa, Eng, SFC, SSYB, PMP
Zhang Fengxiao
Felipe Fernandes Moreira, PMP
Rafael Fernando Ronces Rosas
Gail Ferreira, PhD, SPC5, PMP
Cornelius Fichtner, CSM, PMP
William Flanagan
Luis Alberto Flores, PhD, PMI-ACP, PMI-RMP, PMP
Gustavo Flouret, DBA, PMP
Les Foley, MPM, MBA, PMP
Mitchell Fong, PEng, PMP
Luis Eduardo Franca, PMO-CP, PMI-ACP, PMP
Kellen Sabrina Rodrigues Francisco,
    MBA, PSM I, PMP
Douglas Franco
Carla Frazier
Michael Frenette, SMC, ITCP, PMP
Ray Frohnhoefer, MBA, CCP, PMP
Michelle Fuale
Steven Fullmer, MBA, CQ, PMP
Jeff Furman, CompTIA, CTT+, PMP

Nestor Gabarda Jr., ECE, PMI-ACP, PMP
Marius Gaitan, Eng, PMI-PBA, PMP
Zsolt G. Gálfalvi, MSP, SCM, PRINCE2
Sara Gallagher, PSM1, PMP
Juan Gabriel Gantiva Vergara,
    PMI-ACP, PMI-RMP, PMP
Napoleon Garde, PMP
Artur Gasparyan, CSM, PMO-CP, PMP
Louis-Charles Gauthier
Eng. Fabio Gentilini, Eng, CAPM, PMP
Paul Geraghty, BBS, CPMA
Kian Ghadaksaz, EVP, PMI-SP, PMP
Omar Ghazi Ahmad, PMD Pro, MCAD, PMP
Arijit Ghosh, PGDBA, BCom
Subhajit Ghosh, PMI-ACP, PMP, PgMP
Hisham Ghulam, Eng, MBA, PMI-ACP, PMP
Paul D. Giammalvo, PhD, MScPM, CCE
Carl M. Gilbert, PMI-ACP, PMP, PfMP
Theofanis Giotis, MSc, PMI-ACP, PMP
Jörg Glunde, PMI-ACP, PMP
Dhananjay Gokhale
Henrique Gomes da Silva
Herbert G. Gonder, IPMA B, ACE, PMP
Jaime González Vargas, PMP
Diego Goyes Mosquera, MSc, PMP
Falko Graf, MA, CMC, PMP
Ivan Graff, PE, CCP, PMP
Denis Gritsiyenko, PhD, PMP
Pier Luigi Guida, PMS, PMP, PgM
Antun Guidoni
Nagaraja Gundappa, MTech, CSM, PMP
Nandakumar Guruswamy, PMP, PgMP
Anil Guvenatam, PMI-ACP, PMP
Mohamed Hamad Elneel, Eng, PMP
Nagy Hamamo, MSP, MoP, PMP
Karishma Hans, MBA, PMP
Sharad Harale
Simon Harris
Laura Hart
Mahmoud Hassaballa,
    Eng, CVS, 6SigmaGB, PMP
Akram Hassan, PMI-RMP, PMP
Hossam Hassan Anwar,
    MEng, PM, PMI-RMP, PMP
Shane Hastie, MIM, ICE-AC, ICE-PO
Damah Haubner

Hironori Hayashi, PMI-PBA, PMP, PfMP

Kristine Hayes Munson, CIA, CISM, PMP

Bin He, PMI-ACP, PMP

Antonio Hernández Negrete, MBA, CSM, PMP

Abel Herrera Sillas, DM, PMP

Sergio Herrera-Apestigue, P3O, PRINCE2, PMP

Shirley Hinton, PMI-ACP, PMP

Kenji Hiraishi, MsE, PMP

Michael Hoffpauir

Alberto Holgado, MBA

Eden Holt, PMP

Regina Holzinger, PhD, PMP

George Hord, PMP

Gheorghe Hriscu, CGEIT, PMP

Zayar Htun, ICM.PM, AGTI.IT

Varetta Huggins, MS(IST), PMP, PgMP

Ritchie Hughes, CSM, CSPO, PMP

Edward Hung, MBA, PMI-ACP, PMP

David J. L. Hunter, MA, PMI-ACP, PMP

Sherif Hussein, PMP, PgMP, PfMP

Mohammed Elfatih Hussien Ibrahim,
        Eng, MBA, PMI-RMP, PMP

Hany I. Zahran, SAMC, SSYB, VCA-DCV

Shuichi Ikeda, CBAP, CSM/CSPO, PMP

Dmitrii Ilenkov, PMP

Muhammad A. B. Ilyas, PMI-ACP, PMP, PgMP

Andrea Innocenti, CGEIT, PMP

Suhail Iqbal, PMP, PgMP, PfMP

Ilya Ivanichkin, CSM, CSPO, PMP

Ravi Iyer, MS (M&E), MBA, PE

Can Izgi, PMP

Tony Jacob, C Eng, PMI-PBA, PMP

Md Javeed, BE, PMP

Suresh Jayappa

Srini Jeyakumar, PEng, PMP

Greeshma Johnson, CSM, PMP

John Johnson

Tony Johnson, CSP, PgMP, PfMP

George Jucan, MBA, CMP, PMP

Jonathan Justus, MBA, BCA, PMP

Rami Kaibni, Eng, CBAP, PfMP

Orhan Kalayci, ITIL, DevOps, PMP

Sinbong Kang, PhD, PMP

Antoine Karam, PMP, PMI-RMP

Alankar Karpe, PMI-ACP, PMP

Aras Kartouzian, PhD

Naoki Kasahara

Rohit Kathuria, P.Eng, PMP

Nikhil Srinivasan Kaundinya, PMP

Rachel Keen

Gretta Kelzi, CTT+, EADA, PMP

Harry Kendrick, MPM, CSM, PMP

Suhail Khaled, CSM, PMI-ACP, PMP

Mohamed Khalifa, PMP, PgMP, PfMP

Mehran Khalilnejadi

Alexander Khaydarov

Diwakar Killamsetty, CSM, PMP

Ariel Kirshbom, CSP, PMI-ACP, PMP

Hiroshi Kise

Aparna R. Kishore, MCA, CSM, PMP

Konstantinos Kirytopoulos,
        Dr Eng, MEng, PMP

Hadi Kiyoumarsi

Henry Kondo, PMP, PgMP, PfMP

Steven Kopischke, MSPM, ITIL, PMP

Markus Kopko, PMP, PSM

Maciej Koszykowski, PgMP, PMP, PMI-RMP

Srikanth Kota

Rouzbeh Kotobzadeh, PMI-ACP, PMP, PfMP

Kevin Kovalic, MCP, CSSGB, PMP

Wayne Kremling

Mohsen Krichi, Eng, COBIT, ITIL 4, PMP

Ravindrakumar Kshirsagar, SPC, PMP, PgMP

Ashis Kumar Garg

Kathy Kuypers

Thierry Labriet, Prosci, PMP

Cédric Laffitte, PMP

Marylene Lafon, PMP

Marc Lafontrinz

Harisha Lakkavalli, PMP, PgMP, PfMP

G Lakshmi Sekhar, PMI-PBA, PMI-SP, PMP

Arun Lal, PMP

Soheil Lamei, PhD, PMP, PgMP, PfMP

Hagit Landman, MBA, PMI-SP, PMP

Olivier Lazar, PMP, PgMP, PfMP

Chia Kuang Lee, PhD, CQRM, PMP

Oliver F. Lehmann, MSc, ACE, PMP

Raman Lemtsiuhou, PSM II, PMP

Harvey Levine

Richard Lewis, MBA, PMP

Bing Li, PMP

Xujie Liang

Mei Lin, PMI-ACP, PMI-PBA, PMP
Kong Linghai, MD, PMP
An Liu
Kai Liu
Haishan Liu
Tong Liu
Pablo Lledó, MSc, MBA, PMP
Anand Lokhande, PSM, PMI-PBA, PMP
Stefania Lombardi, PhD, PMP
Carlos López Javier, MBA, ME, PMP
Marisa Andrea Lostumbo, MScPM, PMP
Hugo K. M. Lourenço, PMI-ACP, PMI-RMP, PMP
Sérgio Lourenço, PMI-RMP, PMP
Erin Danica Lovell, MBA, BRMP, PMP
Sophie Lowery, MBA, PMP
Paolo Lucena
Francesco Ludovico, Eng, PMP
Sergio Oswaldo Lugo, MBA, SSMC, PMP
Ionel Lumezianu
Michele Lusciano
Azam M. Zaqzouq, MCT, PMP
M. Bhuvaneswari, BE
Alejandro Maceda
Jan Magdi, MSc
Ganesh Mahalingam, CSM, PMP
Patrick Maillard, MBA, PMP
Abhijit Maity, CBAP, PMP, PgMP
Kieran Major, MBA, PMP
Richard Maltzman, PMP
Arun Mandalika, PMI-ACP, PMP
Hussam Mandil, MBA, PMI-ACP, PMP
Nicole Mangona, PMP
Nandhini Manikhavel, CSM, MBA, CAPM
Rasa Manikkam, PMP
Erasma Mariano, ESP GP, ICP, ITIL
Antonio Marino, Eng, PSM, PMI-ACP, PMP
Photoula Markou-Voskou, PMP
Orlando Marone, PMI-ACP, PMP
Bernardo Marques, PMI-ACP, PMI-RMP, PMP
Lucía Márquez de la Plata, MBA, ACC, PMP
Douglas Martin, CSP-SM, PMI-ACP, PMP
Cesar Ulises Martinez Garcia,
        SAFe SSM, PMI-ACP, PMP
Mercedes Martinez Sanz, PMP
Ulises Martins
Ronnie Maschk, ASM, PMI-ACP, PMP

Faraz Masood, MS-EE, MBA, PMP
Abid Masood Ali, Eng
Puian Masudi Far, PhD, PMP
Mayte Mata Sivera, PMP
Todd Materazzi, PMI-ACP, PMP
Komal Mathur, PMP, CSM
Mohit Mathur, PMP
Cristiane da Silva Matos
David Maynard, MBA, PMP
David McDonald, MA, MBA, CSPO
Jon McGlothian, MBA, PMI-ACP, PMP
Alain Patrick Medenou, MSc, PRINCE2, PMP
Maite Meijide Montes, MS-Eng, MBA, PMP
Orlando Mendieta, CSM, KMP I, PMP
Hamed Mesinehasl
Mohamed MH. Elfouly, PhD, P, PMP
Lubomira Mihailova, MBA, MSP, PMP
Gloria J. Miller, PMI-ACP, PMP
Vladimir Mininel, PMP
Manuel Minute, CPIM, CGEIT, PMP
Amr Miqdadi, CIPM, PMP
Nick Mirabella, PSNI
Kunihiko Mishima
David E. Mitchell, PMP
Stephanie Moffatt
Wolf Dieter Moggert, PMI-ACP, PMI-PBA, PMP
Walid Mohamed Ahmed
Eman Mohamed El Rashidy, PMP, PgMP
Omar Mohamed Sallam, PMI-RMP, PMI-SP, PMP
Islam Mohamed Soliman, Eng, PMP
Ahmed Ishage Mohammed Musa,
        MBA, PMI-RMP, PMP
Shoeb Mohammed Nadeem Uddin, PMP
Mohamed Mohsen Mohamed Hussein, PMP
Jose Morales, DBA, PMP
Paola Morgese, PMP
Alessandro Moro, PSM-I, PMP
Chuck Morton, CSM, PMI-ACP, PMP
Henrique Moura, PMI-ACP, PMI-RMP
Nitin Mukesh, PMP
Gaurav Mukherjee, CSM, PMP
Stephen Murefu
Wanja Murekio, MBA, PMP
Jennifer Murphy, B.Comm(Int), MBS, MSc
Syed Ahsan Mustaqeem, PE, PMP
Yassir Nagy, PMI-ACP, PMP, PgMP

Devan Naidu, MBA, PMP, PfMP

Brijesh Nair, CEng, PMP, PgMP

Asaya Nakasone, PMP

Saed Namazi, MBA, PRINCE2, PMP

Sareesh Narayanan

Sripriya V Narayanasamy, MCA, PMP

Zabihollah Nasehi

Faig Nasibov, PMP

Mahmoud Nasr, Eng., MSc, CPM

Asad Naveed, MS-Eng, MEF-CECP, PMP

Karthikeyan NB, MCA, CSM, PMP

Gundo Nevhutalu, MSc, PMP

Kian Ching Ng, MSc, PMP

Sam Nicholson

Eric Nielsen, PMP, CDA

Manisha Nigam, CSM, TOGAF 9, PMP

Aleksei Nikitin, PMI-ACP, PMI-RMP, PMP

Mohammad Ali Niroomand Rad, MArch, PMP

Jose Noguera, 6SBB, CSP0, PMP

Michael Nollet, MBA, PMI-ACP, PMP

Eric Norman, PMP, PgMP, Fellow

Patryk Nosalik, EMBA, AgilePM, PMP

Toru Oda, PMP

Antonio Oliva González, SMPC, SCPO, PMP

Ernesto Olivares

Matheus Angelini Vidigal de Oliveira

Tiago Chaves Oliveira, PMP

Antonio Olivieri, PMI-ACP, PMI-RMP, PMP

Habeeb Omar, PMP, PgMP, PfMP

Austin Baraza Omonyo, PhD, P2 Pr, PMP

Stefan Ondek, PMP

Arivazhagan Ondiappan,
        PhD(hon), MBB, PMI-RMP, PMP

Michael Ord, AccMIVMA, CPEng, RPEQ

Stefano Orfei, PMI-PBA, PMP

Henrique Ortega-Tenorio, MBA, PMP

Cristiano Ottavian, PRINCE2P, PMP

Ramesh P B, CAIIB, PMI-ACP, PMP

Antonio Pagano

Vijayalakshmi S. Pai, PRINCE2, PMP

Ravindranath Palahalli, BE, PG ADR, PMP

Jorge Palomino Garcia, Eng, MBA, PMP

Hariyo Pangarso

Emmanouil Papadakis, PhD, MSc, PMP

Paul Paquette, MBA, PMI-RMP, PMP

Divya Pareek, BTech, GMP-YLP (IIMB Alumna)

Stéphane Parent, PMI-RMP, PMI-SP, PMP

Reginald Paul Parker, MS, CAS, PMP

Cristina Parodi

Satyabrata Pati, PMP

Laura Paton, MBA, PMI-PBA, PMP

Marcus Paulus, MBA, P2P, PMP

Neil Pearson, PhD, PMP

Srinivasa Rao Pentapalli,
        CMQ/OE, LEED AP, PMP

Craig A. Perue, MBA, CMQ/OE, PMP

Dana Persada, MBA, PMP

Pradeep Perumparambil

Mark Peterson

Yvan Petit

Brian Phillips

Durga P Phuyal, MA, CDA, PMP

Paolo Pierani, PSM, 6 Sigma, PMP

Kavita Pikle, PMP

Crispin Kik Piney, PMP, PfMP

Jose Angelo Pinto, PMP

Daniel Fernandes Pinto, MSc, PMP

Massimo Pirozzi, MSc Eng, PrinPM, PMI-ACP

Frank Polack

Alejandro Polanco, SCPM, LPM, PMP

Aaron Porter

Napoleon Posada, MBA, PMP

Svetlana Prahova, PMP, CSPO

B K Subramanya Prasad, CSM, PMP

Adi Prasetyo, PrinPM, MEng, PRINCE2, PMP

Pedro Pretorius, MCom, PMP

Claudia Prince, PMP

Carl Pritchard, PMI-RMP, PMP

Carl Pro

Hossein Radmehr

Medhat Ragab Metwaly, PMI-RMP, PMP

Sriramasundararajan Rajagopalan, PgMP, PfMP

Anne Niroshi Rajamohan, MSc

Swetha Rajesh, ITIL, CSM, PMP

Karthik Ramamurthy, MCA, MBA, PMP

Gurdev Randhawa, MBA, BE, PMP

Alakananda Rao, MSc, PGDBA, PMP

S. Raghavendra Rao, SAFe(Agi), CSM, PMP

Reda Rashwan, Eng, MCP, AmiChemE, PMP

Rahul Rathod, MSPM, MBA, PMP

Steve Ratkaj

P. Ravikumar, PMI-ACP, PMP, PgMP

Kris Ravuvari, BSc Tech, M. Tech, PMP
Mohammad Yawar Raza, Eng., PMI-ACP
Krupakara Reddy, PRINCE2, SMC, PMP
S. Sreenivasula Reddy, MTech., MIE
Lucas Rocha Rego
Nabeel Ur Rehman,
     Eng, PMI-ACP, PMI-PBA, PMP
Alexander V. Revin, PMP
Roman Reznikov, PRINCE2, ITIL, PMP
Tashfeen Riaz, PgMP, PMP, PMI-ACP
Juan Carlos Ribero Gómez, Ing, PMP
Andre Luis Fonseca Ricardi, PMP
Fabio Rigamonti, PMP
Ivan Rincon, PMP, PgMP, CISA
Laurajean Rispens, PMP, PMI-ACP
Hasnain Rizvi, PhD, SPC, CSP, PMP
Kenneth Robson, PMP
Ruy Rodriguez-Roman, CPA, PMP
Sergio Rojas A., Eng, MBA, PMP
Dan S. Roman, CSSBB, PMI-ACP, PMP
Sadegh Roozbehi, DBA PMP
María Rosas, PMO-CP, SA, PMP
J. Travis Rose, PMP
Michela Ruffa, PMI-RMP, PMP
Tim Rumbaugh
Brian Rush
Philip Russell, PMP
Mike Ryal, PMP
Nagy Saad, ITIL, PMI-ACP, PMP
Mohammed Salaheddien Saad, Ph, PMP
Gopal Sahai, MSP, PMI-PBA, PMP
Ahmad Said, MM, PMP
Savio Saldanha, BE, CTFL, PMP
Ahmed Omer Saleh Mubarak, Eng, MBA, PMP
Sarvenaz Salimitabar
Ing. Roger Salinas-Robalino, MSIG, PMP
Emre Salmanoglu, PMP
Mario Salmona, PMI-PBA, PMI-RMP, PMP
Omar Samaniego
Abubaker Sami, MoP, PgMP, PfMP
Yishai Sandak, MSc, PMI-ACP, PMP
Shankar Sankaran
Prithvinand P. Sarode, BE, PMP
Sachlani Sarono, P3OF, PSM I, PMP
Muhammad Sauood ur Rauf, PMP
Bipin Savant, MTech, CBM, PMP

Jean-Charles Savornin, PMP
Guy Schleffer, PMP, PgMP, PfMP
Gary Schmitz, PMI-ACP PMI-PBA, PMP
David Schwantes, MBA, CSM, PMP
Dayashankara Sedashivappa
Arun Seetharaman
Grégoire Semelet
Yad Senapathy, MS, PMP
Carl Sergeant, PMP
Nikita Sergeev, PhD, MBA, IPMA, PM
Daisy Sg
Casey Shank, PEng, PMP
Giridhar Shankavaram
Ali Sheikhbahaei, PE, PMI-RMP, PMP
Lokman Shental, PMP, TOGAF
Dennis Sherman, PhD, PMP
Hatim Sid Ahmed, MBBS, PMP
Sameer Siddhanti, MSc, PMP, PMP
Gary Sikma, PMI-ACP, PMP
Marcos Felix Silva
Marisa Silva, MSc, PMP
Michael Sims, MBA
Mayank Veer Singh, Eng
Ravinder Singh, PSM I, PRINCE2, PMP
Ashwani Kumar Sinha, MBA, MSc
Gitika Sinha, ITIL, PMI-ACP, PMP
Ann Skinner, PhD, PMP
Daniel Sklar, PMP
Jen Skrabak, PMP, PfMP
Steven Skratulja
Martin J Smit, PhD, PMP
Daniele Almeida Sodré
Victor S. Sohmen, EdD, MBA
Boon Soon Lam
Joseph Sopko
Mauro Sotille, MBA, PMI-RMP, PMP
Fernando Souza, CSM, CSPO, PMP
Russel Souza, PMP
Michael Spatola, MSSM, MS, PMP
Clifford Sprague, PSPO1, PMP
Mario Špundak, PhD, PfMP
Sreeshaj Sreedhar, SS, BBELT, PMP
Nitesh Srivantava
Gunawan ST, PMI-RMP, PMP
Klaus J. Stadlbauer, PMP
Chris Stevens, PhD

Cameron Stewart, PMI-ACP, PMP
Jim Stewart, CSM, PMI-ACP, PMP
Ian R. Stokes, PMP
Nathan Subramaniam, ITIL4, TOGAF 9, PMP
Premkumar Subramanian, MBA, PMP
Yasuji Suzuki, PMI-ACP, PMP
Lisa Sweeney, PMP
Grzegorz Szalajiko
Ahmed Taha, PhD, PRINCE2, PMI-RMP, PMP
Mohammad Mehdi Tahan, MSc, PMP
Mohamed Taher Arafa, PMI-ACP, PMI-RMP, PMP
Shoji Tajima, ITC, ITIL, PMP
Nilton Takagi, MSc, PMP
Peter Wee Seng Tan, CPP, CISSP, PMP
Tetsuya Tani, CBAP, PMP
Chelsea Tanimura, MPA, PMP
Awadalsaid Tara, Eng, MScE, SFC, PMP
Usama Tariq, Eng, PMP
Carsten Tautz
Jose Teixeira De Paulo, PMI-RMP, PMI-SP, PMP
Iván Samuel Tejera Santana, PSM, PMI-ACP, PMP
Gerhard Tekes, Dipl Inf, PMOVR-CP, PMP
Maria Temchina, PMI-ACP, PMP
Daniel Tennison, PE, PMP
Hector Teran, PMP
Gino Terentim, PMI-ACP, PMP, PfMP
Carlos Tessore, PhD, PMI-RMP, PMP
Mohammed Thoufeeq
Shuang Tian, PMI-ACP, PMP
Claudia Tocantins, MSc, PMP
Mark Tolbert
Dyana Torquato, PMI-ACP, PMP
Süleyman Tosun, PhD, PSM I, ITIL, PMP
Sayed Tousif, BE, PMCP
Bella Trenkova, ICP-ACC, SPC4, PgMP
Mario Trentim, PMI-PBA, PMP, PfMP
John N. Tse, MBA, CDA, PMP
Georg Turban, PMP
Daniel Ubilla Baier, MBA, PMI-RMP, PMP
Yoon Sup Um, PMI-ACP, PMI-RMP, PMP
Hafiz Umar
Judith W. Umlas, SVP, IIL
Joseph Ursone, CSM, MCP, PMP
Ebenezer Uy, SSBB, PMI-ACP, PMP
Ali Vahedi, PMP, PgMP, PfMP
Madrony Valdivia Ponce, ING, ITIL

Andre Bittencourt do Valle, PhD, SAPM
Henk-Jan van der Klis, MSc, PMP
Tom Van Medegael, PMP
Raymond van Tonder, PMP, PMI-ACP
Ricardo Vargas, PhD, SAFe SPC, PMP
Enid T. Vargas Maldonado,
      PMI-ACP, PMI-PBA, PMP
Santosh Varma, PDGCA, ITIL, PMP
Norm Veen, MBA, PMP
Jean Velasco, MBA, PMP
Vijay Vemana, SAFe, PMP, PgMP
Nagesh Venkataramanappa, PMP
Charu Venkatararaman, CSM, CSPO, PMP
Vanessa Ventura
Eddy Vertil, PhD (ABD), PMI-RMP, PMP
Anand Vijayakumar, PMI-RMP, PMP, PgMP
Roberto Villa, PMP
Tiziano Villa, PMI-ACP, PMP
Aura Villagrana, MBA, SPC, PMP
Esteban Villegas, PMI-ACP, PMP
Andrea Vismara, MBA, PMI-PBA, PMP
Lislal Viswam, MSc, CSM, PMP
Yiannis Vithynos, PRINCE2P, PMI-ACP, PMP
Vijay Vittalam, PMI-ACP, PMI-RMP, PMP
Aline Vono
Thomas Walenta, PMP, PgMP
Qun Wang, CSPO, CSM, PMP
Gorakhanath Wankhede, PMP
J. LeRoy Ward, PMP, PgMP, PfMP
Muhammad Waseem, MS(PM), PMP
Toshiyuki Henry Watanabe, PE.JP, PMR.JP, PMP
Barb Waters, MBA, PMP
John Watson, PMP, PMI-ACP
Darrell Glen Watson Jr., MPM, PMP
Ganesh Watve, MBA, SMC, PMP
Patrick Weaver, FAICD, PMI-SP, PMP
Xu Wei, PMP
Lars Wendestam, MSc, PMP
Michal Wieteska, ASEP, PMP
Bronsen Wijaya
Angela Wiley, PMP
Edward Williams
Doug Winters, CSSBB, PMP
Louise Worsley, MA
Te Wu, PhD, PMP, PgMP, PfMP
Yang Xiao, MBA, SCOR-P, PMP

Rajesh K. Yadav, MTech
Aliaa Yahia Elshamy, PharmD, PMP, MQM, TQM
Zhang Yanxiang
Bill Yates
Auguste Yeboue, MBA, DBA, PMP
Fu Yongkang
Cynthia Young, DBA, LSSMBB, CMQ/OE, PMP
Daniel Alfredo Zamudio López, SMC, PgMP, PMP
Stefano Mario Zanantoni, PMP

Emanuele Zanotti, PhD, PMP
Ken Zemrowski, ESEP, MSTM
Cristina Zerpa, MC, PMP
Bin Zhao
Fangcun Zhao
Jutta Edith Zilian, CISA, CISM, CGEIT
Priscila Tavares da Sliva Zouback
Alan Zucker, DAC, PMI-ACP, PMP

X1.2 PMI STAFF

Special mention is due to the following employees of PMI:

Marvin Nelson, DBA, SCPM
Danielle Ritter, MLIS, CSPO
Kim Shinners
Roberta Storer

Stephen A. Townsend
Barbara Walsh, CSPO
Daniel Wiser

Appendix X2
Sponsor

X2.1 INTRODUCTION

Research shows that an active project sponsor is a critical success factor in achieving positive outcomes from projects. This appendix describes the actions and impacts of sponsors and how these factors contribute to the overall success of the project.

X2.2 THE SPONSOR ROLE

Depending on the organization, a project typically has a sponsor. The project sponsor provides decision leadership that is outside of the authority and position power of the project manager and project team. Active engagement and oversight by a project sponsor supports the project manager, the project team, and ultimately drives project outcomes. The sponsor also links the project team with the strategy and big-picture view at the executive level of the organization.

Sponsors perform the following functions, among others:

▶ Communicate the vision, goals, and expectations to the team.

▶ Advocate for the project and the team.

▶ Facilitate executive-level decisions.

▶ Help secure resources.

▶ Keep projects aligned to business objectives.

▶ Remove obstacles.

▶ Address issues outside the project team's authority.

▶ Bring opportunities that arise within the project to senior management.

▶ Monitor project outcomes after closure to ensure intended business benefits are realized.

The sponsor's position within the organization and the perspective from that level enable the sponsor to provide key support to the team in the following areas:

▶ **Vision.** Establish and/or communicate the vision and direction for the project.

▶ **Business value.** Work with the team consistently to maintain alignment with the strategic and business objectives. When the market, competition, and strategy are volatile and evolving, this may require frequent interactions to adjust project work to meet the evolving direction.

▶ **Customer focus.** Balance various stakeholder needs and priorities. When there are multiple stakeholders, especially stakeholders with conflicting needs, it may be necessary to prioritize stakeholder needs and make trade-offs.

▶ **Decisions.** Make decisions or direct decisions to the appropriate individual or group when there are decisions to be made that are outside of the project team's authority. If the team cannot come to a decision or if the team is in conflict, sponsors can mediate conflict and facilitate the decision-making process.

▶ **Motivation.** Sponsors serve as a source of motivation for the project team by actively engaging with and supporting them.

▶ **Accountability.** Depending on the authority level of the role, sponsors are often accountable for the project outcomes. In this role, they may accept or reject the deliverables for the project.

X2.3 LACK OF ENGAGEMENT

When the sponsor is not engaged or when that role is vacant, many of the benefits associated with the activities listed in Section X2.2 are missing. This may have a negative impact on project effectiveness. Project performance suffers because there are often longer decision time frames and conflicting priorities. If the sponsor is not helping to secure resources, that gap can impact access to necessary team members or acquisition of physical resources. When there is no direct sponsor support, team members may be removed or switched out. These changes can cause negative impacts to scope, quality, schedule, and budget and diminish the probability of achieving intended outcomes and stakeholder satisfaction.

X2.4 SPONSOR BEHAVIORS

There are certain behaviors that sponsors display that can help teams perform effectively and thus improve project outcomes:

▶ **Resource.** Liaise with the organization to ensure the team has the necessary skill sets and the physical resources needed to deliver the project.

▶ **Guide.** Provide a motivating vision around which the team can rally.

▶ **Align.** Maintain alignment between the organization's strategic goals and the project outcomes. If the market changes or the organization's goals shift, work with the project team to pivot the direction of the project to meet the current needs.

▶ **Tailor.** Work alongside the team to tailor the structure, culture, processes, roles, and work to optimize outcomes.

▶ **Influence.** Enable the needed changes for adoption to the post-project operations. This includes leadership, engagement, and collaboration with stakeholders throughout the organization.

▶ **Communicate.** Provide an ongoing exchange of information from the organization to the team and from the team to the organization.

▶ **Partner.** Partner with the team in achieving success. This can include coaching, mentoring, and demonstrating a personal commitment to the project goal.

▶ **Check.** Engage with the team to stimulate critical thinking by asking questions, challenging assumptions, and fostering innovation.

▶ **Unblock.** Remove impediments and barriers and resolve issues that are outside the team's authority or ability to address.

X2.5 CONCLUSION

The strategic link that the sponsor provides both empowers and enables the project team to optimize its performance by maintaining alignment with the organization's strategy. The sponsor facilitates engagement and decision making and ensures that the skills and resources needed are available. These activities and behaviors increase the likelihood of achieving the desired project outcomes.

X2.6 SUGGESTED RESOURCES

Ahmed, R., Mohamad, N. A. B., & Ahmad, M. S. 2016. Effect of multidimensional top management support on project success: An empirical investigation. *Quality & Quantity, 50*(1), 151–176. https://doi.org/10.1007/s11135-014-0142-4

Kloppenborg, T. J., Tesch, D., & Manolis, C. 2014. Project success and executive sponsor behaviors: Empirical life cycle stage investigations. *Project Management Journal, 45*(1), 9–20. https://doi.org/10.1002/pmj.21396

Project Management Institute (PMI). 2012. *Executive engagement: The role of the sponsor.* Retrieved from https://www.pmi.org/business-solutions/white-papers/executive-engagement-sponsor-role.

Project Management Institute. 2014. Pulse of the Profession® Report, *Executive sponsor engagement: Top driver of project and program success.* Retrieved from https://www.pmi.org/-/media/pmi/documents/public/pdf/learning/thought-leadership/pulse/executive-sponsor-engagement.pdf?v=411b7196-1cb4-4b29-b8d2-2764513bd175&sc_lang_temp=en

Zwikael, O. 2008. Top management involvement in project management: Exclusive support practices for different project scenarios. *International Journal of Managing Projects in Business, 1*(3), 387–403. https://doi.org/10.1108/17538370810883837

Appendix X3
The Project Management Office

X3.1 INTRODUCTION

The acronym "PMO" can refer to a portfolio, program, or project management office. In the context of the *PMBOK® Guide* – Seventh Edition, the project management office (PMO) represents a management structure that standardizes project-related governance processes and facilitates the sharing of resources, tools, methodologies, and techniques. Recognizing that the character and function of a PMO varies between organizations, and even within the same organization, this appendix outlines common attributes among PMOs and discusses how PMOs support project work.

X3.2 THE PMO VALUE PROPOSITION—WHY HAVE ONE?

Organizations establish PMOs for a variety of reasons but with one core benefit in mind: improved project management in terms of schedule, cost, quality, risk, and other facets. PMOs have many potential roles in aligning work with strategic goals: engaging and collaborating with stakeholders, developing talent, and realizing value from investments in projects.

PMOs can take multiple forms. Understanding how PMOs are utilized in organizations as well as assigned roles and responsibilities sheds light on the range of benefits PMOs can deliver:

▶ Some PMOs provide project management guidance that supports consistency in how projects are delivered. These PMOs may provide guidelines, templates, and examples of good practices along with training and coaching. Standardized approaches and tools promote a common business picture across projects and facilitate decisions that transcend individual project concerns. This type of PMO often exists in organizations that are just starting to improve their project management capabilities.

▶ A PMO may offer project support services for planning activities, risk management, project performance tracking, and similar activities. This shared services model of a PMO often exists in organizations with independent or diverse business units that want support with delivery while maintaining more direct control over their projects.

▶ PMOs can be part of a department or business unit and oversee a portfolio of projects. Oversight can include such activities as requiring a business case to initiate a project, allocating financial and other resources to deliver the project, approving requests to change project scope or activities, and similar functions. This type of PMO provides centralized management of projects. This structure exists in organizations that have departments with multiple projects and that deliver strategically important results, such as IT capabilities or new product development.

▶ An organization may have an enterprise-level PMO (EPMO) that links implementation of organizational strategy with portfolio-level investments in programs and projects that deliver specific results, changes, or products. This structure exists in organizations with well-established project management capabilities that are directly linked to achieving organizational strategy and broad business objectives.

▶ Organizations with flatter structures, customer-centered initiatives, and more adaptive delivery approaches may adopt an Agile Center of Excellence (ACoE) or Value Delivery Office (VDO) structure. The ACoE/VDO serves an enabling role, rather than a management or oversight function. It focuses on coaching teams, building agile skills and capabilities throughout the organization, and mentoring sponsors and product owners to be more effective in those roles. This type of structure is emerging within organizations adopting more decentralized structures where teams need to respond quickly to changing customer needs.

PMOs may be layered. For example, an EPMO may have subordinate PMOs and VDOs that reside within specific departments. Such layering supports strategic alignment at the EPMO level and specific project management capabilities within the departmental PMO or VDO.

The formation of any type of PMO or VDO is based on organizational needs. Key influencers that help to shape the PMO or VDO include the types of projects being delivered, the size of the organization, its structure(s), the degree of centralized/decentralized decision making, and corporate culture. As organizational needs change over time, PMOs and VDOs evolve in response. For example, a PMO may transform into a VDO or the PMO may be closed after fulfilling its charter.

X3.3 KEY PMO CAPABILITIES

The Standard for Project Management states that projects are part of a system for value delivery within organizations. PMOs can support that system and are a part of the system. Just as project teams need specific capabilities to deliver results, so do PMOs. Effective PMOs make three key contributions that support value delivery:

▶ **Fostering delivery and outcomes-oriented capabilities.** PMOs foster project management capabilities. They ensure that employees, contractors, partners, etc., who are within and outside of the PMO, understand, develop, apply, and value a range of project management skills and competencies. They focus on right-sizing processes and governance, based on the unique characteristics of each project to produce high-quality results efficiently, quickly, and effectively.

▶ **Keeping the "big picture" perspective.** Staying true to the goals of a project remains a key element of success. Scope creep and new priorities not aligned to strategic or business goals can allow projects to drift off course. Strong PMOs evaluate the performance of projects with an eye toward continuous improvement. They evaluate work in the context of the organization's overall success rather than maximizing a specific project's results. They provide project teams, senior management, and business leaders with information and guidance that help them understand current circumstances and options in support of decision making.

▶ **Continuous improvement, knowledge transfer, and change management.** Strong PMOs regularly share project results across the organization to transfer valuable knowledge gained from each project. Learning and sharing activities inform strategic and business objectives while improving activities that strengthen future project delivery. Effective organizational change management builds and sustains alignment with process updates, capability enhancements, and new skills that support project management.

X3.4 EVOLVING FOR STRONGER BENEFITS REALIZATION

For many businesses, greater uncertainty, an accelerated pace of change, increased competition, and more empowered customers mean organizations produce value in an increasingly complex environment. The ability to implement new strategic initiatives and change rapidly is becoming a key differentiator. These changes are also exerting greater pressure on PMOs to demonstrate their contributions to benefits realization and value creation. PMOs are evolving to meet these challenges by:

▶ **Focusing on critical initiatives.** While all projects are important, strategic initiatives can significantly impact the organization's future, its relationship with its stakeholders, and its capabilities. PMOs are shifting from being project watchdogs to orchestrating conversations between senior leaders, business unit heads, product owners, and project teams. These conversations provide accurate insights into project performance, threats, and opportunities that can affect important strategic initiatives. Such focus promotes clarity and course correction around emerging issues and the fullest possible realization of business outcomes.

▶ **Instituting smart and simple processes.** PMOs are right sizing their organization's capabilities by establishing just enough process and practice discipline to enable effective communication, collaboration, and continuous improvement without adding wasteful steps or overriding processes that are producing value.

▶ **Fostering talent and capabilities.** PMOs are playing a more proactive role in recruiting and retaining talented team members. They are developing and nurturing technical, strategic, management, and leadership skills within project teams and across the organization.

▶ **Encouraging and enabling a culture of change.** PMOs are becoming change leaders by actively building organization-wide support for and commitment to outcomes and benefits-focused performance and organizational change management as competitive differentiators.

X3.5 LEARN MORE ABOUT PMOS

These PMI standards and guides provide additional information about the role of the PMO from different perspectives. They may offer additional insights and useful information.

Project Management Institute. 2017. *The Standard for Organizational Project Management.* Newtown Square, PA: Author.

Project Management Institute. 2017. *The Standard for Portfolio Management.* Newtown Square, PA: Author.

Project Management Institute. 2017. *The Standard for Program Management.* Newtown Square, PA: Author.

Project Management Institute. 2017. *The Standard for Business Analysis.* 2017. Newtown Square, PA: Author.

Project Management Institute. 2017. *Agile Practice Guide.* Newtown Square, PA: Author.

Project Management Institute. 2016. *Governance of Portfolios, Programs, and Projects: A Practice Guide.* Newtown Square, PA: Author.

X3.6 SUGGESTED RESOURCES

Project Management Institute. 2013. *Strategic Initiative Management: The PMO Imperative.* Available at https://www.pmi.org/learning/thought-leadership/pulse/strategic-initiative-management-the-pmo-imperative.

Project Management Institute. 2013. *The Impact of PMOs on Strategy Implementation.* Available at https://www.pmi.org/learning/thought-leadership/pulse/impact-pmo-strategy-in-depth.

Project Management Institute. 2013. *PMO Frameworks.* Available at https://www.pmi.org/learning/thought-leadership/pulse/pmo-frameworks.

Appendix X4
Product

X4.1 INTRODUCTION

There has been a gradual transition in project management concepts over the last decade. Views such as defining success as meeting scope, schedule, and budget objectives have transitioned to measuring value and the outcomes (not the outputs) of the project. Product management is aligned with this value view and adds a longer time frame perspective. These concepts are shown in Table X4-1.

Table X4-1. Views of Project and Product Management

Attribute	Project View	Product View
Focus	Outcomes	Outcomes
Typical metrics	Value	Business value
Staffing model	Temporary teams	Stable teams
Delivery emphasis	"Deliver value" accountability	"Inception to retirement" accountability

This appendix provides information about product development that raises tailoring considerations for teams to consider. It describes how products and services continue to develop and evolve through their use and over their lifetime. For purposes of this appendix, products, product management, and product life cycle are defined as:

Product. A product is an artifact that is produced, is quantifiable, and can be either an end item in itself or a component item.

Product management. Product management is the integration of people, data, processes, and business systems to create, maintain, and evolve a product or service throughout its life cycle.

Product life cycle. A product life cycle is a series of phases that represents the evolution of a product, from concept through delivery, growth, maturity, and to retirement.

Given these definitions, products extend beyond a project life cycle. They operate more like long-running programs that focus on maximizing benefits realization. For example:

▶ The Apple iPhone® product has been through multiple versions with future updates on someone's drawing board.

▶ Once they are finished, buildings and homes require ongoing maintenance to keep them functioning correctly and, at specific points, they may be refurbished or expanded for different uses.

Continuous development has impacts on many factors including, but not limited to, funding models, staffing models, development, and sustainment practices.

X4.2 GLOBAL MARKET SHIFTS

Three global trends are disrupting traditional business models and transforming products and services (see Figure X4-1).

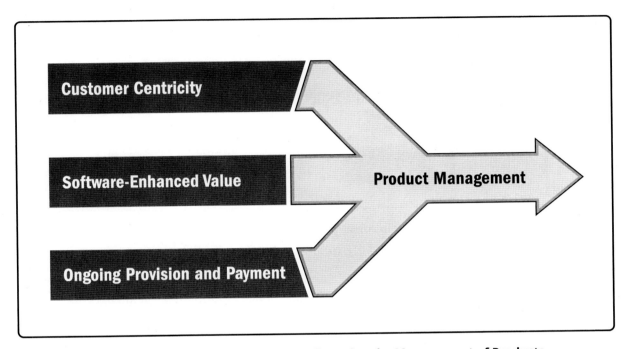

Figure X4-1. Global Business Trends Influencing the Management of Products

▶ **Customer centricity.** Customer centricity inverts the traditional model of organizations developing products and pushing them out to customers. Today, organizations are changing to better understand, serve, and maintain customer loyalty (see Figure X4-2). Today's technology can capture a range of customer data and requirements that organizations analyze and use for potential product enhancements, cross-selling opportunities, new product ideas, etc.

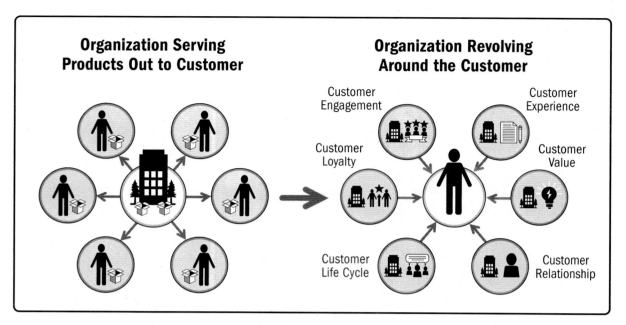

Figure X4-2. The Changing Relationship Between an Organization and Its Customers

▶ **Software-enhanced value.** Software and the capabilities it can provide have become key differentiators in a range of products and services today. Thirty years ago, software ran predominantly on dedicated computers. Ten years ago, software was embedded in control systems for vehicles and homes as a result of enhanced wireless and satellite communication systems. Now, even the most mundane appliances run software that adds new capabilities and captures usage data.

Most organizations conduct at least some portion of their transactional business electronically through websites and applications. Due to the ongoing need to upgrade and maintain these systems, these services are only truly finished with development when the product or service is retired.

▶ **Ongoing provision and payment.** Changes to established economic models are transforming many organizations. Single-transaction services are being replaced with continuous provision and payment. Examples include:

- ▷ *Publishing.* Self-publishing, direct distribution, and electronic books that allow ongoing refinement and development after publication.

- ▷ *Finance.* The shift away from local branches and toward microlending with funding in smaller batches is based on evaluation of value delivered.

- ▷ *Start-ups.* With the increase in the gig economy and custom markets, there are more start-ups and small businesses today than ever. Work is more distributed, fragmented, and fluid than with traditional models.

- ▷ *Media.* A move away from buying DVDs and CDs from centralized outlets; instead, a rise in subscription services with ongoing funding and delivery of benefits.

X4.3 IMPACT ON PROJECT DELIVERY PRACTICES

As markets shift from a single project delivery model to an ongoing delivery model, some organizations are looking for alternatives to temporary project structures that deliver a single product, change, or service. Instead, they are looking for delivery constructs that have a strong customer focus, recognize the rapid evolution of technology, and align with the ongoing service and revenue streams of loyal customers.

These factors have led to an increased interest in and shift toward product management life cycles for value delivery. Product management takes a longer life cycle view that encompasses support, sustainment, and ongoing evolution with the same team. Stable teams are especially valuable in complex and unique domains, such as systems with embedded software where knowledge transfer is time-consuming and costly. The shifting focus to product management is prompting some project-oriented organizations to adapt their delivery models.

X4.4 ORGANIZATIONAL CONSIDERATIONS FOR PRODUCT MANAGEMENT

Organizations that are shifting to long-running, product-based environments can utilize several strategies to align and coordinate product management. Three strategies include, but are not limited to, the following (see also Figure X4-3):

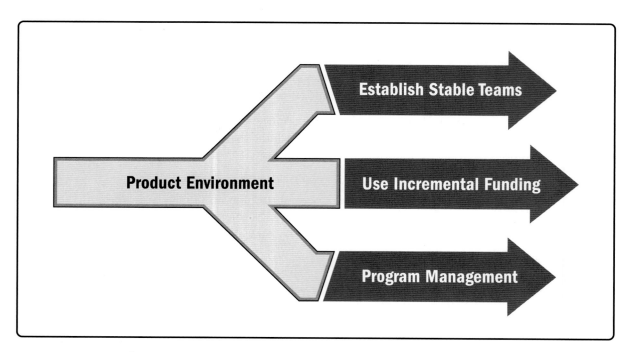

Figure X4-3. Supporting Strategies for Continuous Value Delivery

▶ **Establish stable teams.** Instead of disbanding the team when initial development is complete, use that team to sustain and evolve the product with the designated product owner or person within the team reflecting the customer perspective. This removes the need for knowledge transfer and reduces the risk of future enhancements being delayed due to a loss of tacit knowledge.

Long-standing teams also develop better market awareness, customer insights, and customer empathy than short-term teams. This helps with maintaining customer focus and customer loyalty and builds competitive advantage. When people know they will be responsible for maintaining and enhancing a product, they are less likely to take shortcuts to get something ready for release. As a result, quality, maintainability, and extensibility are often improved with long-serving teams rather than with teams that develop then handover products. These factors, in turn, contribute to creating value and sustaining value delivery.

Partners or contractors who develop initial products for deployment on a customer site incorporate effective change management to ensure customers have the capabilities to maintain the product once it is transitioned. Part of transition planning can include discussions on building a team within the receiving organization that can support and evolve the product over its life cycle.

▶ **Use incremental guidance and funding.** Instead of predefined project durations or annual budgets, consider more frequent reviews (such as quarterly) and funding for the next quarter. With more frequent evaluations and funding, the business is in closer control of overall progress, direction, and decision making.

Similar to venture capital funding, regular reviews of delivered value allow direct funding toward products that are providing expected value and reduce or curtail investment in underperforming initiatives. Such funding models enable organizations to pursue new market opportunities and capitalize on successful endeavors while limiting exposure to the inevitable percentage of new initiatives that fail.

▶ **Utilize program management structures.** Practitioners operating with stable teams that support customer-centric products can apply program management constructs for managing long-running initiatives. Programs align well with adjusting to market changes and focusing on customer benefits. They are also typically much longer running than a single project.

The Standard for Program Management addresses ongoing priority changes as follows: "The primary difference between projects and programs is based on the recognition within programs that the strategies for delivering benefits may need to be optimized adaptively as the outcomes of components are individually realized. The best mechanisms for delivering a program's benefits may initially be ambiguous or uncertain."

This acceptance of up-front uncertainty, need for adaptation, focus on benefits, and longer time frames may make programs a better fit than projects for many organizations managing product delivery.

Many traditional product industries, such as infrastructure, aerospace, and automotive, use program management guides and frameworks. These industries utilize programs for directional alignment and integration of component activities, such as programs, subprograms, and project activities. For example, an organization with a technology platform can use program and product management to prioritize and oversee capabilities that will maximize the platform's return on investment over its lifetime. A stable, continuous development team can work on customer-focused, value-adding features and functions. Project teams then deliver equipment upgrades and interfaces with new or enhanced systems. Operational teams can troubleshoot user interface issues and help customers adapt to new features. When program structures already exist in organizations, shifting to those structures for product management does not require reorienting everyone to a new way of thinking or working.

Table X4-2. Unique Characteristics of Projects, Programs, and Products

Characteristic	Project	Program	Product
Duration	Short term, temporary	Longer term	Long term
Scope	Projects have defined objectives. Scope is progressively elaborated throughout the life cycle.	Programs produce aggregate benefits delivered through multiple components.	Products are customer focused and benefits driven.
Change	Project teams expect changes and implement processes to address the changes, as needed.	Program teams explore changes and adapt to optimize the delivery of benefits.	Product teams explore changes to optimize the delivery of benefits.
Success	Success is measured by product and project quality, time lines, budget, customer satisfaction, and achievement of intended outcomes.	Success is measured by the realization of intended benefits and the efficiency and effectiveness of delivering those benefits.	Success is measured by the ability to deliver intended benefits and ongoing viability for continued funding.
Funding	Funding is largely determined up front based on ROI projections and initial estimates. Funding is updated based on actual performance and change requests.	Funding is up front and ongoing. Funding is updated with results showing how benefits are being delivered.	Product teams engage in continuous development via funding, development blocks, and reviews of value delivery.

Organizations taking an integrated view of project and product management can benefit from examining program management frameworks as a stepping stone. Programs are much better aligned with product thinking through their acceptance of up-front uncertainty, need for adaptation, focus on benefits, and longer time frames.

X4.5 SUMMARY

Global markets, increased diversification, and the addition of software to more products are resulting in extended support, sustainment, and time frames for realization of value. Customer-centric and digitally focused organizations are finding advantages in forming stable teams for the lifetime support and growth of these new classes of products.

Product life cycles may appear at odds with traditional project delivery constructs such as the temporary nature of projects. However, they have many overlaps with the evolution of project thinking that includes focusing on customer value.

Organizations in such environments can find alignment and additional resources in creating long-running stable teams, staged funding, and program management constructs.

X4.6 SUGGESTED RESOURCES

Kelly, A. 2018. *Continuous Digital: An Agile Alternative to Projects for Digital Business.* Columbus, OH: Allan Kelly Associates.

Leybourn, E. and Hastie, S. 2019. *#noprojects: A Culture of Continuous Value.* Toronto, Ontario, Canada: C4Media.

Kersten, M. 2018. *Project to Product: How to Survive and Thrive in the Age of Digital Disruption with the Flow Framework.* Portland, OR: IT Revolution Press.

Project Management Institute. 2017. *The Standard for Program Management* – Fourth Edition. Newtown Square, PA: Author.

Appendix X5
Research and Development for
The Standard for Project Management

X5.1 INTRODUCTION

The purpose of this appendix is to provide insight into how the update to *The Standard for Project Management* was developed. Content includes:

- ▶ Rationale for a move to a principle-based standard,

- ▶ Overview of the research conducted prior to the development of the standard,

- ▶ Description of how the standard was developed, and

- ▶ Information on how the content in the standard was validated.

X5.2 THE MOVE TO A PRINCIPLE-BASED STANDARD

Since 2010, PMI's standards program has included research in addition to practitioner experience to develop standards. Academic research, market research, focus groups, and practitioner experience have been inputs when updating many of the standards documents, including *The Standard for Project Management.*

As early as 2012, research suggested a move away from a prescriptive, process-oriented standard toward one that requires reflection to apply in practice. Since that time, many of PMI's standards have moved to a principle-based format, such as *The Standard for Program Management* – Third Edition and *The Standard for Portfolio Management* – Fourth Edition. In addition, as part of supporting the development of ISO standards, PMI participated in discussions within ISO TC258[1] regarding the need to shift to a narrative- or principle-based approach and away from a process-based approach.

---

[1] International Organization for Standardization Technical Committee 258, Project, Programme, and Portfolio Management.

Comments by the review teams and exposure draft participants collectively affirmed the shift of *The Standard for Project Management* away from a process-based approach to a principle-based standard in keeping with research findings and practitioner need.

X5.3 RESEARCH FOR *THE STANDARD FOR PROJECT MANAGEMENT*

Prior to updating *The Standard for Project Management*, significant research and review were conducted, including:

▶ International project management standards or standards-like documents along with lean, agile, and design thinking principles and some of the mostly commonly used frameworks. This research helped to identify common practice areas and themes that served as inputs into developing the principles in the *The Standard for Project Management*.

▶ PMI research, such as *Pulse of the Profession®*, which indicated that more organizations and practitioners are embracing agile and hybrid models along with new ways of working (i.e., tools, frameworks, technologies, etc.).

▶ Review of published white papers, thought leadership articles, and related documents to elicit underlying principles.

▶ Focus groups and workshops to gather stakeholder input for improving the usability of *The Standard for Project Management*.

Analysis of the research led to the conclusion that more organizations are embracing a variety of project management approaches. Some organizations are moving toward a hybrid approach which mixes predictive and adaptive practices. Organizations and project teams are tailoring their approaches to the needs of the industry, organization, and project. These findings indicated that the PMI standard needed to reflect a more holistic and inclusive view of project management applicable to predictive, hybrid, and adaptive approaches.

All of this information contributed insights to the development process for exploring:

▶ A shift from a process- to a principle-based focus that would reflect the full spectrum of the various ways that projects are managed.

▶ Potential new content areas for inclusion, such as benefits realization management, organizational change management, and complexity, in alignment with the practice guides in those areas.

▶ Moving any "how to" content to a more interactive and adaptive medium and adapting that content to better reflect a range of considerations based on industry, type of project, and other important characteristics.

▶ Broadening the focus of the standard to be inclusive of all projects and placing more emphasis on the desired outcomes from the project.

X5.4 STANDARD DEVELOPMENT PROCESS

Developing the standard included ensuring global stakeholder representation from a broad range of industries and the various approaches to managing projects.

X5.4.1 DEVELOPMENT AND REVIEW TEAMS

Prior to developing the content for the standard, a Development Team and two review teams were formed. Approximately 450 individuals applied to participate on the teams. Twelve people were selected for the Development Team and approximately 70 were selected to participate in one of two review teams. The Development Team and review teams were comprised of stakeholders from around the globe and across industry segments and roles (e.g., government, practitioners, academic, consulting, and organizational providers). The teams included expertise in delivering projects using predictive, hybrid, and adaptive approaches.

X5.4.2 CONTENT

The standard is comprised of three sections: Introduction, A System for Value Delivery, and Project Management Principles.

The Introduction includes key terms and concepts associated with project management. Much of this information is consistent with previous editions.

Content in the section on A System for Value Delivery draws on content from PMI foundational standards[2] as well as research on benefits realization management and organizational agility. The content is presented with a focus on delivering value and is inclusive of the various ways in which value is created.

The Project Management Principles section evolved throughout the development and validation process. The initial concepts for the principles were identified through the research discussed previously. The Development Team worked individually and collaboratively to identify potential principles and then grouped them into affinity categories. Each category was further analyzed and decomposed to include a list of keywords associated with each category. The potential categories and keywords were composed into an initial draft, which was then reviewed and commented on by the entire Development Team to ensure the intent of the principles was reflected in the draft.

It is important to note that the principles are intended to be broadly based. Nothing in the principles is intended to be dogmatic, restrictive, or prescriptive. The principles are aligned with, but not duplicative of, the content in the *PMI Code of Ethics and Professional Conduct*.

It is not possible to generate the "right principles" as each project and organization is different. Therefore, the principles are designed as a guide for people working on projects. Project professionals and others working on projects can seek to be aligned with the principles, but they are not intended to provide instructions for managing projects.

X5.5 VALIDATING THE STANDARD

Content in the standard was validated using three main approaches: global workshops, iterative development, and public exposure draft.

---

[2] *The Standard for Program Management* – Fourth Edition and *The Standard for Portfolio Management* – Fourth Edition.

X5.5.1 GLOBAL WORKSHOPS

Throughout the development process, global workshops were held where the move to a principle-based standard was presented and workshop participants were asked to explore guiding principles for project management. Workshops were presented in Dublin, Ireland (PMI Global Congress – EMEA); Bangalore, India; Brazilia, Brazil; Ottawa, Canada (PMI Global Executive Council meeting); Philadelphia, Pennsylvania, United States (PMI Global Conference); and Beijing, China. These workshops served as input into the Development Team's work and as validation checkpoints during development.

X5.5.2 ITERATIVE DEVELOPMENT

The Development Team worked in pairs and small teams to develop the initial content for each of the three sections that comprise *The Standard for Project Management*. Once the initial drafts were integrated, the Development Team and Review Team 1 reviewed and commented on the drafts of each section of the standard. These reviews produced over a thousand comments which the Development Team analyzed and addressed to produce a second draft of the full standard. Review Team 2 reviewed the entire draft standard and provided comments with a fresh perspective to the Development Team. Those comments were analyzed and integrated into the content, as appropriate.

X5.5.3 EXPOSURE DRAFT

The draft standard was made available for public review and comment from 15 January to 14 February 2020. Almost 600 individuals submitted comments on the exposure draft. In response to the exposure draft comments, the content was reorganized and edited for clarity. Most comments indicated agreement with the intent of the principle-based standard. The Development Team then reviewed the draft of the standard and gave approval for the draft to go to the Standards Consensus Committee for consensus ballot per *PMI's Policy for the Development and Coordination of American National Standards*.

X5.6 SUMMARY

Continuing changes in the project management profession and the ways in which projects are managed support a less prescriptive standard. Industry research, global participation with broad industry representation, and an iterative review process shaped and validated the move from a process-based standard to a principle-based standard. Future teams can evaluate the impact of the shift in presentation of *The Standard for Project Management* and use that information to enhance or revise future editions.

Glossary

1. INCLUSIONS AND EXCLUSIONS

This combined glossary includes definitions of terms and acronyms from the following:

▶ *The Standard for Project Management*

▶ *A Guide to the Project Management Body of Knowledge (PMBOK® Guide)* – Seventh Edition

This glossary includes terms that are:

▶ Unique or nearly unique to project management (e.g., minimum viable product, work breakdown structure, Gantt chart), and

▶ Not unique to project management but used differently or with a narrower meaning in project management than in general everyday usage (e.g., release planning, contingency reserve).

This glossary generally does not include:

▶ Application-area-specific terms,

▶ Terms used in project management that do not differ in any material way from everyday use (e.g., calendar day, delay),

▶ Compound terms whose meanings are clear from the meanings of the component parts,

▶ Variants when the meaning of the variant is clear from the base term, and

▶ Terms that are used only once and are not critical to understanding the point of the sentence. This can include a list of examples that would not have each term defined in the glossary.

2. COMMON ACRONYMS

AC	actual cost
BAC	budget at completion
CCB	change control board
CFD	cumulative flow diagram
COQ	cost of quality
CPAF	cost plus award fee
CPFF	cost plus fixed fee
CPI	cost performance index
CPIF	cost plus incentive fee
CPM	critical path method
CV	cost variance
DoD	definition of done
EAC	estimate at completion
EEF	enterprise environmental factors
EMV	expected monetary value
ETC	estimate to complete
EV	earned value
EVA	earned value analysis
FFP	firm fixed price
FPEPA	fixed price with economic price adjustment
FPIF	fixed price incentive fee

IDIQ	indefinite delivery indefinite quantity
LCA	life cycle assessment
MVP	minimum viable product
NPS®	Net Promotor Score®
OBS	organizational breakdown structure
OPA	organizational process assets
PMB	performance measurement baseline
PMBOK	Project Management Body of Knowledge
PMO	project management office
PV	planned value
RAM	responsibility assignment matrix
RBS	risk breakdown structure
SOW	statement of work
SPI	schedule performance index
SV	schedule variance
SWOT	strengths, weaknesses, opportunities, and threats
T&M	time and materials contract
VAC	variance at completion
VDO	value delivery office
WBS	work breakdown structure

PMBOK® Guide

3. DEFINITIONS

Many of the words defined here have broader, and in some cases, different dictionary definitions. In some cases, a single glossary term consists of multiple words (e.g., root cause analysis).

Acceptance Criteria. A set of conditions that is required to be met before deliverables are accepted.

Accuracy. Within the quality management system, accuracy is an assessment of correctness.

Activity List. A documented tabulation of schedule activities that shows the activity description, activity identifier, and a sufficiently detailed scope of work description so project team members understand what work is to be performed.

Actual Cost (AC). The realized cost incurred for the work performed on an activity during a specific time period.

Adaptive Approach. A development approach in which the requirements are subject to a high level of uncertainty and volatility and are likely to change throughout the project.

Affinity Diagram. A diagram that shows large numbers of ideas classified into groups for review and analysis.

Affinity Grouping. The process of classifying items into similar categories or collections on the basis of their likeness.

Agile. A term used to describe a mindset of values and principles as set forth in the Agile Manifesto.

Alternatives Analysis. A method used to evaluate identified options in order to select the options or approaches to use to perform the work of the project.

Ambiguity. A state of being unclear, having difficulty in identifying the cause of events, or having multiple options from which to choose.

Analogous Estimating. A method for estimating the duration or cost of an activity or a project using historical data from a similar activity or project.

Artifact. A template, document, output, or project deliverable.

Assumption. A factor in the planning process that is considered to be true, real, or certain, without proof or demonstration.

Assumption and Constraint Analysis. An assessment that ensures assumptions and constraints are integrated into the project plans and documents, and that there is consistency among them.

Assumption Log. A project document used to record all assumptions and constraints throughout the project.

Authority. The right to apply project resources, expend funds, make decisions, or give approvals.

Backlog. An ordered list of work to be done.

Backlog Refinement. Progressive elaboration of the content in the backlog and (re)prioritization of it to identify the work that can be accomplished in an upcoming iteration.

Baseline. The approved version of a work product, used as a basis for comparison to actual results.

Basis of Estimates. Supporting documentation outlining the details used in establishing project estimates such as assumptions, constraints, level of detail, ranges, and confidence levels.

Benchmarking. The comparison of actual or planned products, processes, and practices to those of comparable organizations to identify best practices, generate ideas for improvement, and provide a basis for measuring performance.

Benefits Management Plan. The documented explanation defining the processes for creating, maximizing, and sustaining the benefits provided by a project or program.

Bid Documents. All documents used to solicit information, quotations, or proposals from prospective sellers.

Bidder Conference. The meetings with prospective sellers prior to the preparation of a bid or proposal to ensure all prospective vendors have a clear and common understanding of the procurement. Also known as contractor conferences, vendor conferences, or pre-bid conferences.

Blocker. See *impediment*.

Budget. The approved estimate for the project or any work breakdown structure (WBS) component or any schedule activity.

Budget at Completion (BAC). The sum of all budgets established for the work to be performed.

Burn Chart. A graphical representation of the work remaining in a timebox or the work completed toward the release of a product or project deliverable.

Business Case. A value proposition for a proposed project that may include financial and nonfinancial benefits.

Business Model Canvas. A one-page, visual summary that describes the value proposition, infrastructure, customers, and finances. These are often used in Lean Startup situations.

Business Value. The net quantifiable benefit derived from a business endeavor that may be tangible, intangible, or both.

Cadence. A rhythm of activities conducted throughout the project.

Cause-and-Effect Diagram. A visual representation that helps trace an undesirable effect back to its root cause.

Change. A modification to any formally controlled deliverable, project management plan component, or project document.

Change Control. A process whereby modifications to documents, deliverables, or baselines associated with the project are identified, documented, approved, or rejected.

Change Control Board (CCB). A formally chartered group responsible for reviewing, evaluating, approving, delaying, or rejecting changes to the project, and for recording and communicating such decisions.

Change Control Plan. A component of the project management plan that establishes the change control board, documents the extent of its authority, and describes how the change control system will be implemented.

Change Control System. A set of procedures that describes how modifications to the project deliverables and documentation are managed and controlled.

Change Log. A comprehensive list of changes submitted during the project and their current status.

Change Management. A comprehensive, cyclic, and structured approach for transitioning individuals, groups, and organizations from a current state to a future state with intended business benefits.

Change Request. A formal proposal to modify a document, deliverable, or baseline.

Charter. See *project charter*.

Check Sheet. A tally sheet that can be used as a checklist when gathering data.

Closing Process Group. The process(es) performed to formally complete or close a project, phase, or contract.

Communications Management Plan. A component of the project, program, or portfolio management plan that describes how, when, and by whom information about the project will be administered and disseminated.

Complexity. A characteristic of a program or project or its environment that is difficult to manage due to human behavior, system behavior, and ambiguity.

Confirmation Bias. A type of cognitive bias that confirms preexisting beliefs or hypotheses.

Conformance. The degree to which the results meet the set quality requirements.

Constraint. A limiting factor that affects the execution of a project, program, portfolio, or process.

Contingency. An event or occurrence that could affect the execution of the project, which may be accounted for with a reserve.

Contingency Reserve. Time or money allocated in the schedule or cost baseline for known risks with active response strategies.

Continuous Delivery. The practice of delivering feature increments immediately to customers, often through the use of small batches of work and automation technology.

Contract. A mutually binding agreement that obligates the seller to provide the specified product, service, or result and obligates the buyer to pay for it.

Control. The process of comparing actual performance with planned performance, analyzing variances, assessing trends to effect process improvements, evaluating possible alternatives, and recommending appropriate corrective action as needed.

Control Chart. A graphic display of process data over time and against established control limits, which has a centerline that assists in detecting a trend of plotted values toward either control limit.

Cost Baseline. The approved version of the time-phased project budget, excluding any management reserves, which can be changed only through formal change control procedures and is used as a basis for comparison to actual results.

Cost-Benefit Analysis. A financial analysis method used to determine the benefits provided by a project against its costs.

Cost Management Plan. A component of a project or program management plan that describes how costs will be planned, structured, and controlled.

Cost of Quality (COQ). All costs incurred over the life of the product by investment in preventing nonconformance to requirements, appraisal of the product or service for conformance to requirements, and failure to meet requirements.

Cost Performance Index (CPI). A measure of the cost efficiency of budgeted resources expressed as the ratio of earned value to actual cost.

Cost Plus Award Fee Contract (CPAF). A category of contract that involves payments to the seller for all legitimate actual costs incurred for completed work, plus an award fee representing seller profit.

Cost Plus Fixed Fee Contract (CPFF). A type of cost-reimbursable contract where the buyer reimburses the seller for the seller's allowable costs (allowable costs are defined by the contract) plus a fixed amount of profit (fee).

Cost Plus Incentive Fee Contract (CPIF). A type of cost-reimbursable contract where the buyer reimburses the seller for the seller's allowable costs (allowable costs are defined by the contract), and the seller earns its profit if it meets defined performance criteria.

Cost-Reimbursable Contract. A type of contract involving payment to the seller for the seller's actual costs, plus a fee typically representing the seller's profit.

Cost Variance (CV). The amount of budget deficit or surplus at a given point in time, expressed as the difference between the earned value and the actual cost.

Crashing. A method used to shorten the schedule duration for the least incremental cost by adding resources.

Criteria. Standards, rules, or tests on which a judgment or decision can be based or by which a product, service, result, or process can be evaluated.

Critical Path. The sequence of activities that represents the longest path through a project, which determines the shortest possible duration.

Critical Path Method (CPM). A method used to estimate the minimum project duration and determine the amount of schedule flexibility on the logical network paths within the schedule model.

Cumulative Flow Diagram (CFD). A chart indicating features completed over time, features in other states of development, and those in the backlog.

Cycle Time. The total elapsed time from the start of a particular activity or work item to its completion.

Cycle Time Chart. A diagram that shows the average cycle time of the work items completed over time.

Daily Standup. A brief, daily collaboration meeting in which the team reviews progress from the previous day, declares intentions for the current day, and highlights any obstacles encountered or anticipated.

Dashboard. A set of charts and graphs showing progress or performance against important measures of the project.

Data Gathering and Analysis Methods. Methods used to collect, assess, and evaluate data and information to gain a deeper understanding of a situation.

Decision Tree Analysis. A diagramming and calculation method for evaluating the implications of a chain of multiple options in the presence of uncertainty.

Decomposition. A method used for dividing and subdividing the project scope and project deliverables into smaller, more manageable parts.

Definition of Done (DoD). A checklist of all the criteria required to be met so that a deliverable can be considered ready for customer use.

Deliverable. Any unique and verifiable product, result, or capability to perform a service that is required to be produced to complete a process, phase, or project.

Delivery Performance Domain. The performance domain that addresses activities and functions associated with delivering the scope and quality that the project was undertaken to achieve.

Development Approach. A method used to create and evolve the product, service, or result during the project life cycle, such as a predictive, iterative, incremental, agile, or hybrid method.

Development Approach and Life Cycle Performance Domain. The performance domain that addresses activities and functions associated with the development approach, cadence, and life cycle phases of the project.

DevOps. A collection of practices for creating a smooth flow of deliveries by improving collaboration between development and operations staff.

Digital Product. A product or service that is delivered, used, and stored in an electronic format.

Discretionary Dependency. A relationship that is based on best practices or project preferences.

Duration. The total number of work periods required to complete an activity or work breakdown structure component, expressed in hours, days, or weeks. Contrast with *effort*.

Earned Value (EV). The measure of work performed expressed in terms of the budget authorized for that work.

Earned Value Analysis (EVA). An analysis method that uses a set of measures associated with scope, schedule, and cost to determine the cost and schedule performance of a project.

Effort. The number of labor units required to complete a schedule activity or work breakdown structure component, often expressed in hours, days, or weeks. Contrast with *duration*.

Emotional Intelligence. The ability to identify, assess, and manage the personal emotions of oneself and other people, as well as the collective emotions of groups of people.

Enterprise Environmental Factors (EEF). Conditions, not under the immediate control of the team, that influence, constrain, or direct the project, program, or portfolio.

Epic. A large, related body of work intended to hierarchically organize a set of requirements and deliver specific business outcomes.

Estimate. A quantitative assessment of the likely amount or outcome of a variable, such as project costs, resources, effort, or durations.

Estimate at Completion (EAC). The expected total cost of completing all work expressed as the sum of the actual cost to date and the estimate to complete.

Estimate to Complete (ETC). The expected cost to finish all the remaining project work.

Estimating Methods. Methods used to develop an approximation of work, time, or cost on a project.

Executing Process Group. Those processes performed to complete the work defined in the project management plan to satisfy the project requirements.

Expected Monetary Value (EMV). The estimated value of an outcome expressed in monetary terms.

Explicit Knowledge. Knowledge that can be codified using symbols such as words, numbers, and pictures.

External Dependency. A relationship between project activities and non-project activities.

Fast Tracking. A schedule compression method in which activities or phases normally done in sequence are performed in parallel for at least a portion of their duration.

Feature. A set of related requirements or functionalities that provides value to an organization.

Firm Fixed Price Contract (FFP). A type of fixed-price contract where the buyer pays the seller a set amount (as defined by the contract), regardless of the seller's costs.

Fixed Duration. A type of activity where the length of time required to complete the activity remains constant regardless of the number of people or resources assigned to the activity.

Fixed-Price Contract. An agreement that sets the fee that will be paid for a defined scope of work regardless of the cost or effort to deliver it.

Fixed Price Incentive Fee Contract (FPIF). A type of contract where the buyer pays the seller a set amount (as defined by the contract), and the seller can earn an additional amount if the seller meets defined performance criteria.

Fixed Price with Economic Price Adjustment Contract (FPEPA). A fixed-price contract, but with a special provision allowing for predefined final adjustments to the contract price due to changed conditions, such as inflation changes, or cost increases (or decreases) for specific commodities.

Flow. The measure of how efficiently work moves through a given process or framework.

Flowchart. The depiction in a diagram format of the inputs, process actions, and outputs of one or more processes within a system.

Forecast. An estimate or prediction of conditions and events in the project's future based on information and knowledge available at the time of the forecast.

Function Point. An estimate of the amount of business functionality in an information system, used to calculate the functional size measurement of a software system.

Gantt Chart. A bar chart of schedule information where activities are listed on the vertical axis, dates are shown on the horizontal axis, and activity durations are shown as horizontal bars placed according to start and finish dates.

Governance. The framework for directing and enabling an organization through its established policies, practices, and other relevant documentation.

Grade. A category or rank used to distinguish items that have the same functional use but do not share the same requirements for quality.

Hierarchy Chart. A chart that begins with high-level information that is progressively decomposed into lower levels of detail.

Histogram. A bar chart that shows the graphical representation of numerical data.

Hybrid Approach. A combination of two or more agile and nonagile elements, having a nonagile end result.

Impact Mapping. A strategic planning method that serves as a visual roadmap for the organization during product development.

Impediment. An obstacle that prevents the team from achieving its objectives. Also known as a *blocker*.

Incremental Approach. An adaptive development approach in which the deliverable is produced successively, adding functionality until the deliverable contains the necessary and sufficient capability to be considered complete.

Indefinite Delivery Indefinite Quantity (IDIQ). A contract that provides for an indefinite quantity of goods or services, with a stated lower and upper limit, within a fixed time period.

Influence Diagram. A graphical representation of situations showing causal influences, time ordering of events, and other relationships among variables and outcomes.

Information Radiator. A visible, physical display that provides information to the rest of the organization, enabling timely knowledge sharing.

Initiating Process Group. Those processes performed to define a new project or a new phase of an existing project by obtaining authorization to start the project or phase.

Internal Dependency. A relationship between two or more project activities.

Interpersonal Skills. Skills used to establish and maintain relationships with other people.

Issue. A current condition or situation that may have an impact on the project objectives.

Issue Log. A project document where information about issues is recorded and monitored.

Iteration. A timeboxed cycle of development on a product or deliverable in which all of the work that is needed to deliver value is performed.

Iteration Plan. A detailed plan for the current iteration.

Iteration Planning. A meeting to clarify the details of the backlog items, acceptance criteria, and work effort required to meet an upcoming iteration commitment.

Iteration Review. A meeting held at the end of an iteration to demonstrate the work that was accomplished during the iteration.

Iterative Approach. A development approach that focuses on an initial, simplified implementation then progressively elaborates adding to the feature set until the final deliverable is complete.

Kanban Board. A visualization tool that shows work in progress to help identify bottlenecks and overcommitments, thereby allowing the team to optimize the workflow.

Kickoff Meeting. A gathering of team members and other key stakeholders at the outset of a project to formally set expectations, gain a common understanding, and commence work.

Knowledge. A mixture of experience, values and beliefs, contextual information, intuition, and insight that people use to make sense of new experiences and information.

Lag. The amount of time whereby a successor activity will be delayed with respect to a predecessor activity.

Last Responsible Moment. The concept of deferring a decision to allow the team to consider multiple options until the cost of further delay would exceed the benefit.

Lead. The amount of time whereby a successor activity can be advanced with respect to a predecessor activity.

Lead Time. The time between a customer request and the actual delivery.

Lead Time Chart. A diagram showing the trend over time of the average lead time of the items completed in work.

Lean Startup Canvas. A one-page template designed to communicate a business plan with key stakeholders in an efficient and effective manner.

Lessons Learned. The knowledge gained during a project, which shows how project events were addressed or should be addressed in the future, for the purpose of improving future performance.

Lessons Learned Register. A project document used to record knowledge gained during a project, phase, or iteration so that it can be used to improve future performance for the team and the organization.

Life Cycle. See *project life cycle*.

Life Cycle Assessment (LCA). A tool used to evaluate the total environmental impact of a product, process, or system.

Log. A document used to record and describe or denote selected items identified during execution of a process or activity. Usually used with a modifier, such as issue, change, or assumption.

Make-or-Buy Analysis. The process of gathering and organizing data about product requirements and analyzing them against available alternatives including the purchase or internal manufacture of the product.

Management Reserve. An amount of the project budget or project schedule held outside of the performance measurement baseline for management control purposes that is reserved for unforeseen work that is within the project scope.

Mandatory Dependency. A relationship that is contractually required or inherent in the nature of the work.

Measurement Performance Domain. The performance domain that addresses activities and functions associated with assessing project performance and taking appropriate actions to maintain acceptable performance.

Measures of Performance. Measures that characterize physical or functional attributes relating to system operation.

Method. A means for achieving an outcome, output, result, or project deliverable.

Methodology. A system of practices, techniques, procedures, and rules used by those who work in a discipline.

Metric. A description of a project or product attribute and how to measure it.

Milestone. A significant point or event in a project, program, or portfolio.

Milestone Schedule. A type of schedule that presents milestones with planned dates.

Minimum Viable Product (MVP). A concept used to define the scope of the first release of a solution to customers by identifying the fewest number of features or requirements that would deliver value.

Modeling. Creating simplified representations of systems, solutions, or deliverables, such as prototypes, diagrams, or storyboards.

Monitor. Collect project performance data, produce performance measures, and report and disseminate performance information.

Monitoring and Controlling Process Group. Those processes required to track, review, and regulate the progress and performance of the project; identify any areas in which changes to the plan are required; and initiate corresponding changes.

Monte Carlo Simulation. A method of identifying the potential impacts of risk and uncertainty using multiple iterations of a computer model to develop a probability distribution of a range of outcomes that could result from a decision or course of action.

Mood Chart. A visualization chart for tracking moods or reactions to identify areas for improvement.

Multipoint Estimating. A method used to estimate cost or duration by applying an average or weighted average of optimistic, pessimistic, and most likely estimates when there is uncertainty with the individual activity estimates.

Net Promoter Score®. An index that measures the willingness of customers to recommend an organization's products or services to others.

Network Path. A sequence of activities connected by logical relationships in a project schedule network diagram.

Objective. Something toward which work is to be directed, a strategic position to be attained, a purpose to be achieved, a result to be obtained, a product to be produced, or a service to be performed.

Opportunity. A risk that would have a positive effect on one or more project objectives.

Organizational Breakdown Structure (OBS). A hierarchical representation of the project organization, which illustrates the relationship between project activities and the organizational units that will perform those activities.

Organizational Process Assets (OPA). Plans, processes, policies, procedures, and knowledge bases that are specific to and used by the performing organization.

Osmotic Communication. Means of receiving information without direct communication by overhearing and through nonverbal cues.

Outcome. An end result or consequence of a process or project.

Parametric Estimating. An estimating method in which an algorithm is used to calculate cost or duration based on historical data and project parameters.

Performance Measurement Baseline (PMB). Integrated scope, schedule, and cost baselines used for comparison to manage, measure, and control project execution.

Phase Gate. A review at the end of a phase in which a decision is made to continue to the next phase, to continue with modification, or to end a project or program.

Plan. A proposed means of accomplishing something.

Planned Value (PV). The authorized budget assigned to scheduled work.

Planning Performance Domain. The performance domain that addresses activities and functions associated with the initial, ongoing, and evolving organization and coordination necessary for delivering project deliverables and results.

Planning Process Group. Those processes required to establish the scope of the project, refine the objectives, and define the course of action required to attain the objectives that the project was undertaken to achieve.

Portfolio. Projects, programs, subsidiary portfolios, and operations managed as a group to achieve strategic objectives.

Portfolio Management. The centralized management of one or more portfolios to achieve strategic objectives.

Precision. Within the quality management system, precision is an assessment of exactness.

Predictive Approach. A development approach in which the project scope, time, and cost are determined in the early phases of the life cycle.

Prioritization Matrix. A scatter diagram that plots effort against value so as to classify items by priority.

Prioritization Schema. Methods used to prioritize portfolio, program, or project components, as well as requirements, risks, features, or other product information.

Probabilistic Estimating. A method used to develop a range of estimates along with the associated probabilities within that range.

Probability and Impact Matrix. A grid for mapping the probability of occurrence of each risk and its impact on project objectives if that risk occurs.

Procurement Management Plan. A component of the project or program management plan that describes how a project team will acquire goods and services from outside of the performing organization.

Product. An artifact that is produced, is quantifiable, and can be either an end item in itself or a component item.

Product Breakdown Structure. A hierarchical structure reflecting a product's components and deliverables.

Product Life Cycle. A series of phases that represent the evolution of a product, from concept through delivery, growth, maturity, and to retirement.

Product Management. The integration of people, data, processes, and business systems to create, maintain, and evolve a product or service throughout its life cycle.

Product Owner. A person responsible for maximizing the value of the product and accountable for the end product.

Product Scope. The features and functions that characterize a product, service, or result.

Program. Related projects, subsidiary programs, and program activities that are managed in a coordinated manner to obtain benefits not available from managing them individually.

Program Management. The application of knowledge, skills, and principles to a program to achieve the program objectives and obtain benefits and control not available by managing program components individually.

Progressive Elaboration. The iterative process of increasing the level of detail in a project management plan as greater amounts of information and more accurate estimates become available.

Project. A temporary endeavor undertaken to create a unique product, service, or result.

Project Brief. A high-level overview of the goals, deliverables, and processes for the project.

Project Calendar. A calendar that identifies working days and shifts that are available for scheduled activities.

Project Charter. A document issued by the project initiator or sponsor that formally authorizes the existence of a project and provides the project manager with the authority to apply organizational resources to project activities.

Project Governance. The framework, functions, and processes that guide project management activities in order to create a unique product, service, or result to meet organizational, strategic, and operational goals.

Project Lead. A person who helps the project team to achieve the project objectives, typically by orchestrating the work of the project. See also *project manager*.

Project Life Cycle. The series of phases that a project passes through from its start to its completion.

Project Management. The application of knowledge, skills, tools, and techniques to project activities to meet the project requirements.

Project Management Body of Knowledge (PMBOK). A term that describes the knowledge within the profession of project management.

Project Management Office (PMO). A management structure that standardizes the project-related governance processes and facilitates the sharing of resources, methodologies, tools, and techniques.

Project Management Plan. The document that describes how the project will be executed, monitored and controlled, and closed.

Project Management Process Group. A logical grouping of project management inputs, tools and techniques, and outputs. The Project Management Process Groups include Initiating processes, Planning processes, Executing processes, Monitoring and Controlling processes, and Closing processes.

Project Management Team. The members of the project team who are directly involved in project management activities.

Project Manager. The person assigned by the performing organization to lead the team that is responsible for achieving the project objectives. See also *project lead*.

Project Phase. A collection of logically related project activities that culminates in the completion of one or more deliverables.

Project Review. An event at the end of a phase or project to assess the status, evaluate the value delivered, and determine if the project is ready to move to the next phase or transition to operations.

Project Schedule. An output of a schedule model that presents linked activities with planned dates, durations, milestones, and resources.

Project Schedule Network Diagram. A graphical representation of the logical relationships among the project schedule activities.

Project Scope. The work performed to deliver a product, service, or result with the specified features and functions.

Project Scope Statement. The description of the project scope, major deliverables, and exclusions.

Project Team. A set of individuals performing the work of the project to achieve its objectives.

Project Vision Statement. A concise, high-level description of the project that states the purpose and inspires the team to contribute to the project.

Project Work Performance Domain. The performance domain that addresses activities and functions associated with establishing project processes, managing physical resources, and fostering a learning environment.

Prototype. A working model used to obtain early feedback on the expected product before actually building it.

Quality. The degree to which a set of inherent characteristics fulfills requirements.

Quality Management Plan. A component of the project or program management plan that describes how applicable policies, procedures, and guidelines will be implemented to achieve the quality objectives.

Quality Metrics. A description of a project or product attribute and how to measure it.

Quality Policy. The basic principles that should govern the organization's actions as it implements its system for quality management.

Quality Report. A project document that includes quality management issues, recommendations for corrective actions, and a summary of findings from quality control activities and may include recommendations for process, project, and product improvements.

Register. A written record of regular entries for evolving aspects of a project, such as risks, stakeholders, or defects.

Regression Analysis. An analytical method where a series of input variables are examined in relation to their corresponding output results in order to develop a mathematical or statistical relationship.

Regulations. Requirements imposed by a governmental body. These requirements can establish product, process, or service characteristics, including applicable administrative provisions that have government-mandated compliance.

Relative Estimating. A method for creating estimates that are derived from performing a comparison against a similar body of work, taking effort, complexity, and uncertainty into consideration.

Release. One or more components of one or more products, which are intended to be put into production at the same time.

Release Plan. The plan that sets expectations for the dates, features, and/or outcomes expected to be delivered over the course of multiple iterations.

Release Planning. The process of identifying a high-level plan for releasing or transitioning a product, deliverable, or increment of value.

Report. A formal record or summary of information.

Requirement. A condition or capability that is necessary to be present in a product, service, or result to satisfy a business need.

Requirements Documentation. A record of product requirements and other product information, along with whatever is recorded to manage it.

Requirements Management Plan. A component of the project or program management plan that describes how requirements will be analyzed, documented, and managed.

Requirements Traceability Matrix. A grid that links product requirements from their origin to the deliverables that satisfy them.

Reserve. A provision in the project management plan to mitigate cost and/or schedule risk, often used with a modifier (e.g., management reserve, contingency reserve) to provide further detail on what types of risk are meant to be mitigated.

Reserve Analysis. A method used to evaluate the amount of risk on the project and the amount of schedule and budget reserve to determine whether the reserve is sufficient for the remaining risk.

Resource Breakdown Structure. A hierarchical representation of resources by category and type.

Resource Management Plan. A component of the project management plan that describes how project resources are acquired, allocated, monitored, and controlled.

Responsibility. An assignment that can be delegated within a project management plan such that the assigned resource incurs a duty to perform the requirements of the assignment.

Responsibility Assignment Matrix (RAM). A grid that shows the project resources assigned to each work package.

Result. An output from performing project management processes and activities. See also *deliverable*.

Retrospective. A regularly occurring workshop in which participants explore their work and results in order to improve both the process and product.

Rework. Action taken to bring a defective or nonconforming component into compliance with requirements or specifications.

Risk. An uncertain event or condition that, if it occurs, has a positive or negative effect on one or more project objectives.

Risk Acceptance. A risk response strategy whereby the project team decides to acknowledge the risk and not take any action unless the risk occurs.

Risk-Adjusted Backlog. A backlog that includes product work and actions to address threats and opportunities.

Risk Appetite. The degree of uncertainty an organization or individual is willing to accept in anticipation of a reward.

Risk Avoidance. A risk response strategy whereby the project team acts to eliminate the threat or protect the project from its impact.

Risk Breakdown Structure (RBS). A hierarchical representation of potential sources of risks.

Risk Enhancement. A risk response strategy whereby the project team acts to increase the probability of occurrence or impact of an opportunity.

Risk Escalation. A risk response strategy whereby the team acknowledges that a risk is outside of its sphere of influence and shifts the ownership of the risk to a higher level of the organization where it is more effectively managed.

Risk Exploiting. A risk response strategy whereby the project team acts to ensure that an opportunity occurs.

Risk Exposure. An aggregate measure of the potential impact of all risks at any given point in time in a project, program, or portfolio.

Risk Management Plan. A component of the project, program, or portfolio management plan that describes how risk management activities will be structured and performed.

Risk Mitigation. A risk response strategy whereby the project team acts to decrease the probability of occurrence or impact of a threat.

Risk Register. A repository in which outputs of risk management processes are recorded.

Risk Report. A project document that summarizes information on individual project risks and the level of overall project risk.

Risk Review. The process of analyzing the status of existing risks and identifying new risks. May also be known as *risk reassessment*.

Risk Sharing. A risk response strategy whereby the project team allocates ownership of an opportunity to a third party who is best able to capture the benefit of that opportunity.

Risk Threshold. The measure of acceptable variation around an objective that reflects the risk appetite of the organization and stakeholders. See also *risk appetite*.

Risk Transference. A risk response strategy whereby the project team shifts the impact of a threat to a third party, together with ownership of the response.

Roadmap. A high-level time line that depicts such things as milestones, significant events, reviews, and decision points.

Role. A defined function to be performed by a project team member, such as testing, filing, inspecting, or coding.

Rolling Wave Planning. An iterative planning method in which the work to be accomplished in the near term is planned in detail, while the work in the future is planned at a higher level.

Root Cause Analysis. An analytical method used to determine the basic underlying reason that causes a variance or a defect or a risk.

Scatter Diagram. A graph that shows the relationship between two variables.

Schedule. See *project schedule*.

Schedule Baseline. The approved version of a schedule model that can be changed using formal change control procedures and is used as the basis for comparison to actual results.

Schedule Compression. A method used to shorten the schedule duration without reducing the project scope.

Schedule Forecasts. Estimates or predictions of conditions and events in the project's future based on information and knowledge available at the time the schedule is calculated.

Schedule Management Plan. A component of the project or program management plan that establishes the criteria and the activities for developing, monitoring, and controlling the schedule.

Schedule Model. A representation of the plan for executing the project's activities including durations, dependencies, and other planning information, used to produce a project schedule along with other scheduling artifacts.

Schedule Performance Index (SPI). A measure of schedule efficiency expressed as the ratio of earned value to planned value.

Schedule Variance (SV). A measure of schedule performance expressed as the difference between the earned value and the planned value.

Scope. The sum of the products, services, and results to be provided as a project. See also *project scope* and *product scope*.

Scope Baseline. The approved version of a scope statement, work breakdown structure (WBS), and its associated WBS dictionary that can be changed using formal change control procedures and is used as the basis for comparison to actual results.

Scope Creep. The uncontrolled expansion to product or project scope without adjustments to time, cost, and resources.

Scope Management Plan. A component of the project or program management plan that describes how the scope will be defined, developed, monitored, controlled, and validated.

S-Curve. A graph that displays cumulative costs over a specified period of time.

Self-Organizing Team. A cross-functional team in which people assume leadership as needed to achieve the team's objectives.

Sensitivity Analysis. An analysis method to determine which individual project risks or other sources of uncertainty have the most potential impact on project outcomes by correlating variations in project outcomes with variations in elements of a quantitative risk analysis model.

Servant Leadership. The practice of leading the team by focusing on understanding and addressing the needs and development of team members in order to enable the highest possible team performance.

Simulation. An analytical method that models the combined effect of uncertainties to evaluate their potential impact on objectives.

Single-Point Estimating. An estimating method that involves using data to calculate a single value which reflects a best guess estimate.

Specification. A precise statement of the needs to be satisfied and the essential characteristics that are required.

Sponsor. A person or group who provides resources and support for the project, program, or portfolio and is accountable for enabling success.

Sprint. A short time interval within a project during which a usable and potentially releasable increment of the product is created. See also *iteration*.

Stakeholder. An individual, group, or organization that may affect, be affected by, or perceive itself to be affected by a decision, activity, or outcome of a project, program, or portfolio.

Stakeholder Analysis. A method of systematically gathering and analyzing quantitative and qualitative information to determine whose interests should be taken into account throughout the project.

Stakeholder Engagement Assessment Matrix. A matrix that compares current and desired stakeholder engagement levels.

Stakeholder Engagement Plan. A component of the project management plan that identifies the strategies and actions required to promote productive involvement of stakeholders in project or program decision making and execution.

Stakeholder Performance Domain. The performance domain that addresses activities and functions associated with stakeholders.

Stakeholder Register. A project document that includes information about project stakeholders including an assessment and classification of project stakeholders.

Standard. A document established by an authority, custom, or general consent as a model or example.

Statement of Work (SOW). A narrative description of products, services, or results to be delivered by the project.

Status Meeting. A regularly scheduled meeting to exchange and analyze information about the current progress of the project and its performance.

Status Report. A report on the current status of the project.

Steering Committee. An advisory body of senior stakeholders who provide direction and support for the project team and make decisions outside the project team's authority.

Story Map. A visual model of all the features and functionality desired for a given product, created to give the team a holistic view of what they are building and why.

Story Point. A unit used to estimate the relative level of effort needed to implement a user story.

Strategic Plan. A high-level document that explains an organization's vision and mission plus the approach that will be adopted to achieve this mission and vision, including the specific goals and objectives to be achieved during the period covered by the document.

Strategy Artifacts. Documents created prior to or at the start of the project that address strategic, business, or high-level information about the project.

Swarm. A method in which multiple team members focus collectively on resolving a specific problem or task.

SWOT Analysis. Analysis of strengths, weaknesses, opportunities, and threats of an organization, project, or option.

Tacit Knowledge. Personal knowledge that can be difficult to articulate and share such as beliefs, experience, and insights.

Tailoring. The deliberate adaptation of approach, governance, and processes to make them more suitable for the given environment and the work at hand.

Task Board. A visual representation of the progress of the planned work that allows everyone to see the status of the tasks.

Team Charter. A document that records the team values, agreements, and operating guidelines, as well as establishes clear expectations regarding acceptable behavior by project team members.

Team Performance Domain. The performance domain that addresses activities and functions associated with the people who are responsible for producing project deliverables that realize business outcomes.

Technical Performance Measures. Quantifiable measures of technical performance that are used to ensure system components meet the technical requirements.

Template. A partially complete document in a predefined format that provides a defined structure for collecting, organizing, and presenting information and data.

Test Plan. A document describing deliverables that will be tested, tests that will be conducted, and the processes that will be used in testing.

Threat. A risk that would have a negative effect on one or more project objectives.

Threshold. A predetermined value of a measurable project variable that represents a limit that requires action to be taken if it is reached.

Throughput. The number of items passing through a process.

Throughput Chart. A diagram that shows the accepted deliverables over time.

Time and Materials Contract (T&M). A type of contract that is a hybrid contractual arrangement containing aspects of both cost-reimbursable and fixed-price contracts.

Timebox. A short, fixed period of time in which work is to be completed.

Tolerance. The quantified description of acceptable variation for a quality requirement.

Trend Analysis. An analytical method that uses mathematical models to forecast future outcomes based on historical results.

Triple Bottom Line. A framework for considering the full cost of doing business by evaluating a company's bottom line from the perspective of profit, people, and the planet.

Uncertainty. A lack of understanding and awareness of issues, events, path to follow, or solutions to pursue.

Uncertainty Domain. The performance domain that addresses activities and functions associated with risk and uncertainty.

Use Case. An artifact for describing and exploring how a user interacts with a system to achieve a specific goal.

User Story. A brief description of an outcome for a specific user, which is a promise for a conversation to clarify details.

Validation. The assurance that a product, service, or result meets the needs of the customer and other identified stakeholders. See also *verification*.

Value. The worth, importance, or usefulness of something.

Value Delivery Office (VDO). A project delivery support structure that focuses on coaching teams; building agile skills and capabilities throughout the organization; and mentoring sponsors and product owners to be more effective in those roles.

Value Delivery System. A collection of strategic business activities aimed at building, sustaining, and/or advancing an organization.

Value Proposition. The value of a product or service that an organization communicates to its customers.

Value Stream Map. A display of the critical steps in a process and the time taken in each step used to identify waste.

Value Stream Mapping. A lean enterprise method used to document, analyze, and improve the flow of information or materials required to produce a product or service for a customer.

Vanity Metric. A measure that appears to show some result but does not provide useful information for making decisions.

Variance. A quantifiable deviation, departure, or divergence away from a known baseline or expected value.

Variance Analysis. A method for determining the cause and degree of difference between the baseline and actual performance.

Variance at Completion (VAC). A projection of the amount of budget deficit or surplus, expressed as the difference between the budget at completion and the estimate at completion.

Velocity. A measure of a team's productivity rate at which the deliverables are produced, validated, and accepted within a predefined interval.

Velocity Chart. A chart that tracks the rate at which the deliverables are produced, validated, and accepted within a predefined interval.

Verification. The evaluation of whether or not a product, service, or result complies with a regulation, requirement, specification, or imposed condition. See also *validation*.

Virtual Team. A group of people with a shared goal who work in different locations and who engage with each other primarily through phone and other electronic communications.

Vision Statement. A summarized, high-level description about the expectations for a product such as target market, users, major benefits, and what differentiates the product from others in the market.

Visual Data and Information. Artifacts that organize and present data and information in a visual format, such as charts, graphs, matrices, and diagrams.

Voice of the Customer. A planning method used to provide products, services, and results that truly reflect customer requirements by translating those customer requirements into the appropriate technical requirements for each phase of project or product development.

Volatility. The possibility for rapid and unpredictable change.

Waste. Activities that consume resources and/or time without adding value.

WBS Dictionary. A document that provides detailed deliverable, activity, and scheduling information about each component in the work breakdown structure.

What-If-Scenario Analysis. The process of evaluating scenarios in order to predict their effect on project objectives.

Wideband Delphi. An estimating method in which subject matter experts go through multiple rounds of producing estimates individually, with a team discussion after each round, until a consensus is achieved.

Work Breakdown Structure (WBS). A hierarchical decomposition of the total scope of work to be carried out by the project team to accomplish the project objectives and create the required deliverables.

Work Package. The work defined at the lowest level of the work breakdown structure for which cost and duration are estimated and managed.

Index

B

BAC. *See* Budget at completion
Backlog, 45, 62, 76, 96, 185
Backlog refinement meeting, 179
Balance
    competing constraints and, 72
    reframing and, 111
Bar chart, 106
Baseline(s), 188. *See also* Cost baseline; Scope
    baseline
    definition, 93
Baseline performance, 100–101
Basic ordering agreement (BOA), 191
Basis of estimates, 20, 54
Behavior
    project management principles and, 146
    sponsors, 209
Benchmarking, 175
Benefit-cost ratio, 102
Benefits realization, PMO and, 214
Best practices, benchmarking and, 175
Bias(es)
    confirmation bias, 112
    conscious and unconscious, 20
Bidder conferences, 70, 75, 179
Bid documents, 70, 75, 192
Bid process, 75
Big picture perspective, 207, 213
Big visible charts (BVCs), 108
Bottlenecks, 71
Brainstorming, 13, 22, 121
Budget
    budget build up, 62–63
    definition, 52, 188
    Planning Performance Domain, 62–63
Budget at completion (BAC), 104–105
Burn charts, 108, 109, 111
Burndown/burnup chart, 188
Burndown chart, 108, 109
Burnup chart, 108, 109, 111
"Business as usual," 163
Business case
    business value and, 102
    definition, 184

    delivery cadence and, 50
    description of, 82
    feasibility phase and, 42
    outcomes and, 175
    planning and, 54
    as strategy artifact, 184
    value and, 82
Business case document, 22
Business justification analysis methods, 175
Business model canvas, 184
Business value, 82
Business value measurements, 82
Buyer
    agreements, contracts and, 191
    bid process and, 75

C

Cadence
    definition, 33
    delivery, 33–34
    Development Approach and Life Cycle
    Performance Domain, 33–34, 46–48
    life cycle, development and, 33, 55
Calendar, project, 192
Capabilities, PMO and, 213, 214
Cause-and-effect diagram, 188
Celebrating success, 21
Change(s)
    cost of, 90–91
    culture of, 214
    ease of, 40
    8-Step Process for Leading, 162, 173
    monitoring new work and, 76–77
    Planning Performance Domain, 66
    transitions associated with, 164
Change control
    changes and, 66
    checking results and, 68
Change control board (CCB), 68, 77, 169, 183, 186
Change control plan, 186
Change control system, 107
Change log, 185
Change management, 213

Document(s)
bid, 70, 75, 192
business, 82
business case document, 82
project, 62
project-authorizing, 82
Documentation
requirements, 83, 192
written communication, 73
Domains. *See* Performance domains; Project
performance domains
Drexler/Sibbet Team Performance Model, 167
Duration, 52, 62, 224
effort and, 100
Duration estimates, 105

E

EAC. *See* Estimate at completion
Earned value (EV), 100, 101
Earned value analysis (EVA)
definition, 176
schedule and cost variance, 101
Earned value management (EVM), 100, 104, 105
Effort, 100
8-Step Process for Leading Change, 162, 173
Emotional intelligence (EI), 25–27
components of, 27
key areas, 26
Empowerment
culture and, 143
high-performing project teams and, 22
tailoring engagement and, 136
EMV. *See* Expected monetary value (EMV)
Encouragement, development opportunities
and, 18
Engage, 121
Engagement. *See also* Stakeholder engagement
communication and, 73
lack of, sponsor and, 208
Project Work Performance Domain, 73
tailoring, 136

Enterprise-level PMO (EPMO), 212
Environment
product, 222
tailoring and, 154
Environmental considerations, 53, 129
Escalation
threats and, 123
Estimate(s). *See also* Basis of estimates
analogous, 178
definition, 52
parametric, 178
Estimate at completion (EAC), 104, 105
Estimate to complete (ETC), 104, 105
Estimating, 55–58
absolute, 57
adjusting estimates for uncertainty, 58
deterministic, 57
flow-based, 58
life cycle phase and, 55
low accuracy, high precision, 56
Planning Performance Domain, 55–58
probabilistic, 57
range decreasing over time, 56
relative, 57, 58
Estimating methods, 178
EVA. *See* Earned value analysis
EVM. *See* Earned value management
Exception plan
definition, 114
triggering of, 113
Executing Process Group, 171
Expected monetary value (EMV), 116, 126, 176
Expert judgment, 104. *See also* Subject matter
experts (SMEs)
Explicit knowledge, 70, 77–78
External dependency, 60
External failure costs, 89
Extrinsic motivation, 159

Indefinite delivery indefinite quantity (IDIQ), 191
Indicators. *See* Key performance indicators (KPIs)
Individual project risk, 177, 190
Industry/industries
  market and, 142
  traditional product, 224
Influence
  development approach and, 39, 40, 41
  leadership and, 29
  sponsors and, 209
Influence diagram, 176
Information
  gathering, 119
  historical, 149
  Measurement Performance Domain, 106–111
  presenting, 106–111
Information radiator, 108, 109
Initiating Process Group, 171
Initiatives, critical, 214
Innovation
  degree of, 39
Input(s)
  flow of deliveries and, 45
  Process Groups and, 171
Inputs, tools/techniques, and outputs (ITTOs), 6
Inspection, 42, 47, 88, 89
Integration
  practice and, 163
  tailoring engagement and, 136
Integrity, 20
Intellectual property, 75
Interactions, performance domains
  Delivery Performance Domain, 91
  Development Approach and Life Cycle Performance Domain, 49–50
  Measurement Performance Domain, 114–115
  Planning Performance Domain, 67
  Project Work Performance Domain, 78
  Stakeholder Performance Domain, 14
  Team Performance Domain, 31
  Uncertainty Performance Domain, 128
Internal dependency, 60
Internal failure costs, 89
Internal rate of return (IRR), 175

Interpersonal skills, 25–29
  soft skills, 12
  stakeholder engagement and, 12
  types of, 23–29
Intrinsic motivation, 159
IRR. *See* Internal rate of return
Issue log, 185
Iterate, 121
Iteration, 44–45, 53
Iteration plan, 61, 186
Iteration planning meeting, 179
Iteration review, 179
Iterative development, 37
Iterative process, 120
ITTOs. *See* Inputs, tools/techniques, and outputs

J

Job shadowing, 78
Judgment. *See* Expert judgment
Just-in-time scheduling approach, 45

K

Kanban boards, 109, 110
Kanban scheduling system, 45
Key performance indicators (KPIs), 95–96
Key stakeholders, 11, 23, 44, 167, 179
Kickoff meeting, 179, 183
Knowledge
  explicit, 70, 77–78
  tacit, 77–78
Knowledge management, 77
Knowledge management repository, 149
Knowledge transfer, 213
KPIs. *See* Key performance indicators

L

Lagging indicators, 96
Lags, leads and, 59
Late start and finish dates, 100

outcomes, checking, 129
outcomes, desired, 116
overview, 116–118
risk, 122–127
tailoring considerations, 150
uncertainty, general, 119
volatility, 122
Understand and analyze, stakeholders and, 11–12
Understanding, shared, 22
Update(s)
    artifacts and, 171
    generic, 183
Use case, 190
User stories
    customer value and, 84
    decomposition and, 54
    definition, 192
    iteration plan and, 61
    story point estimating and, 178

V

VAC. *See* Variance at completion
Value. *See also* Business value
    delivery of, 81–82
    software-enhanced, 220
Value analysis. *See* Earned value analysis (EVA)
Value delivery
    continuous, 222
    Delivery Performance Domain, 81–82
Value delivery office (VDO), 140, 141, 212
Value stream map, 190
Value stream mapping, 177
Vanity metric, 112
Variance(s), 68, 72, 94, 96, 101, 115, 188
Variance analysis, 177
Variance at completion (VAC), 105

Variations, 121, 123, 177
Velocity chart, 190
Vendor conferences. *See* Bidder conferences
Verification, 88
Virginia Satir Change Model, 163
Vision
    defining and sharing, 11
    establishing and maintaining, 23
    objectives and, 18
    sponsors and, 208
Visual controls, 109–111. *See also* Chart(s)
    kanban boards, 110
    task boards, 110
Visual data and information, 188–190
Volatility, 117
    Uncertainty Performance Domain, 122
Voting, 28

W

Warranty claims, 89
Waste, 89
Waterfall approach, 15, 49
WBS. *See* Work breakdown structure (WBS)
WBS dictionary, 85, 188
What-if scenario analysis, 177
Wideband Delphi, 28, 178
Win-win perspective, 169, 170
Work
    new work effort, 58
    non-value-added, 72
Work breakdown structure (WBS)
    decomposition and, 54, 84
    definition, 81, 187
Work packages, 85, 189
Work performance. *See* Project Work Performance Domain
Written communication, 72. *See also* Email